Sanctified Subversives

Sanctified Subversives:

Nuns in Early Modern English and Spanish Literature

By

Horacio Sierra

Cambridge Scholars Publishing

Sanctified Subversives:
Nuns in Early Modern English and Spanish Literature

By Horacio Sierra

This book first published 2016

Cambridge Scholars Publishing

Lady Stephenson Library, Newcastle upon Tyne, NE6 2PA, UK

British Library Cataloguing in Publication Data
A catalogue record for this book is available from the British Library

Copyright © 2016 by Horacio Sierra

All rights for this book reserved. No part of this book may be reproduced, stored in a retrieval system, or transmitted, in any form or by any means, electronic, mechanical, photocopying, recording or otherwise, without the prior permission of the copyright owner.

ISBN (10): 1-4438-9112-6
ISBN (13): 978-1-4438-9112-7

TABLE OF CONTENTS

Acknowledgements vii

Chapter One.. 1
Early Modern Nuns in Context

Chapter Two 31
Reclaiming Isabella, the Queer Virgin: Celebrating Catholicism's
Opportunities in *Measure for Measure*

Chapter Three 69
Convents as Feminist Utopias: Margaret Cavendish's *The Convent
of Pleasure* and the Potential of Closeted Dramas and Communities

Chapter Four.. 109
The *Sarao* as Conventual Rhetorical Space in María De Zayas's
Desengaños amorosos

Chapter Five 149
Straddling the Secular and Spiritual Divide: Sor Juana Inés de la Cruz's
Life and Literature

Chapter Six 189
Extraconventual Escapades: Erstwhile Nuns in Erauso's and Behn's
Fictions

Bibliography 217

Index 233

Acknowledgements

I am eternally grateful to my parents, Horacio and María Sierra, for their unconditional love and support. Their commitment to education and broadening my cultural horizons through trips to Europe, the Caribbean, and Latin America whetted my appetite for the kind of reading, writing, and research that led to this book. ¡Gracias a todos los miembros de mi familia – my sister Lyan, and all the tías, tíos, primos, sobrinos, abuelos, y abuelas – in the Cuban-American paradise that is Miami!

Thank you to my friends for their encouragement and support: David Paul Canelas, Dallas Clay Williams, Michele Alanis Carroll, Aurora del Carmen Quiel, Uwe Michael Dietz, Ellen Joy Letostak, Catherine Elizabeth Hoyser, Randi Marie Smith, Anthony Salvatore Abate, Jonathan Francis Gibbons, Ellen Macbeth Boomer, Rebecca Anne Sheehan, and Anita Jude Savo.

Thank you to the sages, teachers, and professors in my life for the wisdom they have shared and the intellectual horizons to which they have introduced me: Pan Zelenak, Carolina Amram, Hank Eder, Peggy Falagan, María Bouza, Lourdes Moller-Gomez, Mihoko Suzuki, Piotr Gwiazda, Pamela Hammons, Anne Cruz, Sidney Homan, Ira Clark, Shifra Armon, Pamela Gilbert, David Leverenz, Al Shoaf, Kim Emery, Sid Dobrin, Jodi Schorb, and Kenneth Kidd.

Thank you to the institutions that have served as a home away from home and as intellectual safe havens: Bent Tree Elementary, McMillan Middle, Miami Coral Park Senior High, the University of Miami, the University of Florida, the Florida Education Fund's McKnight Doctoral Fellowship Department, the University of Saint Joseph, the National Endowment for the Humanities, the Biblioteca Nacional de España, the Biblioteca Nacional de Portugal, the Folger Shakespeare Library, the British Library, and Bowie State University.

To all the nuns doing God's work: Thanks be to you and God.

Chapter One

Early Modern Nuns in Context

Why are nuns so fascinating? We take a second look when we see them on the streets. We are in awe of them as much as we are mystified by their lifestyle. Their habits, vows, and convents have intrigued us for millennia. Despite their long-standing presence in society, nuns still manage to grab our attention. What draws our interest has been a staple of nunhood since its inception: their perennial status as the other within. Nuns are a paradox in a patriarchal world; they are at once the quintessential embodiment of femininity and incongruous to its very definition. As chaste women devoted to God they are viewed as the purest of the pure. Yet, as females who reject courtship, sex, marriage, child bearing, and materialism, they are anathema to how society has proscribed roles for women: sex object, wife, mother, and capitalist consumer.

People notice when nuns speak up, become political activists, or articulate feminist convictions because the popular expectation is that nuns are meek, mild-mannered, and subservient. As this book fleshes out, nuns have been rebelling for centuries, veering from the normative paths constructed for women thanks to a feminist loophole within the Catholic Church's patriarchal hierarchy: conventual life as a nun. Western ideologies about womanhood and gendered power structures in early modern society can be illuminated by an examination of nuns and how their alternative lifestyles, as described in popular literature of the time, helped reflect and define what it meant to be a woman during the Renaissance.

Given the growing divide between Catholicism and Protestantism during the sixteenth and seventeenth centuries, examinations of the early modern era's literature benefit from an analysis of how authors articulated sentiments about these Christian denominations and their relationship with women. In this book, I pay particular attention to how authors perceive convents and the profession of nuns as either expanding and/or hindering the opportunities of early modern women within English and Spanish cultures.

On one hand, nuns and convents in the works of English authors such as William Shakespeare and Margaret Cavendish express English sympathy and nostalgia for Catholicism, the philanthropic endeavors of the clergy, and the opportunities the Catholic Church afforded women who wanted to circumvent the sexual economy that rendered them chattel. On the other hand, the Spanish Empire's familiarity with Catholic clergy and institutions influenced its authors to offer more complex depictions of conventual life. For example, Catalina de Erauso, better known as the Lieutenant Nun in her self-titled memoir/exploration narrative, runs away from a Basque convent and experiences life as a male soldier in the New World while battling would-be wives, antagonistic indigenous populations, and incredulous church officials. Meanwhile, her contemporary María de Zayas idealizes life in the convent with her collection of astoundingly riveting stories, *Desengaños amorosos* (*The Disenchantments of Love*). Zayas does as much by recognizing, as many female writers of the *querelle des femmes* did, that women could prevail in a female intellectual circle with the help of the Catholic Church and its distinct spatial home for women religious. Catalina, however, much like many other nuns, knew that the more independent-minded women chafed under the strictures of a conventual life whose structure and livelihood was still under the male purview.

If Shakespeare posits *Measure for Measure*'s Isabella as a noble heroine and Zayas envisions the convent as the ultimate escape for women avoiding violent marriage, then what does an actual nun do and write about? For this reason I ask us to cross the Atlantic Ocean to analyze the writing of a real-life nun – Mexico's Sor Juana Inés de la Cruz. A close reading of her poems, prose, and drama demonstrates how the feminist hopes expressed in Shakespeare's and Zayas's works are fulfilled in Sor Juana's engagement with the *querelle des femmes* thanks to the independence she enjoyed within her convent and from the liberties she was granted by the viceregal court of New Spain.

In this book, I employ fictional representations of nuns as a framework through which to interrogate depictions of gender, sexuality, and power structures in early modern English and Spanish societies. I do so by drawing on the scholarly tools of New Historicism, Feminism, and Queer Theory to establish a transnational, transatlantic, and inclusive framework. I utilize this collection of texts to study how popular authors exploited the role of the nun in fiction to challenge notions about gender in Christian nation-states beginning to see the earliest buds of feminist polemical writing. From commercial playwrights such as Shakespeare to feminist[1] authors such as Zayas highly attuned to how the continent-wide *querelle des femmes* was determining women's role in society, English- and Spanish-language writers of the early modern period were aware of the significance of nuns as mirrors, conduits, and trial balloons for their views and theories of gender dynamics, the double standard, and heterosexism.

Nuns have long possessed an exceptional status in Western Civilization in their role as women set apart from the lay female population. Their special standing as women venerated for their ability to renounce worldliness and embrace the vows of poverty, chastity, and obedience renders them relatively anomalous in a patriarchal world that subsumes women into a heteronormative sexual economy that belittles their worth. Nuns are simultaneously the antithesis and epitome of femininity. From a superficial perspective, we can begin this discussion by acknowledging popular conceptions about the choices nuns make when they live a religious life. On the one hand, because nuns are expected by the lay population to be silent, meek, humble, and caring, they fulfill expectations of the nurturing, maternal woman. On the other hand, their vow to renounce marriage, heterosexual intercourse, childbearing, and childrearing establishes them as non-conformists who challenge heteronormativity and reproductive futurity. Nonetheless, this peaceful coexistence of expectations demonstrates how living as nuns allowed many women during the early modern period to lead lives that afforded them a safe environment in which to pray, meditate, learn, and educate others with the blessing of religious and secular male leaders. Similar to the way in which I highlight the paradox inherent in a nun's public persona, Elizabeth Kuhns makes a similar observation about the dichotomous symbolism of nuns' clothing: "the habit serves to shroud the body and to mask the individual, it also dramatically announces its wearer to the world. The habit has the glamour of fashion while being antifashion;

---

[1] I liberally use terms such as "feminist," "queer," "capitalist," and "Marxist" throughout this book so that contemporary readers can efficiently understand the epistemological identities I am examining. I reject the need to always use the prefix "proto-." Historians and literary scholars know that these words were not coined until centuries after the Renaissance, but it does not mean that these ideologies or identities were nonexistent. We have created these words to explain and reify abstract concepts. Thus, I use them to provide a sociohistorically-minded literary analysis of such concepts when they appear in the works under consideration.

it is the antithesis of extravagance and sexual allure, yet it impresses and arouses" (7).

This book illustrates how both English and Spanish authors of the early modern period latched onto the figure of the nun as a way to evaluate feminine identities. As seemingly paradoxical representations of what womanhood could entail, nuns presented writers with the richest of subjectivities to scrutinize. If nuns cannot exist without the states of being they renounce – material richness, sexual coupling, and obedience to secular males – then their expected embodiment of the more virtuous side of femininity's binary allows them to be the perfect conduit through which authors can query and challenge society's assessment of womanhood. A discrete analysis of a nun's moral structure underscores the potential she possesses to subvert and exploit the gendered expectations placed on her when she wishes to transcend them. By eschewing bawdy, lewd, and propagandistic literature about lusty nuns that serve as whores to priests who act as pimps, this book employs mature works to tease out how canonical writers employed the role of the nun to showcase the powerful potential these women possessed in acting as sanctified subversives.

To initiate such a study, this introductory chapter briefly discusses the significance of Catholicism in late Medieval and early modern England. Doing so illustrates how integral nuns were to the everyday politics and culture of these nation-states as they expanded into global empires. Given that the Catholic Church began to lose its grip on wide swaths of Europe during the Renaissance, it is literature from the early modern period that merits a close examination of the fictional interpretations of the archetypal nun.

In an ambivalently Protestant England that saw a half-dozen shifts in political, religious, and cultural direction between the 1530s and the 1660s, authors and other intellectuals were accustomed to contemplating how the textual, political, religious, and sociological commentaries published in their name would play out on the larger cultural landscape. Because Catholicism remained an integral part of England's hallowed history, depictions of a "Romish" past could not escape feelings of nostalgia and/or wishful-thinking for those steeped in the traditions of the Catholic Church and/or aware of how it afforded women opportunities they were denied in Protestant nations. Even without considering scholarly work that posits Shakespeare as a crypto-Catholic, one sees that Shakespeare's personal religious persuasion does not distract from the fact that his England was awash in Catholic residue – architecturally, liturgically, textually, and psychologically. From rood loft edicts attempting to physically cleanse England of its Catholic past to Queen

Elizabeth's support of the "Common Prayer" book, Protestant England's ties to the Catholic Church – through both its contemporary threat and historic importance – are indelible parts even of the secular literature produced in such a religiously-centered era.[2] In fact, the Abbey of the Order of Saint Clare, a convent of the Poor Clares, the community that Isabella in Shakespeare's *Measure for Measure* wishes to join, had been located in Aldgate, the easternmost part of London since it was founded in 1293 by Blanche, Queen of Navarre, wife of Edmund Plantagenet, until its closure during the Reformation. No doubt Londoners seeing this play would have remembered the convent when they first saw Isabella speak with Francisca as she enquires about becoming a Poor Clare nun.

In the case of Golden Age Spain and its global empire, long deemed the official defender and representative of the Catholic faith by popes in awe of the nation's imperialist success and valiant military force, the nation's authors were familiar with living under the splendor and yoke of the Catholic Church. Intellectuals, particularly female authors, decided to challenge the status quo from within the system. Zayas and Sor Juana employed the convent and the figure of the nun to distance themselves from a world ruled by men for men. By subverting stereotypes about nuns as subservient to patristic leaders, these two authors engendered hope among their readers that all-female religious communities could provide a quasi-utopian alternative to a hostile world that usually rendered them inferior objects subject to male control.

Independent Women: Constructions and Identities of Early Modern Nuns as Anomalous Women

Early Christians who sought a respite from the frenzy and vagaries of the world escaped cities for spaces such as the desert, remote caves, or isolated monasteries. These locations offered the requisite tranquility needed for religious devotion and contemplation. Understandably, women

---

[2] The following monographs are essential reads on English Catholic recusancy during the early modern period: Ronald Corthell's, ed., *Catholic Culture in Early Modern England*. Notre Dame: University of Notre Dame Press, 2007. Frances E. Dolan's *Whores of Babylon: Catholicism, Gender, & Seventeenth-Century Print Culture*. Ithaca: Cornell University Press, 1999. Jane Degenhardt & Elizabeth Williamson's *Religion and Drama in Early Modern England: The Performance of Religion on the Renaissance Stage*. Burlington: Ashgate, 2011. Alison Shell's *Catholicism, Controversy and the English Literary Imagination, 1558-1660*. New York: Cambridge University Press, 1999.

and men who flocked to Christianity in its infancy sought clandestine places of worship since their lives depended on it. As Christianity gained political currency and its followers were able to practice the religion more freely, there was still an attraction to transcending worldliness by removing oneself from society. Escaping the bustle of urban life stemmed from a "biblical tradition" wherein a freeing space "meant . . . wild places without limit or definition, which represented withdrawal from worldly engagement, purification, and contact with the divine" (McNamara 61). However, the gradual institutionalization of the Church introduced sexist, hierarchical elements into the philosophies grounding permanent religious communities.

As isolated areas gave way to the construction of formal religious houses, the desire to separate monasteries by sex developed. A woman's vow of chastity was one of the main reasons behind this segregation. A woman's virginity contained a mixed blessing for women who sought to attain spiritual transcendence in a religious world governed by men. Virgins were celebrated for their purity and ability to renounce sexuality in pursuit of living a rigorously ascetic life. Nuns' perceived purity made them integral to Catholic life as lay people paid them reverence and requested that they made intercessory prayers on their behalf. At the same time, the alleged innate weakness of the female sex created an expectation of transgression: "As the descendants of Eve—forever linked to images of carnality and bodily sin—women would always, it would seem, fall short of the mark. Thus, women required rigid safeguards and protection" (Lehfeldt 3). Despite the problematic double bind of freedom and surveillance that these religious houses bestowed on nuns, women who sought to avoid either marriage and/or losing their virginity frequently flocked to convents in search of sanctuary. Both popular legends and historical anecdotes during the Middle Ages tell tales of heroines "fighting to retain their virginity at all costs" and entering "a walled enclosure that would guard them from the lusts of men and the ambitions of their families" (McNamara 99). The four protagonists that flee their family home for a convent in Zayas's *Desengaños amorosos* demonstrate how powerful a pull conventual life held for women in a society that offered them little recourse to abstain from sexual relations with men if they wanted to enjoy the essentials of civilized life.

Despite how attractive the convent seemed to some women, the empowerment accorded to nuns within the convent should not be overstated. As Sor Juana's life story makes clear, nuns took a vow of obedience that rendered them subservient to male superiors and Catholic Church hierarchy. Various applications of canon law required male supervision of convents. Bishops often butted heads with competent and intelligent abbesses who had to justify their actions to the patriarchy. Regular visitations by superiors removed any hope of a life unencumbered by male intrusion. On a more philosophical plane, the women's chasteness inspired outsiders to be continually protective, suspicious, and controlling of nuns' sexuality. As Elizabeth Lehfeldt argues in her study of women religious in early modern Spain, "nuns who accepted the enclosure of the convent had to accept at a certain level an ideology that devalued their worth as women and was suspicious of their ability to protect their own chastity" (13).

Because nuns were most recognized for what made them anomalous – their refusal to engage in sex and procreate – their vow of chastity was always more closely scrutinized, surveilled, and slandered than that of clergymen. Historically, many women who have resisted heterosexual intercourse have been physically abused and raped as punishment for their attempt to defy the sexual status quo. Despite a millennia of Catholics venerating the Blessed Virgin Mary and celebrating the virginal status of nuns and other women religious who chose to take a vow of chastity, by the Middle Ages it was commonplace for "dirty jokes and pornographic fantasies detailing the fictional longings of unwilling nuns" to give "license to the sexual ambitions of young men seeking wives or just a brief diversion by breaking into convents" (McNamara 4).

In fact, some Protestants considered it their duty to target nuns and free them from their enclosure and celibacy. One subgenre within popular anti-Catholic discourse included texts written to advise Protestants how to dissuade friends and family members from being Catholic or taking on a Catholic profession. The French-English Anglican clergyman Peter du Moulin included an example of such a text by adding a "Circulatory Letter to the Fathers of those Virgins that Desert their Families to Turn Nuns" as an epilogue to his 1678 book *The Ruine of Papacy: Or, A Clear Display of the Simony of the Romish Clergy*. The letter begins by saying it is written for the "consolation and attonment" of fathers and to "instruct the Daughter, and to give her such reasons as might be capable to perswade her to leave the Nunnery with as little noise and danger as she enter'd in." (85) The letter launches characteristically Protestant attacks on issues such as Transubstantiation, which the author says would create a paradox wherein if "all the Hosts were the body of Christ, at the same time Christ would be above in one place, and below in another. One body would be large, another small; one would be hot, another cold; one weighty, another light, one would rest in the Church, another be carry'd through the Streets" (92) and contends that "To understand Transubstantiation, there is a necessity of understanding Chimeras, accidents without substances, substances without accidents, Conversions without Communication, and Bodies without quantity" (93). Despite the profound theological subject matters addressed in the letter that belittle the cognitive reasoning abilities of nuns, the author concludes humanely by advising parents that nuns must leave the convent only by their own "free will" (95) rather than by force.

Likewise, Martin Luther wrote a letter to three nuns in the summer of 1524 that enjoined them to leave the convent and quit their profession because chastity was unnatural. Luther argued that "both Scripture and experience teach that among many thousands there is not one to whom God gives the grace to maintain pure chastity. A woman does not have the power [to do this] herself. God created her body to be with a man, bear children and raise them, as Scripture makes clear in Genesis 1" (141). Luther's call for women to quit the early modern equivalent of a work place and return to the kitchen has had far-reaching consequences well into the twentieth and twenty-first centuries.

In contrast to Luther, by rejecting this notion of rescuing women, the ostensibly Protestant authors Shakespeare and Cavendish sought to redress the grievances of English women religious who were forced to relinquish their conventual life during King Henry VIII's Reformation. The tension created by wars between Protestants and Catholics during the early modern period lends support to this study's examination of how authors of fictional narratives employed the figure of the nun and the space of the convent as literary devices to enable discussions about the value of virginity. After all, following Luther's 1517 posting of his Ninety-five Theses on the Wittenberg Cathedral, the voices of those "long silenced by monastic rhetoric rose to condemn celibacy as an occasion of sin and virginity itself as a crime against nature. Protestantism attacked the spirituality most associated with women, denying the redemptive value of prayer and sacrifice" (McNamara 419).

For example, in Shakespeare's *Measure for Measure* the idea of a woman refusing to engage in sexual intercourse and bear children inspires Angelo to homophonically pun on Isabella's choice of vocation and to question her identity when she rejects his obstreperous wooing, "Be that you are, / That is, a woman; if you be more, you're none" (2.4.135-36). Opposing such narrow-mindedness, some early modern Catholic theologians had already developed progressive epistemologies about gender and sex inspired by the Biblical verse that in Christ "There is neither Jew nor Greek: there is neither bond nor free: there is neither male nor female. For you are all one in Christ Jesus" (Galatians 3:28). In fact, "monastic theorists tended to conceptualize a third gender, apart from the two sexually active genders, harking back to the old view that, without active sexual and reproductive activity, gender did not exist" (McNamara 144). When Protestants critiqued the alleged unnaturalness of women who chose not to marry or engage in sexual intercourse, they discounted both the agency and genuine religious beliefs articulated in such a decision[3].

Whereas St. Jerome's notably misogynistic discussion of virgins and women presented virginity as a physiological state, St. Augustine recognized it along moral and spiritual principles that valued the quality of the woman's spirit over any physical actions that might have caused her to lose her virginity against her will. In oral storytelling and manuscript culture, tales of valiant women who resisted male encroachment on their spiritual being gained popularity throughout the Middle Ages as these legendary virgins were celebrated for their devotion to God. The most notable feature about the narratives that surround these women – such as St. Cecilia, Margaret of Antioch, and Catherine of Alexandria – is that while "the heroines are credited with 'meekness' . . . what is truly striking is their extraordinary boldness and defiance of all forms of authority" (Atkinson 136). Thus, it should come as no surprise that Zayas's celebration of the convent as a sanctuary for women who rebel against violent machismo and Shakespeare's laudation of Isabella demonstrates these authors' championing of the most unconventional of literary underdogs in a misogynistic era: the asexual woman.

Periculoso, The Council of Trent, and the Dissolution of Nuns' Agency

Canon law that called for the strict enclosure of nuns reached its apex with *Periculoso*, title sixteen in the third book of *Liber Sextus*, a collection of papal legislation published under Pope Boniface VIII in 1298. Although the sixteenth-century Council of Trent added stiffer penalties to violations of *Periculoso*, the centuries that preceded the council witnessed nuns, clergymen, and canon jurists wrestling with both the ideas and practical

---

[3] Clarissa Atkinson's study on the ideology of virginity in the late Middle Ages and its influence on the early modern period provides various attestations of women's clear understanding of how the maintenance of their virginity afforded them holy significance. Atkinson, Clarissa W. "'Precious Balsam in a Fragile Glass': The Ideology of Virginity in the Late Middle Ages." Journal of Family History 8:2 (Summer 1983) 131-43.

enforcement of strict claustration for nuns.[4] Pope Boniface VIII's edict justified the fears of so many nuns and abbesses about the amount of power that male religious could have over their lives when he legislated that clergymen had to strictly enforce the claustration of nuns within their jurisdiction or face "divini iudicii et interminatione maledictionis aeternae" ["divine judgment and the threat of eternal damnation"][5].

Claustration of nuns has been a part of monastic practice since at least the 300s according to references made in the letters of St. Jerome and in legal texts discussing the earliest communities of women religious in Rome (Makowski 9). During the early Middle Ages the philosophy behind encloistering religious professionals was applied to both men and women. Although not regularly followed by monks or nuns, the encloistering of members was thought of by many orders as engendering a more ideal situation for allowing them to follow their vows and the rules of their order without unnecessary interruptions from the outside world. With the exception of mendicant orders that relied on the charity of others for their sustenance, most religious houses understood that realities – financial and sometimes familial – necessitated some flexibility when it came to enclosure. Thus, when Pope Boniface VIII's legislation was imposed, many abbesses protested that the act would hinder their ability to solicit funds from the outside and to admit laywomen who wanted to retire in the convent (especially those with substantial funds).

Historians of the Catholic Church cannot clearly ascertain why the pope enacted *Periculoso*, especially since it appeared neither in any papal registers before its publication nor in any response to a decretal letter (a papal reply to a specific question of argument by others). A 1605 edition of a standard gloss to *Liber Sextus* by Joannes Andreae reports the alleged reason for *Periculoso*'s origin as shockingly simple: "A certain person in the presence of Boniface VIII asked the pope to tell him how nuns ought to live; *Periculoso* was the pope's extemporaneous reply" (Makowski 21). We should not dismiss the possible validity of such a marginal reason for enacting new canon law. However, there were some sociohistorical undercurrents that might have informed the pope's desire to more closely monitor the activities of nuns.

---

[4] Elizabeth Makowski's *Canon Law and Cloistered Women: Periculoso and Its Commentators, 1298-1545*, Washington, D.C.: Catholic University of America Press, 1997, is essential reading for this topic.
[5] Bracketed translations throughout the book are mine.

Because the early Middle Ages saw formal religious roles for women in the Catholic Church open to an exclusive well-to-do group of women, many pious women sought more diverse relationships with their faith. The elitism of some religious communities resulted in a disproportionately high number of women (compared to men) that were attracted to heretical movements of the thirteenth century, especially those that promised leadership roles for women. For example, the Guglielimites, which developed after the death of their namesake Guglielma of Bohemia, based its structure on the leadership of women. Consequently, as Elizabeth Makowski asserts, "the variety of religious roles for women in the late thirteenth century" seems to have inspired *Periculoso* as a way to "cordon off women . . . from that growing welter of groups, sects, and individuals" (14).

The practical needs of cloistered life also troubled patristic administrative leaders, since necessity rendered women quasi-autonomous in what occurred within the confines of their convent[6]. Bishops and abbots attempted to ameliorate problematic situations with regular ecclesiastical visits, yet the continual outflow of official literature about the expected comportment and home environment of nuns implies that nuns were not always abiding by the rules handed down by the hierarchy. As early as the twelfth century, Peter of Abelard was advising monasteries to follow the Rule of St. Benedict by ensuring that a religious house contain "within its walls the necessities of everyday life, such as a garden, water, a mill and bakehouse, and places where the sisters could perform their daily tasks, so that no occasion be furnished for straying outside" and so that they may "preserve their bodies from carnal contagion" (qtd. in Makowski 31). The number of utilitarian items and maintenance services required for a self-contained community underscores the realistic need for contact with the extraconventual world.

Despite strident exhortations against the potential for nuns in convents to be tempted and tainted by the worldliness of the outside world, there

---

[6] An area of study that deserves more research for individual and comparative analysis is the role of ribat communities specifically designated for women in Islamic cultures. These ribats functioned as shelters for women, particularly abandonded, divorced, or widowed women, and offered religious guidance, educational services, and personal counseling. Two good sources that discuss ribats include Zainab Alwani's "Muslim Women's Contribution in Building Society" and Adam Sabra's *Poverty and Charity in Medieval Islam: Mamluk Egype, 1250-1517*.

continued to be stern calls for careful surveillance of women religious who seemed to circumvent patristic control and find pleasure in worldly goods. In the mid-1580s, Johannes Franciscus de Pavinis, auditor to Pope Paul II, published his treatise *De visitatione episcoporum*, which encouraged church leaders to exhort nuns in being more diligent in their rejection of materialism. He wanted to ensure that nuns neither "violate dress regulations by wearing silk, various furs, or sandals; that they not wear their hair long in a horn-shaped style nor put on striped and multicolored caps" nor "attend dances, take part in secular banquets, and go walking through the streets and towns by day or night" (Makowski 96). Although this prohibition against luxuries was concomitant with traditional ascetic practices following Jesus Christ's anti-materialist tenet, leaders of the Roman Catholic Church in the palatial Vatican did not think it necessary for themselves to have to follow such spartan guidelines. Cavendish mocks such a repudiation of material luxuriousness in *The Convent of Pleasure* when she has Lady Happy, the closet drama's would-be abbess, describe her convent as one where she and her followers will wear the "softest Silk, / And Linnen fine as white as milk / . . . / Thus will in Pleasure's Convent I / Live with delight, and with it die" (221). By bestowing her female enclave with the richest of trappings, Cavendish rejects the papal auditor's double standard[7].

Johannes's warning surely relies on knowledge of nuns partaking in such activities as Cavendish satirizes, but annual visits to convents rarely uncovered flagrant or frequent examples of nuns eschewing expected behavior. In fact, some orders of nuns relished the ability to encloister themselves. For example, the order of the St. Clare Franciscans made the act of living a cloistered life as important as their other vows of obedience, poverty, and chastity: "vivendo in obedientia, sine proprio, et in castitate, sub clausura." Despite the order's strict membership guidelines and their nearly unflagging attention to St. Clare's deathbed rule of absolute poverty for individual members as well as the entire order, the Poor Clares experienced overwhelming popularity across Europe. Convents were established throughout Italy, France, Spain, Belgium, Bohemia, and Spanish America (Poor, par. 5). The fact that the order reached its peak in 1630 with more than nine hundred religious houses and 34,000 members

---

[7] Lino d'Assumpção's *Frades e Freiras: Chroniquetas Monasticas*'s study of the Clarist nuns in Beja, Portugal, provides a glimpse into the sometimes sumptuous religious and secular festivities and entertainments in which these convents engaged to celebrate holidays.

demonstrates the credibility of Isabella's earnest insistence to enjoy fewer privileges and become a Poor Clare in Shakespeare's *Measure for Measure*: "Yes, truly. I speak not as desiring more, / But rather wishing a more strict restraint / Upon the sisterhood, the votarists of Saint Clare" (1.4.3-5).

Another detrimental effect of the Council of Trent's reapplication of *Periculoso* was that it silenced those who challenged the reification of ideas about the fragile nature of nuns' purity and virtue. The council's effect on the cultural radar was to simultaneously banish nuns from appearing in the daily lives of many and augment the public's fascination with the lives of these women who existed inside of and yet apart from society like some *other within*. Manuela Mourao's discussion of literary representations of nuns after the early modern period confirms that the Council of Trent's strict adherence to *Periculoso* engendered an "aura of mystery" around nuns that in effect created the "opportunity for stereotypes to develop. It certainly opened the way for the fictional representation to become the main vehicle for our experience of nuns" (xx).

This House Is Not a Home: The Dissolution of Monasteries in England

To establish the foundation for English representations of Catholicism, convents, and nuns, this section examines how early modern England responded to its political affiliation with Protestantism. Because the history of convents and monasteries in Spain is part and parcel of the larger history of such institutions in Catholic polities, I will focus only on the watershed dissolution of these houses in the British Isles. For more information on Spanish convents and monasteries, see the monographs noted below.[8]

In descending order of importance, the dissolution of religious houses in England during the 1530s was due to politics, economics, the value of lands, the behavior of same-sex religious communities, and religious belief. With 9,300 male and female religious living in England and Wales in 1530, there was about one person religious for every 375 citizens

---

[8] Concha Torres Sanchez's *La clausura femenina del siglo XVII: Dominicas y Carmelitas Descalzas*. Salamanca: Universidad de Salamanca, 1991 and Angela Muñoz Fernández's *Acciones e intenciones de mujeres: vida religiosa de las madrileñas (ss. XV-XVI)*. Madrid: Horas y Horas: Comunidad de Madrid, Direccíon General de la Mujer, 1995.

(Woodward 2). To argue that English citizens thought of clergymen and women religious solely as burdens, nuisances, or Romish intruders would be to discount their importance in the daily lives of English men and women.

The primary purpose for the existence of convents revolved around prayer, praise, and offering Masses for the deceased. Secondary purposes for these eleemosynary convents included education, housing travelers, and healing the sick. Although there is not much evidence to suggest that English religious houses educated children — with the exception of novices and those who meant to become men and women religious as adults — surveys of the religious homes show that they were efficient in offering hospitality to travelers and giving alms to the poor (Woodward 21).

Despite whatever charitable causes the residents of these homes supported, for centuries there existed an anti-clerical tradition that questioned the amount of property owned by the Catholic Church. Simon Fish asserted in his 1529 tract to King Henry VIII, *A Supplication for the Beggars*, that the clergy "haue gotten ynto theyre hondes more then the therd part of all youre Realme" (1). This claim was often repeated by other anti-clerical writers throughout the time period. Thus, the combination of the crown's financial troubles in the 1530s and the rising anti-Catholic sentiment of certain members of the court created a situation that made the religious homes of the Catholic clergy a prime target for financial appropriation. The crown even began to view monastic lands as foreign enclaves on English soil because the "monies paid to their mother houses often looked like subsidies to England's enemies" (McNamara 423).

Usurping the lands of the religious was not a new idea. During King Henry V's war with France, certain homes were dissolved because of their connections with French peers. Even in Spain during the late 1400s, male church leaders dissolved convents if they deemed their size too small. However, since King Henry VIII's version of Protestantism was not as theologically grounded as that of advisers such as Thomas Cromwell, ardent anti-Catholic forces needed to establish good reasons for the dissolution of the monasteries. Following in the footsteps of Catholic Church officials' periodical ecclesiastic visits to each monastery and convent, the crown conducted its own survey of more than one hundred religious homes between 1535 and 1536. The top-down hierarchy and tightly controlled bureaucracy of the project has led historians to assert that the outcome was determined before the survey was conducted: "Their principal task was to gather material for a campaign designed to bring celibacy and relics into disrepute, and the religious orders with them" (Woodward 33).

The closure of the monasteries began by focusing on those houses whose annual income was less than £200. The crown was able to avoid direct confrontation with the more politically powerful large houses by focusing on small abbeys. Publicizing the crown's financial motivations was not the most prudent way of accomplishing the goal of securing more funds. Consequently, charges against the immorality of those who lived in the religious houses needed to be established. Cromwell employed his own men rather than the local gentry to conduct the visitations of the religious homes. Thomas Legh and Richard Layton were two of the men chosen for this endeavor, and the best known authors of the study's final report, *Compendium Compertorum*. Layton betrayed his unwavering loyalty and lack of neutrality in the matter when he wrote to Cromwell asking to be a member of the expedition attesting that no other applicant would be "so trusty, true and faithful . . . doing all things diligently for your purpose" (qtd. in Woodward 60). Coupling the numerous vague, unsealed entries in the report with the fact that Legh and Layton's travels should have resulted in an impossible visit to two religious houses a day, despite the wide and perilous travel required between such visits, casts doubt on the authenticity of all of their entries. The document reported only four cases of serious crimes and sexual irregularities out of 120 visits – comparable to results by periodical ecclesiastic visits – but still called for the dissolution of all monasteries inhabited by monks and nuns. In a telling example of the crown's predetermined conclusion about the survey, the *Compendium Compertorum* had not even been completed when the bill calling for the dissolution of the monasteries was introduced to the "Reformation Parliament" that met between February 4 and April 14, 1536[9].

The report found the larger abbeys to be more often guilty of immorality, a fact that was carefully excised from public readings of the report since the crown wanted to avoid direct confrontation with the prominent political clout of these houses. The preamble to the Suppression Act of 1536 argued for the transfer of sinful male and female religious to larger houses wherein they could be more easily controlled:

> Forasmuch as manifest sin, vicious, carnal and abominable living is daily used and committed amongst the little and small abbeys, priories, and

---

[9]Anthony N. Shaw's 2003 doctoral thesis "The *Compendium Compertorum* and the making of the Suppression Act of 1536" from the University of Warwick offers a stunningly detailed study of this issue.

other religious houses of monks, canons, and nuns . . . so that without such small houses be utterly suppressed, and the religious persons therein committed to great and honourable monasteries of religion in this realm, where they may be compelled to live religiously for reformation of their lives . . . (qtd. in Gee and Hardy 257-58)

Historians have interpreted the relatively quick closure of dozens of monasteries as a sign of the providential nature of the English Reformation's success. Such historians characterize the time period in a manner that argues for a "decay of Catholicism (which must have decayed, because it lost)" and a "growth of popular Protestantism (which must have been popular, because it won)" (Haigh 15). Facts, however, demonstrate that the dissolution was more haphazard and faced more resistance than popularly remembered. Some organized resistance manifested itself in the northern parishes of Yorkshire and Cheshire, although it is still arguable whether priests and monks coerced the lay people into supporting their cause or whether the local parishioners were genuinely inspired to resist the crown's usurpation of the Catholic Church's property. The seizure of so much church property helped fuel the people-powered Pilgrimage of Grace in the fall of 1536. In the short term, the pilgrimage caused the crown to reestablish religious houses and respect for the pope's supremacy.

Francis Aidan Hibbert is one of many recent scholars who have begun to study the dissolution of the monasteries through the lens of regional case studies. Hibbert examines the County of Staffordshire and offers a localized view of the dissolution's effects on one area and comes to the conclusion that "the suppression by Henry VIII and Cromwell was prompted far less by anti-papal necessities than by sheer cupidity, and not at all for moral reasons" (vi). Hibbert's research shows that far from having the wealthiest monasteries in England, Staffordshire had a monastic wealth of some £1,600 in annual net income with respect to property, real estate, and agricultural lands. His case study can be seen as an illustrative example of the suppression of "ordinary religious houses" (8). Staffordshire included a variety of religious orders such as Benedictines, Austins, Cluniacs, Dominicans, Franciscans, and Cistercians. His study is filled with an appendix listing the items appropriated by the crown from the monasteries and convents. Hibbert wisely argues that it "is the exceptional which attracts attention, but it is the ordinary which better represents the truth" (18). Hence, as one reads through the list as it ranges from "one table of alabaster" and "particions of carvyd woode" in the inventory of sales at the Brewood Nunnery (225) to "all the tyle, shingle, tymber, stone, glasse and iron, one marble grave stone, the pavementes of the church, quyer, and chapelles, with rode lofte, the pyctures of Cryst, Mary and John, beyng in the church and chauncell" of the Austin Friars in Stafford (250) we see how rapaciously the crown and its aristocratic supporters appropriated the holdings of the Catholic Church and the places of worship that so many enjoyed for centuries.

In line with Hibbert's work, Nicholas Dogget analyzes the dissolution's effects on the County of Hertfordshire. His case study focuses on monastic lands, particularly buildings, and discusses the reasons listed by the crown for their dissolution. Dogget then details an inventory of monastic property, catalogs their residents, and describes how the lands were appropriated, capitalized, utilized, and oftentimes destroyed by later owners. His study ranges from "the minor adaptation of existing buildings as sites like St Margaret's, Nettleden, and King's Langley to the transformation of monastic buildings into major country houses as at Ashridge and Sopwell" (15). Buildings were converted by Protestants as well as recusant/closeted Catholics. Dogget hypothesizes that Catholics saw "in the re-use of the buildings themselves some continuity with its monastic past" while Protestants regarded the "secularization of the buildings as the triumph of reason and reform over the perceived ignorance superstition of medieval religion" (69).

It was the crown's assault on the cultural accoutrements of the Catholic Church that most angered laymen: "there were attacks on saints' days and pilgrimages . . . and there were royal officers throwing monks and nuns from their houses, paying off their servants, pulling lead from their roofs, and packing up cartloads of valuables for transport to London" (Haigh 143). The crown's hostile actions against the parishioners' familiar clergymen and the royal officers' obvious concern for appropriating valuable items from the churches offended the people who had been raised Catholic and knew not where this Reformation would go, much less what its religious tenets were, since the king himself had yet to articulate them thoroughly. Recent research into Catholic recusants during the English Reformation even singles out entire geographic areas for their adherence to the Old Faith, such as Lancashire, which is noted as an "intensely recusant county" brimming with Catholic architectural heritage and residue to this day (Davidson 35). Mary Erler's case studies of the writings of male and female religious during the dissolution found varying responses to the Reformation. Several former friars, monks, and nuns retired to life with their families and indicated an openness to Reformation theology. Intriguingly enough, Morpheta Kingsmill, Abbess of Wherwell, Hampshire, left bequests in her will to seven of her nuns, which suggest "the existence of a post-dissolution female living community" (Erler 8).

Some nuns seemed to have left willingly, especially when they had a support system in the secular world.

Overall, however, the situation for nuns being evicted was direr than that of monks. Given the dearth of professional and financial opportunities for women, most nuns clamored to join the larger abbeys, which soon became so overcrowded that the smaller houses had to be exempted from being dissolved in order to accommodate the women. As Parliament acted to include more religious houses under its jurisdiction, rumors spread about how to deal with the crown. It soon became clear that surrendering without a fight would make the terms more favorable for the male and female religious involved in negotiations, since the amount of pensions was at the discretion of the crown. The financial aspect of a quick surrender endowed the crown with a "helpful hold over the monks and nuns who did not take long to learn that a ready compliance with the wishes of the crown would be rewarded more generously than stubborn resistance to all persuasions" (Woodward 108). Male and female religious' new-found awareness about the financial interest at stake coincided with the news that they would no longer have the option of continuing their traditional lifestyle, as even the largest of homes were now being appropriated.

It is difficult to ascertain if the clergy's knowledge caused the crown to change their reasoning regarding the continuing dissolution of religious houses. Whereas the original, official agenda of the crown aimed to eradicate the immorality rampant in such houses, by 1538 and 1540 the preambles of numerous deeds of surrender "spoke of the earnest desire of the religious to be released from a life of idleness and superstition" – a clear attack on the founding philosophy of monastic life (Woodward 108). Historians have also noted that the Reformation Acts of the 1530s served as the impetus for many English intellectuals and religious to flee for the Low Countries. Erler argues that it was the writings of exiles during the ascension of Queen Elizabeth that "made the exchange [of controversial writings] between England and the continent somewhat more visible" (107). Again and again we see evidence that English Catholics did not simply reform overnight or even over the course of decades.

By March 1540 the religious orders were virtually extinct in England and Wales. Thousands of monks lived off comfortable pensions as they became secular clergy, worked within the newly founded Anglican Church, or entered other fields. Nuns did not fare as well since their pensions were usually paltry compared to that given to men, and they could not enjoy an equal level of involvement within the Anglican Church. Some were forced to return to their families, while others married so as to remain financially secure. Nonetheless, a small group of male and female religious, noted for their exceptionality more than for their representativeness, determined to live the common life with each other, such as the monks of Bretton, near Barnsley, and the nuns from Kirklees, a nunnery in the Calder valley (Woodward 153-54). These discrete groups combined their small assets and libraries to continue a religious and contemplative life. Unable to attract new postulants, these communities soon disintegrated with the death of their members.[10]

This gradual, piecemeal dissolution of the English and Welsh monasteries during the 1530s demonstrates that the transition to Protestantism was not as fluid as academic surveys of the period claim. Although many male and female religious slid into their new lives without much protest, the scarcity of written records from the time period raises questions about the number of clergy that genuinely wanted to leave the religious environment they now shamefully confessed to consisting of "dumb ceremonies, wearing of a grey coat, disguising ourself after strange fashions, and other like papistical ceremonies" (Woodward 119).

Haigh asserts that "those who lived in Tudor England experienced Reformation as obedience rather than conversion; they obeyed a monarch's new laws rather than swallowed a preacher's new message" (21). This claim is supported by events such as the Pilgrimage of Grace and the acknowledgment that monks and nuns did not freely abandon their profession because of differences with the Catholic Church. Rather, most English citizens went along with the reformations of the time period as a pragmatic matter. In fact, King Henry VIII's own resistance to some of Cromwell's more radical ideas reflects the English people's comfort with Catholicism even when they did not agree with all of its tenets and its political involvement with the English nation-state. After all, King Henry VIII wrote "Affirmation of the Seven Sacraments" in 1521 to rebut Luther's doctrines, which led to Pope Leo X conferring the king with the title "Defender of the Faith."

From a Catholic perspective, England's loss was the Continent's gain. In the 1560s Spain's King Phillip II created and supported a Catholic

---

[10] See Amy M. Froide's "The Religious Lives of Singlewomen in the Anglo-Atlantic World: Quaker Missionaries, Protestant Nuns, and Covert Catholics" in *Women, Religion, and the Atlantic World (1600–1800)*, edited by Daniella Kostroun and Lisa Vollendorf, Toronto: University of Toronto Press, 2009: 60–78, for more information of covert Catholic nunneries and the attempts of Protestant women to establish a religious community for retired single women.

seminary in Douay, which was then part of the Spanish Empire's dominion in the Netherlands, that attracted many English Catholics. The English College at Douay led to the publication of the influential Douay-Rhemis Bible, an English translation of the Latin Vulgate. The success of this institution inspired the creation of similar ones in Rome, Valladolid, Sevilla, and Lisboa that attracted Catholic dissidents from England and other principilaties that had become overwhelmingly Protestant and hostile to Catholics. Father William Newman wrote to Spain's King Phillip IV in 1621 and cited Douay as a model for the English seminary in Lisboa, the intention of which was to "formar sacerdotes que possam pregar a santa fé católica aos heres ingleses" ["form priests that can preach the holy Catholic faith to the English heretics"] (Homem 30)[11].

Accordingly, Robert Persons, a British priest at the English College in Valladolid, Spain, described in a 1592 letter to a fellow countryman that the students at his college would dedicate a portion of each afternoon in the church praying for England's need: "Luego despues desto vienen todos à la yglesia, donde se dizen unas letanias de nustra Señora por las necessidades de Inglaterra" ["After this they all go to church, where they say some litanies to our Mother for England's needs"] (24). Likewise, once a week they "hallan todos por dos horas a unas disputas, o conclusiones de controversias contra los hereges, principlamente contra los q aora ay en Inglaterra" ["gather together for two hours for debates, or conclusions about controversies against the heretics, principally against those that are now in England"] (26). Upon completion of their studies, the majority of students returned to England to minister to Catholic recusants and attempt to bring others into the Catholic fold: "se partan a Inglaterra a ayudar à la conversion de aquellas almas, hasta dar la vida en la demanda" ["they depart for England to help in the conversion of those souls, even to give their life if so demanded"] (78).

---

[11] The college received funds from the Portuguese crown under King John IV at the same time that his daughter, Catarina de Bragança, was wedded to England's King Charles II. What was affectionately called the Convento Dos Inglesinhos by Lisboans trained priests until 1973, well after Catholicism was once again freely practiced in England.

The Council of Trent

Facing powerful charges of corruption, ineptitude, and a failure to live up to its core religious beliefs, the Roman Catholic Church responded to the exponential growth of the Protestant Reformation by designing an organized Counter-Reformation with the Council of Trent. The importance of this nineteenth ecumenical council can be gleaned from the fact that it met for eighteen years, from 1545 to 1563, more than a decade longer than any other council. Pope Paul III oversaw the first phase of the Council of Trent and established its goals as defining Catholic doctrine, correcting the morality of the clergy and laity, restoring ecumenical peace within Christianity, and fighting infidels. By the time the council was adjourned in 1563, it had been overseen by five different popes and had issued dozens of decrees throughout its twenty-five sessions.

Jo Ann Kay McNamara, a historian of Catholic nuns, argues that the council "hastily" issued its decree regarding nuns and enclosure during its final meeting on December 3, 1563 (461). Compared to lengthier chapters dedicated to clarifying church doctrine on the veneration of relics and saints and the use of sacred books, the fifth chapter of the twenty-fifth session's published decrees tersely renews the rules of *Periculoso* without discussing the necessity for the strict enclosure of nuns. The language strongly rebukes critics of the enclosure of nuns and even calls for secular interference to ensure that the rule is carried out:

> The holy Synod . . . enjoins on all bishops . . . that the enclosure of nuns be carefully restored, wheresoever it has been violated, and that it be preserved, wheresoever it has not been violated; repressing, by ecclesiastical censures and other penalties, without regarding any appeal whatsoever, the disobedient and gainsayers, and calling in for this end, if need be, the aid of the Secular arm. (Waterworth 240)

Although the enforcement of the Council of Trent's decrees on the local level usually took a few generations to take full effect by way of papal nuncios forwarding the new rules, by 1566 Pope Pius V, who never oversaw the council during its different phases, "ruled that the law applied to all professed nuns . . . those who had not taken solemn vows were instructed to do so or have their communities closed" (McNamara 461).

The renewed call for the physical closure of communities of women religious continued the atmosphere of seclusion and isolation that permeated the ideology of conventual life. The Council of Trent simply rehashed *Periculoso*'s argument about the need to protect weak nuns by calling for the forced displacement of nuns in rural areas where they "are exposed, often without any protection, to the robberies and other crimes of wicked men" to safer, more urban areas (Waterworth 240). As such, the Catholic Church patriarchy reinforced the idea that whereas chastity and seclusion were beneficial for clergymen, they were indispensable to the spiritual progress of nuns' lives.

Building a Mystery: The Symbolic Significance of Nuns

Despite whatever original enjoyment women may have felt about their ability to lead more spiritually and intellectually fruitful lives inside a monastery, the increasingly negligible amount of power they possessed within the Catholic Church rendered them passive and subject to the seemingly infallible rules enacted by patristic decrees. As the symbolic importance of the virginal female body that acquired ascetically-derived spiritual significance became gradually transformed into a more rigid interpretation of female subjectivity, nuns were pressured to renounce and repress awareness of their corporal agency. This construction engendered an "inherently misogynist ideal that intended to essentialize the female body and cast it as the locus of society's redemption from sin" (Kirk 4).

This rejection of the female body's agency reached an apex in a guidebook written for nuns in New Spain by the Jesuit priest Antonio Núñez de Miranda in the mid-seventeenth century. The book extends conventional arguments about nuns giving their bodies to God, exaggerating the Baroque fascination with the figurative construction of nuns' bodies as dead, to render them as the "ultimate docile bodies—dead bodies—unable to contaminate and infect" the bodies of other nuns "with their propensity to sin" (Kirk 44).

As can be garnered from the sometimes violent ideologies that patristic writers employed to describe nuns, progressive scholars should not rejoice in the opportunities afforded to nuns in their enclosed, single-sex communities without considering the pressures and restrictions church leaders placed on female convents during the early modern period. Nonetheless, we must acknowledge that the potential for nearly unfettered feminine power in the convent was a tantalizing and promising prospect for thousands of women who sought to circumvent the patriarchy at any costs – even if it meant near continual regulation from male church figures. These women were willing to accept the sometimes spartan aesthetics and dogmatic asceticism that a nun's life required. Theodora Jankowski argues that a nun was able to usurp the power and identity of a man by taking masculine privilege into her own hands and "embracing power and life choices that were traditionally restricted to men" thanks to her ability to resist childbearing and "choosing not to let her body be used as a *woman's* body" (64). Thus "the virgin nun or abbess was, for all intents and purposes, perceived as a 'man' who assumed powers usually reserved for" patristic leaders (Jankowski 64).

The idealization of convent life transcended religious divisions among branches of Christianity. As King Henry VIII's version of Protestantism gradually inculcated itself in English life, some nuns chose to convert to Protestantism rather than give up their life as a community of women religious. Even facing usurpation of their property rights, they could continue their life as women unattached to the heterosexual economy: "Many nuns . . . placed their communal life above their theological commitments. The abbess of Godstow hoped to save her community from Henry VIII's attack when she wrote that they did not respect pope or purgatory, did not pray to images, did not go on pilgrimage, and did not praise dead saints" (McNamara 421). By clinging to their status as women apart from those without professed vows, nuns used their spiritual status as pure women to espouse feminist rhetoric that combined their spirituality with a Marxist-like rejection of materialism.

The most illustrative example of such anti-materialist sentiment can be found in Sor Juana's sonnet "In my pursuit, World," in which she employs her status as a nun who has taken a vow of poverty to criticize not only the objectification of women, "I worship beauty not, but vilify / that spoil of time that mocks eternity," but also the materialistic obsessions of moneyed women who use their financial power to improve their physical appearance to please men, "I have no love of riches or finánce / and thus do I most happily, I find, / expend finances to enrich my mind / and not mind expend upon finánce" (171). Fictional nuns follow philosophies similar to that of Sor Juana by uniting messages about humility and the importance of spiritual richness over material wealth with their desire to be nuns. Illustratively, Isabella wishes to follow strict orders in *Measure for Measure*, and Lady Happy in *The Convent of Pleasure* announces that she will sponsor all the women "whose Births are greater then [sic] their Fortunes" that her "Estate can plentifully maintain" (Cavendish 220).

Each of the authors discussed in this book is aware of both the advantages and drawbacks of life within the convent. Nevertheless, since each of them demonstrates cognizance of the limited opportunities for women in both Protestant and Catholic nations alike, each author focuses on how the convent affords women the chance to live lives more similar to their own with educational opportunities and the freedom to think, meditate, and write without the burden of childrearing and spousal duties. With a room of her own, each nun could choose whether to devote her life to religious piety (*vita contemplativa*), or to action (*vita activa*): she could critique the patriarchy simply by withdrawing from it, or she could take up the pen and use her status as a virtuous woman to express feminist concerns to a world that all too often relegated her to the role of Eve's mischievous daughter.

The following section previews the book's remaining chapters and the way in which I examine literary texts through the lenses of New Historicism, Feminism, Queer Theory, and religious studies to argue for the importance of considering nuns in the literature of the early modern period.

William Shakespeare's *Measure for Measure*

The central figure of William Shakespeare's *Measure for Measure* is Isabella, a would-be nun of the Order of Saint Clare who must delay her novitiate when her brother has been sentenced to death. His crime? Premarital sex with his girlfriend. Who better than the innocent Isabella to save his life? This is the thinking when she is summoned to plea on his behalf to Angelo, a stand-in for the Duke of Vienna. Shakespeare ingeniously transforms his source material, George Whetstone's 1578 *Promos and Cassandra*, by having Isabella, who despite not yet being a professed nun is viewed by the audience as an austere nun, serve as the catalyst for a discussion of sexual ethics and the dichotomy between justice and mercy. Angelo demands that Isabella sleep with him in order to spare her brother's life. Shakespeare cleverly renovates Whetstone's Cassandra into the ultimate avatar for female purity – a nun. Isabella's insistent denials only further excite Angelo. As the complexities of the drama's rising action unfold, readers are given the opportunity to consider how the Catholic Church's religious vocations for women challenged early modern Protestant ideals of womanhood. For a Jacobean audience still anxious about King James I's commitment to a Protestant England, Isabella's presence helps this "problem play" question conventional ideas about the supposed freedoms followers of Protestantism enjoyed and the alleged oppression Catholics suffered.

By studying dynamics between the sexes and gendered power structures in early modern England, this chapter examines how ideas about nuns invite the play's characters and audience to consider Isabella's dialogue and actions as representative of the queer female agency that Catholicism, ironically, affords Isabella as she challenges conventional notions about female identity and patriarchal prerogative. Isabella's decision to reject traditional family structures and expectations that she become a wife and a mother positions her as someone who challenges heteronormativity. Isabella's desire to take a vow of chastity marks her as asexual. She denies her sexual reproductive abilities, and she distances herself from women who follow a path of reproductive futurity. Doing so renders her as non-heterosexual or asexual; if we see acts constituting identities, however anachronistic some critics may deem such labeling, Isabella thus fits within Judith Halberstam's inclusive reclamation of "queer"[12] as a term befitting those who reject mainstream culture through sexual practices, or, in this instance, lack thereof.

Margaret Cavendish's *The Convent of Pleasure*

This chapter examines how Margaret Cavendish's aristocratic status and the closing of public theaters during the Interregnum enabled her to skillfully create fictional realms rooted in the sociopolitical realities of her time. In *The Convent of Pleasure*, Cavendish does this by employing the convent as a spatial location for women to safely retreat into a same-sex community and simultaneously support and challenge the sanctity and effectiveness of such religious enclaves.

Cavendish is careful to not make her convent a Christian one – either Catholic or Protestant – with its various references to "gods" and paying tribute to "Nature." But the very nature of the convent – its inhabitants and architectural space – cannot help but evoke images of Catholic convents in the minds of readers. Cavendish subversively makes political use of this imagery to destabilize ideas about heteronormativity, secluded religious life, and gender roles. I use Cavendish's audacious protagonist, Lady Happy, to examine issues of English nostalgia for Catholic opportunities for women and to examine how Cavendish negotiates female agency via a same-sex community in opposition to the patriarchal extra-conventual world. After all, the Protestant emphasis on marriage as the ultimate institution for women estranged English women from their Catholic counterparts who lived in a culture that valued the virginal nun as being purer and more ideal than the married woman. Cavendish's appropriation of the convent is both a nostalgic device and an exploration of the freedom women could enjoy, albeit rather limited, in Catholic nations.

Cavendish's employment of the convent as a setting in her play offers an entertaining comparison to more traditional narratives about religious

---

[12] Halberstam, Judith. *In a Queer Time and Place: Transgender Bodies, Subcultural Lives*. New York: New York University Press, 2005.

homes because of the way she subverts readers' expectations. While Cavendish indulges in the ascetic empowerment of nuns in *The Convent of Pleasure*, she rejects the austere accommodations and lifestyle of the monastery. Cavendish's fascination with this Catholic architecture is in line with recent developments in sociology and gender studies as the fields recognize how social meanings are attached to places so that feminist geographers can elaborate on the "diversity and solidarity of sisterhood" (Williams 31). Such a recognition and analysis cannot be riper than in the all-female community that is a convent, particularly when Cavendish employs it to explore same-sex romantic desire[13].

María de Zayas's *Desengaños amorosos*

With María de Zayas's *Desengaños amorosos*, I look at the use of the *sarao* as a convent-like rhetorical space that engenders the free discussion of women's issues. I examine these disenchantments through close readings and a sociohistorical context that pays attention to the influence of Alfonso the Wise's *Siete Partidas*, popular conceptions of infamy and man's honor, and the power of women's gossip in Golden Age Spain. I emphasize how Zayas exposes the hypocrisies of a patriarchal society by creating a discursive community of women's voices that functions like a convent. Zayas employs the nun as a literary trope for a critical examination of gendered power structures and engaging in a *querelle des femmes* discussion that rejects all forms of domestic abuse by including characters both in the novellas and in the frame narrative that circumvent their role in the sexual economy by retiring to a convent.

The frame narrative's female storytellers and protagonists entertain the noble men and women gathered at a three-night long *sarao* celebrating Lisis's betrothal to Diego. The co-ed gathering enables each of the collection's stories to function on a metafictional level that makes readers feel as if they are one of the nobles gathered at Lisis's home. Because each of the tales in the frame narrative is supposed to disenchant women about men's falsehoods, Zayas's feminism takes a markedly strident tone against men. Women are routinely neglected, abused, raped, and/or murdered in these tales. Out of the collection's ten stories, six conclude with the

---

[13] An earlier, condensed version of this chapter was published as "Convents as Feminist Utopias: Margaret Cavendish's *The Convent of Pleasure* and the Potential of Closeted Dramas and Communities" in *Women's Studies: An Interdisciplinary Journal*. 38.6 (2009): 647-69.

woman dying and in the other four stories women seek refuge in a convent – sometimes to become a nun and sometimes with other friends or family members that follow them.

This chapter revolves around the four stories that end with the protagonists entering the convent. Each tale offers unique reasons for women's need to abandon the secular world in favor of a same-sex, religious community. Although some women are widows, the majority are virgins or women who are raped. The convent's status as a place of refuge for these women dovetails with Zayas's interpretation of the convent as a place that allows women to circumvent the patriarchy and its burdens. Although Zayas's stories do not detail the lives of nuns in the convents, the idea of the convent and the power of the nun as a singularly independent woman serve as poignant symbols of female empowerment throughout the collection's stories.

Sor Juana's Life and Literature

If Shakespeare's Isabella, Cavendish's Lady Happy, and Zayas's various protagonists sought the all-female convent as a refuge from the world of male rule and female submission, what could a real nun accomplish within the confines of a convent? Sor Juana Inés de la Cruz's prolific writings offer readers the best opportunity for understanding how a nun could exploit her status as a woman confined and ostensibly governed by male church leaders by using Virginia Woolf's coveted spatial possession – a room of one's own. Nuns who were authors, such as Sor Juana, effectively employed their spatial freedom to create a lifestyle that engendered broad intellectual, spiritual, and cultural horizons for learned woman with no other place or means to exert control over their artistic development.

This chapter analyzes Sor Juana's unparalleled literary skills by elucidating the poetic style in which she was able to express disillusionment with the patriarchy and espouse bold feminist rhetoric while simultaneously living up to the expectations of her religious profession. By thoughtfully reading texts such as the poem "Hombres necios" ("Misguided men"), her famous letter "Respuesta a Sor Filotea" ("The Reply to Sor Filotea"), and her comedic drama *Los empeños de una casa* (*The Trials of a Noble House*) within the context of Sor Juana's life and cultural milieu, I argue that Sor Juana's writing positions her as a hybrid figure – pious nun *and* worldly feminist. Sor Juana amalgamated the secular and spiritual in well-crafted *belles lettres* literature that articulated both the traditional teachings of Christ and feminist rhetoric in laymen's terms. Sor Juana accomplishes this feat by also utilizing her status as a nun to defend herself against the very criticism that she faces for being both a writing-woman and a writing-nun.

Catalina de Erauso's *La monja alférez* and Aphra Behn's *History of the Nun*

This chapter offers a comparative look at representations of nuns in Catalina de Erauso's *La monja alférez* and Aphra Behn's *History of the Nun* to examine how two authors from opposite ends of the Iberian-Anglo divide employ imaginative literature to portray women who entered convents at young ages and left them by their own volition. I analyze how each author's construction of the life religious and retirement from such a life is informed by the discourse surrounding these figures and settings in the Catholic-Protestant literary landscape. Such an examination augments our understanding of the choices real-life nuns made when joining or leaving a convent as it relates to portrayals of their lives in popular literature.

La monja alférez begins with Catalina plotting to leave the community of nuns. Despite the narrative's brief glimpse into her life in the convent, Catalina's role as a former "nun" is integral to not only the novelty of the autobiography but also her travels, adventures, and the respect she earns from the public, the crown, and the Papacy. Her ties with the religious community are paradoxically tenable and tenuous. At one point she even tells the archbishop of New Granada that she has neither "orden ni religión" ["neither order nor religion"]. Yet her upbringing as a novitiate, her vouched-for virginity, and the care given to her by the nuns of Guamanga enable her to negotiate transcontinental voyages with her honor unscathed.

Behn's protagonist, Isabella, wrestles with her attractions for a man soon after she has taken her vows. She eventually elopes with him. Although the tale is fraught with melodramatic events that serve as precursors to today's romance novels, Behn offers a complex rendering of Isabella that belies the story's allegedly moralist ending. Is Isabella punished for breaking her vows and leaving the convent? Is she rendered morally weak and a murderous sociopath by the Church's sexist views of women? The answers are far from concrete.

Both women feel constrained by the vows of conventual and heteronormative married life. Whereas the convent is the safe and consistent space of their youth, their extraconventual life is wrought with strife and uncertainty. This chapter comparatively deconstructs how the stories of these two nuns, as portrayed in imaginative literature, reflect, respond, and inform early modern ideas about nuns in respect to the advantages and pitfalls of extracoventual life along the Catholic-Protestant socio-religious spectrum.

Chapter Two

Reclaiming Isabella, the Queer Virgin: Celebrating Catholicism's Opportunities in *Measure for Measure*

Isabella's role as a novice nun in William Shakespeare's *Measure for Measure* presents readers with an opportunity to consider how the Catholic Church's religious vocations for women challenged early modern Protestant ideals of womanhood. For a Jacobean society anxious about King James I's commitment to a Protestant England, Isabella's presence helps this "problem play" question conventional ideas about the supposed freedoms followers of Protestantism enjoyed and the alleged oppression Catholics suffered at the hands of their respective ecclesiastical institutions. Because of their status as embodied icons of the Catholic Church, nuns help elucidate how secular characters, as well as the drama's audience, can respond to opposing religious discourse.

The main analytic drive of this chapter uses the figure of the nun as a catalyst for shifting the attention of the play's contemporary readers to the theoretical dynamics between the sexes and gendered power structures in early modern England. As such, I examine how epistemologies about nuns invite the play's characters and audience to consider Isabella's dialogue and actions as representative of the queer female agency that Catholicism affords her as she challenges conventional notions about female identity and patriarchal prerogative. I do not argue that Isabella is queer in the sexual sense, but in the post-millennial, deconstructive sense. Judith Halberstam considers "queerness as an outcome of strange temporalities, imaginative life schedules, and eccentric economic practices" (1) and queer time as "a life unscripted by the conventions of family, inheritance, and child rearing" (2). In a similarly helpful postmodern vein, bell hooks argues that self-sufficiency stems from "alternative lifestyles which will run counter to the image of the good life" presented to us by the patriarchy (52). If we keep such purposely provocative theoretical lenses in place, we can see that Isabella's decision to reject becoming a wife and a mother allows her to create an identity for herself as someone who opts out of heteronormativity within a self-sufficient, all-female community. Likewise, a nun's anti-capitalist vow of poverty placed her as an outlier in an early modern world that was becoming increasingly commercialized.

The significance of Isabella's profession cannot be fully appreciated without considering Shakespeare's source for *Measure for Measure*. Shakespeare's source material for this play was George Whetstone's 1578 two-part comedy *Promos and Cassandra*, which itself is a reworking of Giraldi Cinthio's 1565 Boccaccio-like collection of tales *Hecatommithi*. The female protagonists in both works, Cassandra in the former and Epitia in the latter, are not nuns. Although both women initially refuse the indecent proposal from a hypocritical male official, the brothers eventually persuade them to sleep with the blackmailer. In both cases the official still sentences the brother to death even after the women have slept with these duplicitous men.

Whetstone's Cassandra pleads with the official, Promos, with as much earnestness as Isabella does with Angelo about the need for leniency in judgment: "Your glorie will be much the more, in showing him mercie. / The world wil think, how if you do, but grant him grace on cause, / And where cause is, there mercy should abate the force of lawes" (3.2.23-25). Unswayed by her argument, Promos gives her his ultimatum. Like Isabella, when Cassandra meets with her brother and they discuss the two evils she faces, fornication or death, she chooses the latter. Her brother attempts to convince her to sacrifice her chastity through an abstract theory that excuses her act because its sinfulness will be transmuted: "Nay Cassandra, if thou they selfe submyt, / To save my life . . . / Justice will say, thou dost no cryme commit: / For in forct faultes is no intent of yll" (3.4.35-38). Cassandra then responds with a tamer version of Isabella's incredulity and argues about "envious tongues" and the value of her "fame" (3.4.42-43).

In terms of diction, poetry, and rhetorical flourishes, Shakespeare's reinterpretation of the story represents a watershed in the development of English drama. Furthermore, his revised version of Cassandra, a would-be nun of the Order of Saint Clare, imbues *Measure for Measure* with complex ideologies that revolve around religion, women's agency, and men's desires to control women's sexuality. Shakespeare designs Isabella as an evolved version of Cassandra to validate the claims of women who decried the authority of patriarchal leaders who monitored and demarcated their sexual liberty. Isabella's decision to become a nun makes her resistance all the more authoritative because her rebellion is founded upon religious dogma. Angelo, Claudio, and Duke Vincentio cannot dismiss Isabella's agency as easily as Promos can ignore Cassandra's because

Isabella possesses unique qualities for an early modern woman due to her novitiate status: she is learned, she has the protection of the Catholic Church, and she wants to wed Jesus Christ.

Isabella's Catholicism and Queer Virginity

Isabella's status as a would-be novice provides the play's audience with credible reasons to understand her decision to not sleep with and/or marry Angelo. Hence, despite *Measure for Measure*'s thematic concerns for a discourse about the dichotomies between justice and mercy, the play's structure would lack its ideologically engaging plot without Isabella's sanctified body and her reluctance to sexually employ it to save Claudio's life. As such, each character values Isabella's virginity differently – from Isabella's self-assessed priceless evaluation to Angelo's and Claudio's get-out-of-jail-free rating. Angelo revels in the surprise he experiences being attracted to Isabella's chasteness rather than to a woman who tempts men with seductive dress and flirtatious talk: "Can it be / That modesty may more betray our sense / Than woman's lightness?" (2.3.174-76). He would not be as vexed with the equally beautiful but more easily marriageable Cassandra or Epitia. Claudio ultimately tries to exploit his control over his sister to appropriate her attractive body and virtuous state when he realizes that his life is at stake with his Hamlet-light speech on mortality, "Ay, but to die, and go we know not where" (3.1.119). Duke Vincentio wants to wed Isabella for her "lovely sake" (5.1.489), implying that their marriage would benefit her more than joining a convent. He wishes for Isabella to conjoin herself with him, "What's mine is yours, and what is yours is mine" (5.1.535), which could sound intoxicatingly attractive given the inequitable distribution of power between a duke and a female citizen.

Each of these men has different reasons for wanting to control Isabella – sexual, personal, and political – but they all use Isabella's gender and virginity as catalysts for personal goals. Living up to the framework of Stephen Greenblatt's notion of the creative powers of Renaissance self-fashioning, Isabella is imbued with subtle and explicit motivations for maintaining her virginity that endear her to the audience and highlight the play's celebration of Catholicism's abilities, however limited, to bestow on women the power to chart their own path. Greenblatt's classic argument that the creative powers of early modern self-fashioning were due to the period's "change in the intellectual, social, psychological, and aesthetic structures that govern the generation of identities" (1) is poignant when analyzing the drama's heroine. Isabella's ability to carve out her own identity during the early modern period is peculiar because she employs a pre-modern institution, the Catholic Church, to help fashion her persona in direct opposition to the early modern trend of people having "less *autonomy* in self-fashioning" with "family, state, and religious institutions impos[ing] a more rigid and far-reaching discipline upon their middle-class and aristocratic subjects" (Greenblatt 1). Ironically enough, the same religious institution that provided women with the most opportunities outside of marriage faced brutal opposition during the Renaissance thanks to the early modern period's quest for unfettered intellectual inquiry. This analysis of Isabella highlights how *Measure for Measure* exploits the subversively conservative profession of nuns to champion women's agency and to express Catholic sympathies in the literary landscape of an officially Protestant England.

Again, following Greenblatt's discussion of Renaissance self-fashioning and the hypothesis that "self-fashioning occurs at the point of encounter between an authority and an alien" (9), these discrete autopsies of Isabella's relationships with different men, Angelo, Claudio, and Duke Vincentio, mark her as an alien and them as authority figures. The most prominent figure Isabella deals and clashes with is Angelo. Thus, this chapter often deals with the dichotomous views Isabella and Angelo hold about Isabella's identity in the larger realm of *Measure for Measure*'s exploration of the bonds and gaps between mercy and justice.

Although Isabella is introduced to the audience as a would-be nun enquiring about the strictures of convent life, Angelo can conceive of her only as a marketable sexual object. Just as there is nothing new about men fetishizing the sexual unavailability of nuns, it still stands to be said that this is not a condoned desire. Angelo offers a quasi-blazon that celebrates Isabella's beauty after meeting her for the first time in his desire to ". . . hear her speak again / And feast upon her eyes" (2.2.185-86). Most traditional productions of the play feature Isabella dressed in a nun's habit or some other severe, conservative outfit. Nonetheless, she is still physically beautiful and has not gone so far as to disfigure her physical features to render herself unattractive to sexual advances. However, one of Isabella's literary chaste cousins does prefer physical deformation to being sexually defiled by a male aggressor: Celia in Ben Jonson's nearly contemporaneous problem comedy, 1605's *Volpone*. Rejecting the lecherous Volpone's advances, Celia asks him to make her look unappealing so that he won't be tempted to rape her:

> . . . Flay my face
> Or poison it with ointments for seducing
> Your blood to this rebellion. Rub these hands

> With what may cause an eating leprosy
> E'en to my bones and marrow—anything
> That may disfavor me, save in my honor—
> And I will kneel to you, pray for you, pay down
> A thousand hourly vows, sir, for your health.
> (3.8.251-58)

Although Celia is married, she is being whored by her husband Corvino. Corvino's treatment of his wife as property attests to how real and valid Isabella's fears are about marriage. Furthermore, Celia's allusions to nun-like activities in her offer to make "hourly vows" creates the religious imagery of a nun enacting the spiritual practice of praying for the living and forgiving offenses, such as Volpone's attempted rape. Shakespeare's protagonist does the same when Isabella acquiesces to Mariana's request that she entreat the Duke to null the sentence of execution he has just put on Angelo: "Sweet Isabel, take my part! / Lend me your knees . . ." (5.1.426-27).

Despite Celia's plea for physical disfigurement, Isabella's control over her own sexuality does not require such extreme measures. However, she soon finds out that outside of a convent's walls she cannot assure that others will respect her virtue. At the end of the play, Isabella mercifully agrees that Angelo's passions were inflamed by seeing her when she benevolently pleaded for his life to the Duke, "I partly think / A due sincerity governed his deeds, / 'Till he did look on me" (5.1.441-43). Because this problem play provocatively leaves so many character and plot developments unresolved, there is a dissonance between Isabella's work on behalf of Angelo and her former resistance to his entreaties since they always revolve around what she sought to escape in the secular world: the virgin/whore complex. Richard Wheeler's reading of the play buttresses Isabella's cognizance of this dichotomy by discussing Angelo's Oedipal anxieties: "Angelo's ideal of feminine purity and his equation of sexuality with evil originate together; they are polarized derivatives of the preoedipal union of infantile sexual desire and tender regard" (96). As Wheeler illustrates, Angelo's perception of Isabella is warped with an immature paradoxical appreciation for and desire to soil her purity. Angelo is turned on by the illicitness of being attracted to someone who would repudiate these unbecoming desires. The more she protests, the more he implores.

In contrast, in *Volpone* Corvino is not anxious about being cuckolded or his wife's sexual libidinousness. He is ostensibly angry at Celia for throwing her handkerchief out the window at Scoto Mantua (Volpone incognito) and acting like a "whore" (2.5.26) similar to the loose serving wench "Franciscina" of Italian commedia dell'arte fame (2.3.4). However, when Corvino pimps his wife his true fears are revealed: he wants to be the one in control of his wife and her sexuality. Even if it means cuckolding himself, Corvino wants to assert his ownership by trading Celia's sexuality for Volpone's inheritance. The issue is property. In contrast, however much Angelo is criticized for his hypocrisy, lecherousness, and abuse of power, he does not take Isabella against her force – technically. Despite whatever pressures he knows he is exerting on her, Angelo seeks Isabella's consent. Although both Whetstone's and Cinthio's versions of this plot also have the male aggressor seeking the woman's consent, Shakespeare's unique depiction of Isabella as a nun complicates Angelo's explcitive tendencies. After all, medieval and early modern laws regarding rape in England treated the violation as "a crime against property and a threat to the class structure and thus very much 'between men'" making "little distinction between rape (equated with defloration) on the one hand, and abduction and elopement on the other" (Baines 72). As a nun and bride of Christ, Isabella would be God's property. Tellingly, Angelo continually seeks Isabella's assent in order to avoid committing a crime "between men," himself and God, rather than just against a woman. Angelo's coup would bolster his masculine prowess by being able to seduce her out of her impending marriage to Christ.

A close examination of Isabella's dialogue with Angelo allows us to see her as a woman who constantly exerts her agency by maintaining control of her body and planning to rejoin her would-be sisters in the convent. Critics who describe Isabella as cold and uncaring often cite Isabella's stern rejection of Angelo's proposals. In this uncompromising rejection of Angelo's lecherous advances, Isabella's allusions to the extreme methods of self-flagellation enacted by some clerical men and women allow the audience to view her as one of the storied Catholic extremists derided in polemical Protestant literature: "Th' impression of keen whips I'd wear as rubies, / And strip myself to death as to a bed / That longing have been sick for, ere I'd yield / My body up to shame" (2.4.101-04). Isabella's speech reflects a masochistic delight in her repudiation of a sexual affair with Angelo. The masochistic pleasures that Isabella would derive from the actual flagellation mark her as an insider only in a spiritual, Catholic realm. Her ability to derive pleasure within the walls of a convent, however painfully, presents her as woman outside the limiting, dichotomous Protestant discourse of wife/whore for English women. Whether one sees her as a single woman or a Bride of Christ, Isabella queerly finds her pleasure away from worldly men.

Shakespeare juxtaposes Isabella's masochistic pleasure with Angelo's sadistic tendencies through Angelo's callous and condescending dialogue with Isabella, particularly when he orders Isabella to put "on the destined livery" (2.4.139). This line offers us two examples of Angelo's cruelty as well as two reasons for understanding the logical motivation behind Isabella's repudiation of his immoral proposals. First, the line chides Isabella for not being womanly enough, for the "destined livery" can be interpreted as the innate frailty of women that Angelo wishes Isabella to assume. Angelo's reference to weak women is a distortion of Isabella's former talk about "soft" women who are "credulous to false prints" (2.4.131). These women are not like the incredulous Isabella, for she has invoked Heaven's help by entering a convent to avoid men manipulating her and "profiting" (2.4.129) off her body. Angelo wants Isabella to be like these "frail" women, but his inability to comprehend Isabella's implied contrast between her and other women provides her with more ammunition to resist his demands. Secondly, Angelo's demand that Isabella wear her "destined livery" implies the popular sixteenth- and seventeenth-century definition of "livery" as a "distinctive uniform style of dress worn by a person's servants" according to the Oxford English Dictionary (OED). Again, we see Angelo trying to leave his physical mark on Isabella. Not only would he destroy her maidenhead, but he would also leave her as one marked by his sexual and political power. Isabella's desire to maintain her virginity cannot allow such a mark to stain her virtue.

Despite all the textual evidence that lays the groundwork for seeing Isabella as a heroic figure who resists becoming signified as yet another whore by several men's desires, many critics have taken Isabella's refusal as a selfish and rigid stubbornness. Stacy Magedanz argues that Isabella's "love of her virtue becomes a kind of self-love that cancels out compassion for Claudio" (322). Likewise, Barbara Tovey asserts that "Isabella cannot comprehend that there may be exceptions to the commandment prohibiting fornication. Her fundamental misconception of the nature of morality is the ultimate cause of her moral collapse" (72). Even Carolyn Brown, who attempts to "reconcile the paradoxes in Isabella's character and unravel some of the perplexities that have accorded *Measure for Measure* the status of 'problem' play and Isabella the designation of dramatic failure" (68), asserts that Isabella believes in "punishing adultery or fornication with death and denouncing sexual sinning as more horrible than homicide" (68). Wheeler harshly refers to Isabella's decision to join a "religious sisterhood that institutionalizes the familial taboo on sexuality" as "an infantile resolution of the oedipal situation" (112). Besides utilizing an anachronistic value system, these critics also seem to demonize Isabella for her reluctance to trade her body for her brother's life and thus participate in a misogynistic economy of sexual pleasure that devalues Isabella's prerogative to resist heteronormative expectations of women.

Rule Six for novitiates in the Order of Poor Clares details the way in which the women are to reject vanity and assume a humbler physical appearance. It states that a novitiate shall have "her haire . . . cut of round, & her secular habit shall be taken away, & the Abbesse shal lend her three coates & one cloke, after which time it is not lawful for her to go out of the Monastery without profitable, manifest, & probable cause" (Da Silva 12). Again, although Isabella has not begun the novitiate process, she wishes to and so one would be hard pressed to project on her an image of a coquettish young woman given to vain displays of beauty and wealth.

And yet we do not even need to cite Isabella's pious beliefs to justify her actions, for she exhibits more reason and logic than any of the other characters in the play. Isabella is presented as a heroine to be celebrated and imitated. In fact, Isabella's first reaction to the news of her brother impregnating Juliet expresses pragmatic nonchalance: "O, let him marry her" (1.4.48). Although Isabella explains to Angelo that "There is a vice that most I do abhor, / And most desire should meet the blow of justice" (2.2.32-33), she never tells Angelo that she believes fornicators and adulterers should be executed. Her ability to argue in a reasonable fashion lends weight to seeing these lines as her way of establishing ethos and camaraderie with Angelo. Granted, what she means by "blow of justice" is unclear, but one should not assume that it implies a death sentence. In fact, Isabella soon remarks "O just but severe law!" (2.2.45). The contrasting coordinating conjunction of "but" implies that the law can be seen as "just" for punishing fornicators yet too "severe" in regards to the proportion of the penalty to the transgression.

Throughout the rest of her dialogue with Angelo, Isabella implores Angelo to be merciful. Her invocations of the Christian virtue of mercy are some of the most eloquent passages in the play:

> No ceremony that to great ones 'longs,
> Not the king's crown, nor the deputed sword,
> The marshal's truncheon, nor the judge's robe,
> Become them with one half so good a grace
> As mercy does. (2.2.64-68)

Isabella's reference to the power of monarchs underscores the historical anxieties that Protestants felt about the political loyalties of English

Catholics who were believed to answer to the pope and the Catholic Church's law before the king and English legislation. Isabella's devotion is seen as pure and just with such inspiring verse. Her words underscore the need for a merciful judicial system overseen by monarchs, regardless of religious affiliation. Isabella's ardent speech displays Miltonesque eloquence in its ability to use religious imagery that would humble even the proudest of men:

> Merciful Heaven,
> Thou rather with thy sharp and sulphurous bolt
> Split'st the unwedgeable and gnarled oak
> Than the soft myrtle: but man, proud man,
> Drest in a little brief authority,
> Most ignorant of what he's most assured,
> His glassy essence, like an angry ape,
> Plays such fantastic tricks before high heaven
> As make the angels weep; who, with our spleens,
> Would all themselves laugh mortal. (2.2.119-27)

The reference to man's ephemeral mortal time span, "brief authority," is made even more poignant in light of Angelo's short span as ruler of Vienna in Duke Vincentio's absence.

The "fasting maids whose minds are dedicate / To nothing temporal" (2.2.160-61) in Isabella's closing remarks to Angelo reaffirm her dedication to the cloistered life and values that repudiate secular concerns. When Isabella attempts to sway Angelo by asking him to put himself in Claudio's position, "If he had been as you, and you as he, / You would have slipped like him; but he, like you, / Would not have been so stern" (2.2.69-71), she invokes Jesus Christ's Sermon on the Mount in respect to hypocrisy and judging others. Audience members can easily sympathize with Isabella's religious beliefs and be angered by Angelo's resistance to Christian morality. Additionally, Isabella uses this compassionate and logical speech in a repudiation of Claudio's desire for her to utilize a "speechless dialect" that would expose her body, ripe with erotic potential, to Angelo's male gaze. Considering the other models of womanhood presented in the play – Mariana as would-be wife, Mistress Overdone as whore, and Juliet as an amalgamation of the two (if we accept Angelo's decision to execute Claudio for fornicating with his betrothed) – we learn that Isabella's earlier commitment to preserve her virginity will not only prepare her for the rewards she expects in Heaven but will also remove her from these fates. She simply cannot submit to Angelo's and Claudio's wishes.

Although most audience members, then and now, would agree that Claudio's punishment is draconian and that all of Vienna is suffering from a lack of justice, critics and audience members who fault Isabella for her unbending refusal to fornicate with Angelo forget her role as an early seventeenth-century woman. With limited choices about her future, Isabella decides to leave the world of men, children, and luxuries to dedicate her life to God. Claudio's predicament could not have arrived at a more inopportune time for her. Shakespeare craftily introduces us to Isabella just as she enquires about the convent she plans to join. Her decision to leave the secular realm is underscored so audience members can contemplate the divide between the secular and spiritual world, especially in light of the chaos that erupts in Vienna after the Duke's absence.

"Is't not a kind of incest": Claudio's Request

The most egregious, immediate outcome of the Duke's absence is Claudio's death sentence. Claudio's livelihood depends on his sister's reputation as a sanctified woman for two reasons. Firstly, he entrusts that her use of logic will convince Angelo to release him. Such an estimation of her intelligence bodes well for the reputation of nuns as educated women. Secondly, although Claudio does not initially consider it, Angelo's perverse attraction to Isabella stems from her purity and innocence. Claudio, like the other men in the play, soon begins to value Isabella's body, even though she sees her virtue as priceless.

Shakespeare neither mentions Isabella's biological father nor any parental figure. This gap enables the audience to interpret Claudio as her familial patriarch. Nonetheless, even as a surrogate paternal figure he attempts to exploit his sister's sex and virginity to satisfy personal needs. Claudio reveals his plans for how he will employ his sister's body when he asks Lucio to tell her about his predicament: "I have great hope in that, for in her youth / There is a prone and speechless dialect / Such as move men" (1.2.155-57). The use of the adjective "prone" sounds lascivious in his description of Isabella's body, implying not only a natural inclination concomitant with an innate feminine desire to please men but also a willing body lying flat or bending forward as an empty vessel anticipating penetration. This description of the female figure's vulnerable sexuality exemplifies how Claudio and other male characters in the play employ her body as a symbol of female passivity that can be easily exchanged between men. In contrast, Claudio also hopes that the "prosperous art" Isabella enjoys when she uses "reason and discourse" can "well . . .

persuade" an assumably fair ruler (1.2.157-59). As a protagonist who refuses to use her body as a commodity, Isabella appeals to logic and reason, as well as to Christian mercy, and emphasizes her intellectual abilities. She embodies Shakespeare's celebration of Catholic women's education in learned convents such as those dedicated to Saint Clare.

One wonders how familiar Shakespeare was with the story of Saint Clare and the traditions of Poor Clares. The fact that family obligations beckon Isabella from the convent is reminiscent of the many entreaties Saint Clare withstood from family and friends to reconsider her decision to become a nun. The English version of Marcos Da Silva's 1622 *The Life of the Glorious Virgin Saint Clare* relates how the foundress of the Poor Clares did not find support from those who knew her when she decided to live the life religious:

> Many of the friendes of her Father and Mother assembled, and consulted to prevent this virtuous virgin of her holy resolution; and coming to the monastery of the Religious of Saint Bennet, whither she was retired, they purpose to execute by violence, what they could not compasse by humane policy, trying their forces against the meeke lambe of Jesus Christ, and by their malice & perverse consell seeking to delude that simple dove; there did they make her deceiptful promises, exhorting her to retire herselfe from such base condition, and abjection, demonstrating unto her, that it was a matter unworthy her noble decsent, and that the like never happened in the Citty. (24-25)

Clare's fierce resistance to the petitions of her family and friends must have served as a constant inspiration for Poor Clares who dealt with similar anatagonism when they decided to join the order. Isabella's desire to be part of such a resolute community are severely tested by her brother's need for help and Angelo's conniviving manipulations.

The engaging prison scene that features Isabella informing Claudio that she will not sacrifice her virginity for his life further articulates the vain endeavors of the play's men to control Isabella. Claudio's first reaction to Angelo's demand that Isabella sleep with him to save Claudio's life is the disbelieving "O heavens, it cannot be" (3.1.99), which is then followed by the ambiguous "Thou shalt not do 't" (3.1.103). Because we have no exclamation point denoting surprise from Claudio, actors and audience members must decide whether the sentence is declarative or imperative. If the line is delivered declaratively, then we see Claudio begrudgingly accept the natural outcome of such a situation. However, if an actor were to deliver the line in a strident, imperative tone then we see an incredulous Claudio demand that his sister not acquiesce to Angelo's lascivious demands. Isabella offers her life for Claudio, but Claudio understands that her life is not what Angelo wants. Unassuaged by the talk he receives from

Friar Lodowick (Duke Vincentio incognito) and frightened by the prospect of death, "Death is a fearful thing" (3.1.118), Claudio recants his former understanding of Isabella's decision. Guilty of a sexual sin himself, Claudio apes the section of Saint Augustine's *City of God* about women who have sex against their will in his attempt to convince his sister to sleep with Angelo to save his life: "What sin you do to save a brother's life, / Nature dispenses with the deed so far / That it becomes a virtue" (3.1.136-38).

Although Isabella is not expected to marry Angelo and perform the role of a wife and bearer of a patrilineal line, her sex act with Angelo is still considered as an object to be exchanged. Isabella stresses the mercantile nature of this double entendre with the word "trade": "O, fie, fie, fie! / Thy sin's not accidental, but a trade. / Mercy to thee would prove itself a bawd" (3.1.150-52). The rapid succession of images – fornication, commercial transaction, prostitution – underscores Isabella's contention that her sleeping with Angelo would be a nefarious combination of the three. Likewise, if the "virtue" Claudio alludes to is the birth of a child, even the admittedly positive spin that Lucio places on Claudio and Juliet's situation with healthy agricultural imagery, "As those that feed grow full, as blossoming time / That from the seedness the bare fallow brings / To teeming foison, even so her plenteous womb / Expresseth his full tilth and husbandry" (1.4.41-44), ignores Isabella's craving to avoid such labors – both physical and reproductive.

Furthermore, Claudio's appropriation of Saint Augustine glosses over one key fact – Isabella's agency. Saint Augustine is clear in Book I, Chapter 18 of *City of God* that a woman's chastity depends on the purity of her mind rather than what occurs to her body: "when the quality of modesty resists the indecency of carnal desires the body itself is sanctified, and therefore, when purity resists in its unshaken resolution to these desires, the body's holiness is not lost, because the will to employ the body in holiness endures" (28). Isabella's choice to fornicate with Angelo in exchange for her brother's life would tarnish the quality of her mind and make her a prostitute who knowingly commits a sin. Isabella realizes that her brother wants to employ her sexually, so she protests "Is't not a kind of incest, to take life / From thy own sister's shame? What should I think?" (3.1.141-42). Claudio's repeated requests that Isabella prostitute herself have already been seen not only in his words but also in those of his surrogate, Lucio. For example, during her first meeting with the Duke, Lucio asks Isabella to place herself in a physically inferior and erotically charged position in relation to Angelo and implies that she should use a warmer and feminine approach: "Kneel down before him; hang upon his gown. / You are too cold. If you should need a pin, / You could not with more tame a tongue desire it" (2.2.48-50).

Claudio continues his faulty rationalization by trying to convince Isabella that the end result of her sin, saving his life, would transform the sin into a positive: "Sweet sister, let me live. / What sin you do to save a brother's life, / Nature dispenses with the deed so far / That it becomes a virtue" (3.1.135-38). Such a painless transformation of a sexual affair may be easy for a man like Claudio who does not suffer from society's double standard when it comes to such matters, but Isabella would not only have been whored by Angelo at the expense of her brother, but she also would have damned her soul by popular seventeenth-century Catholic ideologies. Isabella demonstrates her beliefs when she tells Angelo, "Better it were a brother died at once / Than that a sister, by redeeming him, / Should die forever" (2.4.107-09). Isabella even offers her life for Claudio's, but that is not what Angelo desires. His wish to sleep with her and contaminate her with his forced sexuality supersedes any of her offers to take on more easily forgivable offenses, such as when she proposes that she would take on Angelo's "sin" of granting Claudio's pardon as one of her own "faults" (2.4.72).

An important aspect of Isabella's rejection of Angelo that is overlooked is the result to which Claudio alludes. Angelo tells Isabella that her brother will not die if she sleeps with Angelo: "He shall not, Isabel, if you give me love" (2.4.145). Isabella has no reason to believe that what he says is true as she replies, "Ha! Little honor to be much believed" and goes on to demand that he sign her a pardon for Claudio, "Or with an outstretched throat I'll the world aloud / What man thou art" (2.4.153-54). Even if Isabella were to prostitute herself to Angelo, she has no basis to believe that he will honor her request. Isabella is right. Angelo does not nullify Claudio's death sentence after the Mariana-for-Isabella bed trick leaves him thinking he has slept with Isabella. One should note that the bed trick also illustrates Isabella's fear of a world that can so easily replace one woman with another and not have the man be any wiser or care about the commodification and expendability of women's bodies. Isabella knows what she represents for Angelo: a seductively unattainable body. Marliss Desens might agree with such an assessment in her study of the bed trick, which she sees as a prevalent theatrical tool in the early 1600s, as opposed to the 1580s and 1590s, because this was the period when "drama became concerned with exploring love and desire from a less idealized perspective" (35). Shakespeare's use of the bed trick continues to support Isabella's and the drama's anxieties about marriage as a contract arranged and controlled by men rather than a fair agreement between equal partners.

After all, Angelo's duplicitous actions are so disreputable that we never see him issue Claudio's death sentence. Audience members are just as surprised as Claudio when he is informed by the Provost that "by eight tomorrow / Thou must be made immortal" (4.2.48-49). Isabella's sacrifice would not have been worth the price even in an earthly sense, much less in the afterlife. Furthermore, when the Duke's political and personal calculations lead him to lie and inform Isabella that Claudio has been executed, Isabella is reminded why she wants to leave a secular world riddled with men who renege on their word and leaders who lie. Knowing the reality of the world, Isabella leaves Angelo and hopes to prepare Claudio for death. She exposes herself to the sins of the world when she leaves the safety of the convent to enact two Corporal Works of Mercy: ransom the captive and visit the imprisoned. She has him confess so that she can save his soul and fulfill her duty as a nun to comfort the afflicted - one of the Spiritual Works of Mercy. Whatever blunders Isabella makes while trying to save Claudio, her intention is to follow the Catholic doctrine that insists mortals must earn their way to Heaven through good works and not just through faith or words alone. Unfortunately, her egress from the convent threatens her ability to return. This easy access to the convent is the very thing that Lady Happy seeks to avoid in Margaret Cavendish's 1668 closet drama *The Convent of Pleasure* (which is explored in the next chapter of this book) when she explains that her convent will be grateless.

Isabella's woeful speech to Duke Vincentio at the end of the play belies that she does not sleep with Angelo. Her emotional tone makes the audience feel as though it happened, even though we know she does not. Isabella characterizes Angelo's desires as "concupiscible intemperate lust" (5.1.103) and showcases the traumatic mental contortions she allegedly underwent to sleep with him only to have Angelo continue with his earlier sentence on Claudio's life, "after much debatement / My sisterly remorse confutes mine honor, / And I did yield to him. But the next morn betimes, / His purpose surfeiting, he sends a warrant / For my poor brother's head" (5.1.104-08). Angelo's base desires and duplicitous lies highlight the virtue inherent in Isabella's chastity.

Saint Augustine's "On the Sermon of the Mount" has often been used to illustrate why Isabella should have slept with Angelo to save her brother's life. The reference is to the story in Book I, Chapter 16 about the woman who sleeps with a man, after being given permission to do so by her husband, in order to pay her husband's debt. Saint Augustine offers "no opinion either way" about the tale, but asserts "when the story is related, man's instinctive sense does not so revolt against what was done in the case of this woman, at her husband's bidding, as we formerly shuddered when the thing itself was set forth without any example" (par. 50). A key difference overlooked in these comparisons is that Isabella's brother has asked her to perform this favor. She did not choose her brother. In fact, she chooses to remove herself from her brother's rule when she seeks admittance to the convent. Were Isabella to acquiesce to Claudio's pleadings, she would sully the modesty of her mind by working in an economy of pleasure that would benefit everyone but herself. The patriarchy in *Measure for Measure* attempts to guilt Isabella into submission, but it is unable to do so. Postmodern critics often fail to see how Isabella can separate secular concerns from her spiritual dedications. In the same vein as those who view sleeping with Angelo to save Claudio's life as an easy decision, some critics even argue that Isabella's lie about sleeping with Angelo after she helps arrange the Mariana-Angelo bed trick "symbolically defile[s]" her and makes her "suffer for her sexual provocations, however unwitting, as a condition that makes [her and Duke Vincentio's] marriage possible" (Wheeler 129). If we read the play following the traditional comedic trajectory that requires felicitous marriages at the play's conclusion, then we lose sight of Isabella's courageous individualism and her rejection of the patriarchal protocol when it comes to expectations of what she should do with her body and how she should order her priorities. She is a rebellious, queer virgin that requires no marriage to a mortal for the saving of her soul.

This chapter's various references to Saint Augustine showcase Shakespeare's indebtedness to the theology of this Doctor of the Roman Catholic Church. Saint Augustine uses the word "measure" dozens of times in *Confessions*. Shakespeare shrewdly alludes to Saint Augustine because the Patristic Father's writings on the sins of his youth, particularly lust, mesh well with this problem comedy's exploration of the dichotomous relationship of mercy and justice. Saint Augustine eloquently expresses his opinion in Book II about the corruption of his soul at the hands of theft and lust:

> And what was it that I delighted in, but to love, and be loved? But I kept not the measure of love, of mind to mind, friendship's bright boundary: but out of the muddy concupiscence of the flesh, and the bubblings of youth, mists fumed up which beclouded and overcast my heart, that I could not discern the clear brightness of love from the fog of lustfulness. (26)

Saint Augustine's youthful pride, hubris, and moral confusion is not unlike that of Angelo's. His employment of the term "concupiscence of the flesh" is echoed in Isabella's complaint to Duke Vicentio about Angelo's "concupiscible intemperate lust" (5.1.103) and makes readers certain that Shakespeare had Saint Augustine's searing confessions in mind when asking us to evaluate and celebrate Isabella's desire to maintain her purity.

Furthermore, Saint Clare was clear about issues regarding carnal temptation when she established the Rules for the Order of Poor Clares. Chapter XVIII of Da Silva's 1622 report on the order explains as much:

> First she taught them to cleare their soules of all rumors of the world, that they might the more frely attaine to the high secrets of God. She also taught them to have no affection to their carnall kindred, and inteirely to forget their owne house, the better to please Jesus Christ. She admonished them also to surmount and misprise the necessities of their bodies, & to get a habit of repressing the deceiptes, and appetites of the flesh, by the bridle of reason. She likewise taught them that the subtill enemy armed with malice, continually addresseth his hidden snares to surprise the pure soules, and that he tempteth the pious in another sort then worldlings. (86-87)

Like so many other communities of nuns, the Poor Clares were expected to renounce ties to the worldly – from their family to the temptations of the flesh. The threat ot "hidden snares" is embodied in Angelo's specious logic. His role as an authority figure with a reputation for being holy underscores the concern seen in the way Saint Clare's lesson focuses on the special nature of temptation for the "pious" rather than "worldlings."

One Way or Another: Isabella's Choice

Isabella's desire to join a convent demonstrates her willingness to abandon biological "obligations" such as birthing and nurturing children. Furthermore, her vows of chastity and poverty would allow her to circumvent the expectations of a domestic economy that mostly values the reproductive capabilities of women. Ironically, the same virginity that makes Isabella an attractive wife for Duke Vincentio also marks her as a transgressor of heteronormativity because she has chosen to stay a virgin for so long – and, if she has her way, for the rest of her life. We can clearly see how Isabella fits within Theodora Jankowski's definition of queer virgins that "refuse marriage itself and the kind of contaminating sexuality that would render them whores. For these queer characters, virginity becomes the end rather than the means of their lives, and their virgin condition marks them, paradoxically, as deviant" (171). We must see Isabella's refusal to sleep with Angelo as a subversive and heroic act that validates the ability of Catholic nuns to circumvent the normative patriarchal narratives laid out for them. Shakespeare effectively illustrates this double standard when the Duke interrogates Mariana as to what her womanly status is and asks perplexedly, "Why, you are nothing then, neither maid, widow, nor wife?" (5.1.183). Declaring Mariana to be tantamount to "nothing" denigrates women who do not conform to patriarchal expectations by denying their entire existence and defining them with a sexual pun on their genitals.

Lucio, however, responds with a quip that presents an alternative, "My lord, she may be a punk, for many of them are neither maid, widow, nor wife" (5.1.184-85). Lucio's joke may demonstrate the limited roles for women in early modern England, but the role of the prostitute ("punk") is not the only remaining option for Isabella and her Catholic peers. Isabella inhabits the more progressive and deviant alternative of a nun who relinquishes the patriarchal economy for one based on a same-sex community devoted to spiritual contemplation. Angelo admits as much in a pun that slips when he questions Isabella's womanhood after she rejects his advances: "Be that you are, / That is, a woman; if you be more, you're none" (2.4.135-36). The homophonic pun on "none"/"nun" correctly characterizes Isabella's agency and her location in the patriarchal sexual economy – she will have "none" of it as a "nun" who avoids male control. Furthermore, Angelo's comment reflects an English Protestant literary community that often satirizes women's lack of options when it comes to men. Since marriage to Christ was no longer an option and the new flood of single women seeking husbands inundated the smaller number of available men, the literary scenario of "too many women competing for too few men" was engendered as a "scene ripe for satire" (Hull 110).

Shakespeare's audience is never given an explicit reason for Isabella's decision to become a nun, but her zealous desire to live a spartan and humble life is reflected in her conversation with the nun Francisca:

> ISABELLA.   And have you nuns no farther privileges?
> FRANCISCA. Are not these large enough?
> ISABELLA.   Yes, truly. I speak not as desiring more,
>   But rather wishing a more strict restraint
>   Upon the sisterhood, the votarists of Saint Clare. (1.4.1-5)

Shakespeare is careful to differentiate Isabella from the wealthy widows, aged spinsters, rebellious daughters, and other women who joined convents to escape the drudgeries of everyday life or their roles as wives and mothers in society. Isabella's attempt to join the order is not a desire to repair to an idyllic, same-sex community of leisure. Studies of the history of nuns and convents constantly demonstrate that each woman's motive for joining a convent determined how she would behave within the walls of the community. Women who became "nuns of their own volition because of a strong religious vocation" found the nunnery "the ideal place for a spiritual communion with God" (Daichman 12). The men who seek to control Isabella have even less hope of dissuading her from entering the convent by enticing her with marriage or sexual intercourse since she joined the convent based on her own decision and thus exhibits a lack of interest in the secular world.

Some misguided readings of Isabella often see her as a young woman vexed with her station in life, especially as a woman: "Isabella shares in the deep distrust of women, of female sexuality, diffused throughout the entire play" (Wheeler 114). As a daughter and as sister to Claudio, who is condemned for fornication, Isabella would be familiar with the various ways a woman could express her sexuality. Her rejection of such sexualities does not make her distrustful of her own sexual agency; she simply rejects their possibilities and desires a more Heaven-bound employment of her body. Although Isabella's compassion for her brother forces her to leave the convent even though she has not yet "receive[d] her approbation" (1.2.168) and is "yet unsworn" (1.4.10), for all intents and purposes, the other characters, and, most importantly, the theatrical audience, view Isabella as a nun since the norm is for her to be don a full habit in the play[1].

The markedly austere habit of Clarists, Isabella's order, is "a loose fitting garment of gray frieze; the cord is of linen rope about one-half inch in thickness having four knots representing the four vows; the sandals are of cloth" (O'Hara, par. 9). The visual iconography enacted by Isabella's ascetic costume embodies the integral importance of Shakespeare's decision to make Epitia→Cassandra→ Isabella a would-be member of the Order of Saint Clare. This order, which grew in numbers from its thirteenth-century founding in Italy to a peak of 34,000 sisters throughout the Western World by 1630, was one of the most well-known orders of nuns and had up to 129 members in England alone as late as 1909.

Keeping Isabella's spiritual motivation to join the convent in mind, Shakespeare's Protestant audience could easily see this play as a nostalgic exploration of Catholicism. After all, Catholic England was a pre-Elizabethan relic of the 1520s, not counting the brief years of Queen Mary's reign (1553-58). In fact, for many of Shakespeare's female

---

[1] Stuart Hampton-Reeves's *Measure for Measure: A Guide to the Text and Its Theatrical Life,* New York: Palgrave MacMillan, 2007, offers a great summary of the play's performance potential.

audience members, Isabella's ability to avoid marriage and still lead a socially respectable livelihood was a reminder of a positive option many women had in pre-Reformation times when other single women such as old maids and widows were, according to Sung-Won Cho, "rarely favorably regarded in their communities" and "often referred to as vagrants, criminals, witches, or prostitutes" (567). However, Cho's claim that the play's "religious atmosphere" is "deliberately pre-Reformational, if not entirely medieval" (570) fails to acknowledge the existence of memory, Catholic architectural residue, and the large presence of Catholic recusants in England. More importantly, because the play is set on the Continent, audience members are aware of Catholicism's strength as it was, at the time, the most politically and numerically dominant denomination of Christianity throughout Europe. Thus, the English audience could also view the play's setting as simultaneously contemporary in recognition of Catholic foreign nations and the large number of English men and women who flocked there to join monasteries and convents during the early modern period. Likewise, the similarities between the Duke and King James I as well as the plethora of English names such as Thomas, Peter, Elbow, Froth, and Mistress Overdone engender enough similarities to remind the audience of the play's verisimilitude to their own lives.

Isabella's virginity serves various purposes in the play, but we must not forget that its primary function for Isabella is her spiritual elevation and salvation. Similarly, our twenty-first century ethics and perspectives on a woman's ability to control her sexuality and our questioning of what constitutes a "virgin" are diametrically opposed to the minute anatomization of the subject by early modern writers. It is imperative to remember Isabella's historical setting. Still heavily influenced by the writings of the patristic leaders of the Catholic Church, Isabella functions under a discourse that schizophrenically celebrates and admonishes female virgins for their purity. Such anxious texts likened a woman's virginity to monetary treasures that tempt men. In his "Letter to Eustochium," Saint Jerome warns female virgins about rape if they leave their enclosed environments. Isabella faces such a situation when she leaves the convent to aid her brother. Thus, Jerome's warning that "although God can do all things, He cannot raise up a virgin after she has fallen" (Schulenburg 33) would echo in Isabella's mind if she were admitted to the convent after losing her virginity – even as a result of pressure from her brother and Angelo.

After all, Shakespeare craftily introduces us to Isabella by duping us into believing that she won't follow the harshest of abstemious guidelines as a nun. Isabella's first question to Francisca briefly teases the audience to think that she might seek a pampered retreat with non-spiritual "privileges," but her desire for a "more strict restraint" within the Order of Saint Clare underscores her intention to dedicate her life to spiritual service and contemplation. Just as Francisca's name links the order to its roots in Saint Francis of Assisi, Isabella's name evokes the spirit of Saint Isabel, daughter of Louis VIII of France, who broke a wedding engagement and rejected various suitors in her determination to remain a virgin in order to establish a convent of the order of Saint Clare[2]. This convent, the Humility of the Blessed Virgin Mary at Longchamp, followed the Rule of the Second Order, which was named the Isabella Rule after the French Isabel (Holmes and Slights 272). This rule emphasizes obedience, chastity, and silence. Shakespeare emphasizes his knowledge about this austere rule in Francisca's chiasmus, "Then if you speak you must not show your face, / Or if you show your face you must not speak" (1.4.12-13). The Bishop of Oporto's 1620 report on the Poor Clares stresses that "there was never seene a strictire observance of silence than amongst them, nor a greater form, and example of virtue" (88). Poor Clares were known for their devotion to austere practices. Pope Innocent IV issued a Papal Bull in 1253 "declaring that Clare's nuns could never be forced against their will to break their vow of poverty," which marked "the only example of a female religious order receiving the protection of the Holy See to pursue a lifestyle chosen by the community" (Kuhns 96).

Isabella's well-established commitment to her order exhibits how different her value system is from more secular citizens such as Claudio and Angelo. She values her soul more than her body, so the assurance that a sin that pagan Nature may dispense with and transform into "a virtue" (3.1.136-37) holds little weight for a devout, early seventeenth-century novice such as Isabella. Critics who demonize Isabella for her reluctance to trade her body for her brother's life not only participate in a misogynistic economy of sexual pleasure, but they also employ an anachronistic value system of sexual liberation in an early modern world that was still more concerned with spiritual rewards than transient, earth-bound justice systems, especially corrupt ones. As Jo Ann Kay McNamara explains, even in "our own libertarian age we still refuse to recognize the

---

[2] Nirti Ben-Aryeh Debby's *The Cult of St Clare of Assisi in Early Modern Italy*, Aldershot: Ashgate, 2014, offers a fascinating study on the growth of cultic devotion to Saint Clare, which reached its peak in the seventeenth century. Debby notes that images of Saint Clare transitioned from the Medieval portrayal of her as a humble virgin to that of an abbess. Sometimes she was depicted with a crozier, the symbol of bishops, to demonstrate her leadership skills.

legitimacy of choosing chaste celibacy, linking it to caricatures of nuns as ignorant classroom tyrants and feminists as angry hags" (5). Misogynist critics might even agree with Angelo's rationalization that ". . . Our compelled sins / Stand more for number than for account" (2.4.57-58). Such reasoning abuses Saint Augustine's discussion of rape because it excuses the male exploiter by comforting the rape victim that "it doesn't matter" because she did not consent to have sex. Granted, Isabella and other novices would still be welcomed into nunhood even if they lost their virginity, but such an acceptance of rape would make the world even riper for hypocritical sexual aggressors like Angelo. The fact that Saint Cyprian, a third century Bishop of Carthage, described virgins who broke their vows as adulteresses demonstrates the ancient tradition of hypervigilance over the sexuality of women as well as nuns (Kuhns 27).

"To sin in loving virtue": Angelo and Isabella as Extremists

Despite Angelo's baseness and Isabella's superior moral status, Shakespeare's creation of characters such as Isabella and Angelo does not occur simply for the sake of the plot. These two strong-headed characters are equally naïve, idealistic, and extreme. Forced to interact in two heated scenes, both characters display a ferocity and conviction about their beliefs that no other characters in the play possess. In fact, were the scenario and their ranks different, one could imagine this couple falling in love with each other's resoluteness and forming a politically dynamic marriage. Much has been written about the play's interest in the pairs of substitutions of one character for another. Equally important is the presentation of the self-righteous pair of the seemingly unmalleable Isabella with the apparently unpersuadable Angelo.

Another contrast between the characters exists in their relationships to geospatial communities. Whereas Isabella chooses to withdraw from the world into the convent, Angelo unfairly imprisons others. The enclosed spatial figurations of such settings, convent and prison, place characters' desires under the watchful eyes of others. On one hand, Isabella's surveillance is one of choice under the understanding and merciful eyes of God. On the other hand, Angelo denies his own desires and sublimates his need for reconciliation and penance by sentencing others to suffer under the uncaring eyes of prison guards and hangmen. If we view Isabella's desire for a "strict restraint" and self-flagellation as perverse masochism, at least it is her choice and more palatable to a live-and-let-live attitude than Angelo's sadistic need to punish others. Critics who decry Isabella for her selfishness should find little sympathy for Angelo. Shakespeare underscores Angelo's and authority figures' ability to infect others with their desires by showcasing how Angelo's reputation as an austere man transforms into "concupiscible intemperate lust" (5.1.103) with his desire to contaminate an innocent Isabella, "Shall we desire to raze the sanctuary / And pitch our evils there?" (2.2.206-07). The phallic undertones of Angelo's wish to "pitch" Isabella's "sanctuary"—that is, thrust a pointed object into her fertile ground—showcases his perverse attraction to sully what is pure and to defile one of the holiest of mortal Catholic vessels, a nun.

Angelo's repressed sexuality forces him to act violent and lust-driven during his second meeting with Isabella. Illustrating the framework of how his power as the Duke's deputy and his desires have ensconced his thoughts within a sexual framework, Angelo replies to Isabella's innocent "I am come to know your pleasure" by perversely reading into the potential sexual connotations of her words by responding, "That you might know it would much better please me" (2.4.30-31). Although a few postmodern directors have molded Isabella as a sexy, coquettish character, such castings are as unconcerned with Isabella's self-identification as a nun as those critics who deride her as cold and uncaring[3]. Just as Angelo looks past the novice's calling, such directors and critics downplay the fervent spiritual joy and belief Isabella and other nuns celebrate within the convent. The ironic juxtaposition of Angelo's ethereal name and his devilish stratagems underscores the play's lampooning of Puritans through him. Although never called a Puritan, as Maria does when she criticizes Malvolio as "a kind of puritan" who "cons state without book and utters it by great swaths: the best persuaded of himself" in *Twelfth Night* (2.3.133-42), Angelo's reputation as an austere and morally righteous man convinces the Duke that Angelo has "a kind of character" that unfolds his history "to th' observer" (1.1.29-30).

The Duke's decision to pass over the venerable and moderate Escalus rings alarms for audience members, but until we get a fuller view of Angelo away from the chatter about him throughout Act I, we have little reason to believe that Angelo is not an upstanding individual. After Angelo's lustful desires are exposed and the talk about his being

---

[3] In 2013 the District of Columbia's Shakespeare Theatre Company's production of *Measure for Measure* was set in 1930s Vienna and featured what Peter Marks of *The Washington Post* described as "disrobing dancing nuns" in a 20-minute preshow. The show promoted itself throughout the city with nine-foot high banners affixed to lampposts featuring a nun in a sexually compromising position.

unnaturally unsympathetic, ". . . a man whose blood / Is very snow broth; one who never feels / The wanton stings and motions of the sense, / But doth rebate and blunt his natural edge / With profits of the mind, study, and fast" (1.4.57-61), is confirmed in front of the audience, Isabella threatens to publicly decry his hypocrisy and lechery. Like the stereotypical Puritan criticized by so many Renaissance playwrights, Angelo attempts to use his reputation as a holier-than-thou man to intimidate Isabella: "My unsoiled name, th' austereness of my life, / My vouch against you, and my place i' the state / Will so your accusation overweigh / That you shall stifle in your own report / And smell of calumny" (2.4.155-60). Isabella sees through Angelo's whited sepulcher of a reputation when she describes him as an "outward-sainted deputy" (3.1.89). Isabella's understandable frustration bespeaks the limited legal rights women possessed in early seventeenth-century Europe, especially when compared to that of a man with authority defending his honor against the word of a woman. Disgusted by her impotence in the situation, Isabella decides to visit her brother and prepare him for death.

Isabella's soliloquy at the end of Act II places her values in the spotlight as she reminds herself about her priorities: "Then, Isabel, live chaste, and brother die; / More than our brother is our chastity" (2.3.185-86). Much like Lucio's comment about unfeeling Angelo's monk-like adherence to "the mind, study, and fast," Isabella quickly decides that there is no remedy but to give Claudio the news about her meeting with Angelo. In the verbal tug-of-war in which these two opposites engage, Isabella wins as the underdog with her fiery rhetoric, impassioned language, and sympathetic position. Yet blind to their similarities, Isabella asks Angelo to bend rules that are as important to him as those that she refuses to toy with at Angelo's behest are to her. Even when the audience sees these two characters as extremists, whether one sees Angelo as Puritan-like or not, Isabella's religious biases should hold more weight for both Renaissance and contemporary audience members. Her religious convictions are amalgamated with her moral values in a way that leads even cynical, postmodern audience members to admire her ability to "stand for what she believes in." "Believe" is the key word with its connotations of religious faith, especially when juxtaposed with Angelo's legalistic argumentation and judicial reasoning.

Illustratively, in their first meeting Isabella informs Angelo that "neither heaven nor man" would "grieve at the mercy" he would show in pardoning Claudio (2.2.53). Angelo's reticence to show mercy marks him as un-Christian when compared to the forgiving Isabella. As previously mentioned, Angelo's resemblance to Protestants, especially Puritans, comes to light with how often he falls back on the "word" – the text of the law. We see Angelo realize how pliable and constructed the law is in a world rife with corrupt authority figures when he expresses his unadulterated thoughts and emotions, conflicted as they are, during a soliloquy: ". . . O, let her brother live! / Thieves for their robbery have authority / When judges steal themselves" (2.2.182-84). Following Protestantism's insistence on faith as a path to salvation, Angelo's faith in the law stands in stark contrast to Isabella's supplication for mercy as she attempts to live her life by working her way to Heaven through good works. Angelo does have the law on his side; fornication is to be punished with the death of the fornicator in *Measure for Measure*'s Vienna.

However, given the Duke's past leniency on such matters, even a simple citizen such as Claudio sees through Angelo's display of authoritarianism and questions whether he is putting on a show:

> Whether it be the fault and glimpse of newness,
> Or whether that the body public be
> A horse whereon the governor doth ride,
> Who, newly in the seat, that it may know
> He can command, lets it straight feel the spur. (1.2.130-34).

Shakespeare surely had King James's 1599 treatise on monarchical rule, *Basilikon Doron*, in mind with Claudio's criticism of new rulers who believe they must be feared when they begin their tenure and later show leniency rather than be merciful from the onset. This subtle, anti-monarchical critique is thus transplanted to a "comedy" set on foreign, Catholic soil to offset the censors. Whenever Angelo attempts to stand by the rules he must enforce, rules that he and possibly the Duke never made, he bases his decisions on man-made laws that Isabella often criticizes from her religious perspective. These criticisms have a two-fold purpose: they show how secular laws often fail in their attempt to be like God's laws and how Catholicism's tenets of redemption through Christ and entrance to Heaven through good works supersede Angelo's claims.

Such faith-based dichotomies are also articulated through Shakespeare's use of rhetorical strategies. As Ira Clark demonstrates in his study of language in the drama, "By presenting associations and identities that lay open definitions, and antitheses and commensurabilities that lay out exchanges, chiasmus focuses our attention on many problems adjudicating strict applications of law and grants of clemency in *Measure for Measure*" (51). Angelo attempts to convince Isabella that her denial of his indecent proposal and Claudio's reprieve are equal to his original sentencing of her brother: "Were not you then as cruel as the sentence / That you have slandered so?" (2.4.110-11). His admission of his cruelty continues to impugn his integrity in the audience's eyes. Consequently, all of Isabella's pleadings for Angelo to put himself in her brother's shoes, such as the chiasmus-rich "If you had been as you and you as he, / You would have slipped like him, but he, like you, / Would not have been so stern" (2.2.66-68), redeem her spiritual concerns as superior to Angelo's by-the-book interpretations of secular laws.

Isabella's background as a postulant well-versed in the Christian faith fuels her eloquent response to Angelo when, Pontius Pilate-like, he tries to wipe his hands clean of Claudio's blood by blaming the law for his death sentence:

> ANGELO. Your brother is a forfeit of the law,
> And you but waste your words.
> ISABELLA. Alas, alas!
> Why, all the souls that were were forfeit once;
> And He that might the vantage best have took
> Found out the remedy. How would you be,
> If He, which is the top of judgment, should
> But judge you as you are? O, think on that;
> And mercy then will breathe within your lips,
> Like man new made. (2.2.76-83)

Once again, Angelo attempts to dismiss Isabella, her intelligence, and her faith by belittling her speech in saying that the issue is moot. However, Shakespeare provides Isabella with an exclamation point and the last four syllables needed to complete Angelo's iambic pentameter, thus prodding the actor portraying Isabella to quickly and vehemently rebut Angelo's reasoning with an awe-inspiring response that would humble the most powerful of men.

The two extremists are also positioned alongside one another because of their naïve belief in their ability to persuade other people to agree with their position. As already mentioned, Isabella has religious foundations to support her arguments, and so when she agrees to help her brother she tells Lucio that she will send her brother "certain word of my success" (1.4.90) after meeting with Angelo. Most editors gloss "success" following the OED's primary definition of the noun as "That which happens in the sequel; the termination (favourable or otherwise) of affairs." Isabella's intellectual abilities are evidenced by her desire to join one of the only communities where women can be independently educated. Likewise, Claudio's commendation of his sister as having "... prosperous art / When she will play with reason and discourse, / And well she can persuade"

(1.2.157-59) encourages her that she will be successful. Our twenty-first century meaning of the word, "The prosperous achievement of something attempted; the attainment of an object according to one's desire: now often with particular reference to the attainment of wealth or position," was used as early as 1586 according to the OED. Thus, while Angelo banks his skills of persuasion on his prestige and political power, Isabella is confident in her rhetorical skills and her status as a learned novice with Christian guidelines to have mercy on her side. As always, Isabella has the upper hand. The pairing of these two characters ostensibly provides a mirror upon which both Angelo and Isabella can reflect in respect to their extreme personality traits and unwillingness to alter their rules. However, Isabella's role as an educated, would-be nun imbues her with not only the finesse of the Aristotelian rhetorical triangle, but also the moral Catholic doctrine that an early seventeenth-century audience would understand as valuing the afterlife more than Angelo's blind adherence to archaic secular laws.

"Ignominy in Ransom" or "Free Pardon"?: Isabella's Two Faults

Two cruxes present themselves in this reclamation of Isabella's character: her agreement to arrange the Mariana-for-Isabella bed trick and Isabella's ambiguously silent acceptance of Duke Vincentio's wedding proposal.

The first predicament must be analyzed while keeping in mind that Isabella believes (when she is visiting her brother in prison) that she is speaking to a friar and not a disguised secular ruler with political motives. Isabella does not verbally acknowledge the friar's presence when she enters the prison to visit Claudio in Act III. Despite the Catholic Church's patriarchal hierarchy, which would insist upon a nun like Isabella placing herself in an inferior position respective to a male cleric, Isabella continues to evade male authority figures whenever she can. When the Duke approaches Isabella, she reveals her determination to stay in control by demanding "What is your will?" (3.1.156) and then informs him that she can only grant him a small amount of her precious time, "I have no superfluous leisure – my stay must be stolen out of other affairs – but I will attend you a while" (3.1.160-61). This brusque formal exchange mirrors Isabella's earlier conversation with Lucio when he asks her to intercede on her brother's behalf. Isabella's terse responses are juxtaposed with Lucio's loquaciousness to emphasize her attempts to adhere to the rule of silence followed by the sisters of Saint Clare, especially when it comes to interactions with men.

Audience members continually see Isabella's attempt to assert as much control as she can, especially when male usurpers of her power are in proximity. Isabella listens to the "friar" explain the history between Mariana and Angelo. He assures her that they were "affianced . . . by oath, and the nuptial appointed" (3.1.203-04). The fact that Mariana lost her dowry with her brother's death strikes a heavy chord with Isabella, who is well aware of the plight of a woman without either a dowry or a male heir to defend her honor. Isabella instantly sympathizes with Mariana. The fact that Angelo abandoned Mariana because she lost her dowry emphasizes his superficial nature. Consequently, the bed trick plan appeals to Isabella because it not only saves her virginity and her brother's life, but it also ensures that a spurned woman avenges the man who abandoned her. To boot, Isabella supports another queer virgin (however briefly she may be one) as Mariana goes on to become a "nothing"– neither "maid" nor "punk" (5.1.183) – because she does not easily fit "into any of the acceptable categories women are supposed to occupy in the patriarchal sexual economy" (Jankowski 189).

Granted, Isabella's agreement to the bed trick shows her breaking the Eighth Commandment against bearing false witness against your neighbor. Given her incredulous responses to Claudio's rationalization that fornication "is the least" of the seven deadly sins, "Which is the least?" and "What says my brother?" (3.1.113 and .117), Isabella's acceptance of what is arguably "less sinful" than murder and adultery according to most Christians taints her purity as one "enskied and sainted" (1.4.34). The fact that her trick will restore Mariana's integrity and aid her in marrying Angelo showcases how Isabella is willing to commit a sin as long as it "appears not fould in the truth of my spirit" in order to save others (3.1.196-97). An integral element of this deception to which Isabella consents is the fact that Mariana's plight saddens and infuriates Isabella. Mariana's situation as a woman jilted by her betrothed because she has lost her dowry only adds fuel to Isabella's determination to avoid marrying within a patriarchal sexual economy that monetizes women's worth. Additionally, Isabella witnesses how the innocent and slighted Mariana continues to suffer because of her involvement with Angelo when the Duke informs her that Angelo broke his vows to Mariana by "pretending in her discoveries of dishonor" (3.1.213).

Angelo repeats similar lies when the Duke confronts him later in the play. He admits that he left Mariana not only because of her dowry loss but also due to her "reputation" that was "disvalued / In levity" (5.1.227-

28). According to the OED, "levity" is used to denote "'Light' or undignified behaviour; unbecoming freedom of conduct" in reference to a woman and her virtues, or lack thereof. Given his constant moral failings throughout the play, little need be said about Angelo's hypocritical use of the double standard for falsely accusing Mariana of sexual impropriety. Mirroring her own extreme offer to sacrifice her life for Claudio's, Isabella, who views the life religious and the afterlife with God as superior to a secular existence, briefly wishes death for Mariana as a form of salvation: "What a merit were it in death to take this poor maid from the world!" (3.1.216).

Despite her melodramatic death wish, Isabella comes through for Mariana by way of feminist ideologies that stem from her idealization of the all-female convent community. Isabella's intercession on Angelo's behalf does not come without repeated prodding from Mariana: "Sweet Isabel, take my part! / Lend me your knees . . ." (5.1.426-27) and "Isabel / Sweet Isabel, do yet but kneel by me! / Hold up your hands, say nothing; I'll speak all / . . . / O Isabel, will you not lend a knee?" (5.1.433-38). Mariana's request that Isabella kneel beside her convinces Isabella to do so because of the imagery such an appeal creates in the mind of a woman dedicated not only to a spiritual sisterhood but also a possible extraconventual, feminist collective fighting against Angelo and other misogynists in the daily battles of the *querelle des femmes*. When Isabella goes beyond the call of duty and speaks, she stresses her commitment to life as a nun who enacts the mercy of forgiveness, even though few in the audience would expect her to intercede on Angelo's behalf. Although Isabella supports Mariana's marriage to Angelo, her own thoughts on marriage for herself are another issue.

The matter of Isabella's betrothal to Duke Vincetio has led her to be compared to *Twelfth Night*'s Viola because of her inability to speak after an authoritative male figure (a duke in both instances) insists that she marry him. Just as Duke Orsino asserts his dominance over Viola in marriage, "Here is my hand. You shall from this time be / Your master's mistress" (*TN* 5.1.303-04), Duke Vincentio commands Isabella to wed him, "Give me your hand and say you will be mine" (*MM* 5.1.491). Both lines exhibit the man's ownership of the woman, "master's mistress" and "be mine," and both lines are followed by not even a single word from these women. This comparison between Isabella and Viola implies that they accept the marriages, but it belies the diametrical ideas both characters hold of marriage and their would-be spouses throughout their respective plays. Viola's love for Duke Orsino is a dominant theme throughout the more conventional of the two comedies, especially in such scenes as when she tells Olivia that she is going after he whom she loves: "More than I love these eyes, more than my life" (*TN* 5.1.125). Consequently, readers can easily assume that she will accept Duke Orsino's proposal. In contrast, Isabella's negation of Angelo's lusty demands and her determination to maintain her virginity to ensure her place in the convent demonstrates her commitment to avoid marriage. After all, although the Duke asks for Isabella's "hand" and requests for her to "say" she "will be" his, Isabella remains mute and unmoving according to stage directions. Are audience members to assume that Isabella marries Duke Vincentio? It depends on whom you ask and how the play is performed. Thanks to the lack of explicit stage directions, which perhaps were left unwritten by Shakespeare due to his reverence for the fluid nature of stage work and the theatrical potential of things left unsaid, the possibility of a marriage depends on the staging decision made during each performance.

Ivo Kamps and Karen Raber use Henry Swinburne's early seventeenth-century *A Treatise of Spusals [sic], or Matrimonial Contracts: Wherein All the Questions Relating to That Subject Are Ingeniously Debated and Resolved* to hypothesize on Isabella's ability to consent to the marriage by using non-verbal signifiers: "If she does in any way gesture her assent, however, we may consider her 'pre-contracted' to the Duke" (200). Kamps and Raber reference Section XV of Swinburne's treatise, which includes the line "That which cannot be expressed by words, may be declared by signs," to discuss the contracting of spouses by non-verbal signs (216). Although they cite sundry examples of silent gestures signaling the acceptance of a marriage proposal that Swinburne provides as evidence for this practice being "fairly common," one finds it hard to believe that so many people would willingly enter marriages without verbally expressing their desire to do so. Furthermore, such gestures on which Kamps and Raber base this argument are not found in the stage directions of Shakespeare's play. The actor who plays Isabella would need to improvise this telling signal.

Isabella's silence speaks volumes. Given that Shakespeare has bestowed Isabella with dozens of powerful sections of speech throughout the play, one is hard-pressed to imagine him not providing her with a fitting way to escape the confines of marriage to Duke Vincentio. Continuing to read Isabella as a deviant, queer virgin would allow us to agree with Jankowski's assertion that Isabella's silence shows her "refus[ing] integration into the sexual economy. Silence does not necessarily mean acquiescence; one cannot be married by remaining silent during the ceremony" (163). Jankowski's assertion is more fitting with the Catholic setting of the play. Catholic Canon Law emphasizes the necessity of words from the husband and wife to consent to marriage. Catholicism's prolific set of dogmas and laws allows Isabella to queerly circumvent marrying the Duke. Shakespeare cleverly emphasizes Isabella's nuptial silence by giving her the iconic marital phrase of consent, "I do," but only in reference to finding solace in the fact that her brother can enjoy his afterlife:

> DUKE. But peace be with him!
> That life is better life past fearing death
> Than that which lives to fear. Make it your comfort,
> So happy is your brother.
> ISABELLA. I do, my lord. (5.1.392-95)

Again, Isabella's allegiances are spiritual ones. She believes in the Christian afterlife and finds solace in knowing that her brother is no longer tormented by mortal fears. Her marital assent is a spiritual one, marking her as a Bride of Christ rather than as Duke Vincentio's spouse.

Nonetheless, many critics continue to argue that Isabella is definitively married off at the end of play without any mention of Isabella's literal and textual lack of consent. For example, David Bevington matter-of-factly informs readers in his influential *Norton Anthology of English Renaissance Drama* that Margaret in Robert Greene's *Friar Bacon and Friar Bungay* rejects nunhood just "like Isabella" since "the heroine of this romantic comedy concludes that the pleasures of this world are to be embraced" (131). *Measure for Measure*'s well-earned and well-known status as one of Shakespeare's problem plays surely removes it from the list of such Renaissance-era, run-of-the-mill romantic comedies that celebrate marriage as an easy solution to life's dilemmas.

In fact, Isabella expresses her continued determination to live as a votarist of Saint Clare when she pleads for Angelo's life, the one time she does kneel according to most stage directions, because his thoughts do not constitute a crime: "His act did not o'ertake his bad intent, / And must be buried but as an intent / That perished by the way. Thoughts are no subjects, / Intents but merely thoughts" (5.1.447-49). Because Isabella can be seen arguing against the "boundaries between licit and illicit desire and behaviors [becoming] ever more regulated and defined by government intervention" (Holmes and Slights 290), her use of the term "subjects" can be interpreted as having a double meaning. On the one hand it is an object, and on the other hand it is an individual under the dominion of a monarch. The joining of these hands in Isabella's vague employment of the word "subjects" allows Isabella to claim that Angelo's thoughts cannot be subject to the Duke, and then to metonymically transform "intents" into "thoughts," so that her intent to enter a convent cannot be under the dominion of the Duke. Furthermore, Isabella's kneeling puts her in a venerable line of women who kneel in religious drama and visual art, such as the Virgin Mary and Mary Magdalene. This physical posturing highlights not only the play's indebtedness to Catholic Medieval drama such as the Chester Cycle's *Raising of Lazarus* (Groves 163), but also to Isabella's insistence on pleading for mercy regardless of the person's sins, as would befit a nun.

Clearly, Isabella's complete silence about marriage after this florid supplication for Angelo's life problematizes both Duke Vincentio's plans and the drama's fulfillment of the expectations of a comedy. A reformed view of Isabella as virtuous nun rather than a selfish woman indicates that Shakespeare strove to present readers with a positive depiction of Catholicism in regards to the options it afforded early modern women. Likewise, Isabella's boldness represents the capabilities of an intelligent woman with a certain degree of agency, which, in this case, is dependent on the options available to Catholic women. Given that some of Shakespeare's contemporaries, such as Thomas Heywood, "argued that plays could inspire imitation . . . on the basis that what they had to teach was moral conduct" (Clark, S. 13), it would not be far-fetched to imagine that Shakespeare offers Isabella as a role model for female theatergoers to emulate. On the same note, Puritanical anti-theater polemicists could argue that Isabella's perverse rejection of marriage and childbearing highlights not only one of the evils of Catholicism but also the theatrical world's corrupt morals. Or, having gone this far in his positive portrayal of Catholic virtues, Shakespeare avoids sending the young and attractive Isabella back to the convent instead of the marriage altar.

Whatever the case may be, as many readers of the problem play's unique structure infer, *Measure for Measure*'s pseudo-comedic ending leaves more issues unresolved about personal identities and decisions as well as public policy than not - including the Duke's unrequited marriage proposal. If we interpret the Duke as a stand-in for King James, then we can see Shakespeare lightly nudge the monarch to keep women out of convents and uphold the Protestant makeup of England. Nonetheless, there is no firm resolution; Shakespeare attempts to have it both ways. Isabella's rejection of marriage throughout the play presents her as a contrast to women in his other comedies who gradually warm up to the prospect of marriage, such as Portia in *The Merchant of Venice* and Beatrice in *Much Ado About Nothing*.

Duke Vincentio's return as a King James-like ruler problematizes Isabella's future. The Duke's view of marriage as an economic exchange is highlighted when Mariana bewails the impending death of her husband, Angelo, and the Duke consoles her with monetary language: ". . . For his possessions, / Although by confiscation they are ours, / We do instate and widow you withal, / To buy you a better husband" (5.1.418-21). While the Duke enriches Mariana and even gives her the freedom to find another husband, his crass use of the verb "buy" denotes the lucrative resale value of widows. This coarse response to Mariana's heartfelt protests showcases the Duke's inability to act like the average citizens of Vienna or to be a virtuous husband to Isabella, were she to ever accept his offer.

"The Life Removed": Fey and Fraudulent Friars

The second key figure in this appropriation of *Measure for Measure*'s Catholic sympathies is Duke Vincentio. The audience can employ the Duke's disguise as a friar to examine the performance of friars as public figures in the Catholic community. Just as Shakespeare creates a nun by updating his sources' characters, he also invents the friar figure as another way to inject more complex religious and cultural commentary into the play's multifaceted exploration of the dynamics between secular law and religious law as well as between justice and mercy.

Friars were given more liberties in their interactions with the public because of their sex, especially after the Council of Trent (1545-63) reinforced 1298's *Periculoso*, the Medieval rule of enclosure for nuns. One of the messages inherent in *Measure for Measure* revolves around the duke's portrayal of a friar to reflect the distinctions between secular and spiritual leaders and the ways in which both are expected to treat their subjects. The parallels between Duke Vincentio and King James I mark the English monarch as an administrator who, despite his power in the hierarchy of the Church of England, cannot function as a true spiritual leader because of his distinction from the masses as a royal and political figure. The king's seeming inability to relate to the English people or to be popularly loved was well-known. When Duke Vincentio asks Friar Thomas how to mimic a friar in order to "Visit both prince and people" (1.4.45) in his plan to observe Angelo, audience members can see how the Duke will perform in the role of the comparably more likeable Catholic friar. The Duke's request for help from the friar demonstrates the inability of royal figures, such as dukes, to mingle with the common people. Friars could easily walk the streets and nonchalantly speak with lay people while a royal figure never could.

This idea of the "people's friar" celebrates the humble nature of dedicated friars and their knack for relating with the masses. Alexander Leggatt argues that the Duke's counsel to Claudio as a friar, more Stoic than Christian, and the fact that he hears confession even though he is not a priest show him as "blandly unconcerned" with the legitimate instance of fraud that he is committing. Therefore, he is "meant to horrify us with an image of power abused and the abuse accepted" (Leggatt 357). The Duke's disguise functions as a testimony to the potential amount of goodness and abuse that was inherent in clergymen. As Sidney Homan asserts, "Like Prospero, the Duke is too removed and bookish to be an effective leader. He must also participate in experience, even if it be at the lofty but covert position of a controlling figure" (144).

This portrayal of friars' dedication to the spiritual guidance of believers showcases itself in Duke Vincentio's dialogue with the Provost, who jovially greets the Duke as a "good friar" (2.3.2) in the prison, even though he has never met him:

> Bound by my charity and my blest order,
> I come to visit the afflicted spirits
> Here in the prison. Do me the common right
> To let me see them and to make me know
> The nature of their crimes, that I may minister
> To them accordingly (2.3.4-7).

Duke Vincentio's subsequent conversations with Juliet and Claudio console the two lovers with his wise spiritual guidance. Shakespeare juxtaposes Duke Vincentio's soothing *memento mori* counsel to Claudio, "Be absolute for death. Either death or life / Shall thereby be the sweeter. Reason thus with life: / If I do lose thee, I do lose a thing / That none but fools would keep" (3.1.5-8), with the duke's starker assessment of Claudio's fate following his eavesdropping on Claudio and Isabella's conversation: "Do not satisfy your resolution with hopes that are fallible. Tomorrow you must die. Go to your knees and make ready" (3.1.168-69). This change from metered verse to prose denotes the eloquence of his former speech as well as the change in his role from a spiritual counselor to a friar with political connections and objectives. This change can be seen in his allusions to being Angelo's confessor. Unlike pro-Catholic criticism that sees Shakespeare's development of the duke-as-friar as "yet another portrait of a saintly member of a monastic order" (Mutschmann and Wentersdorf 280), the political discourse underlying "Friar Lodowick"'s guidance reminds the audience of Vincentio's true role, a duke, and his incompatibility with the life of a genuine friar dedicated to spiritual service.

The Duke's Machiavellian machinations posit his employment of religion only as a way to garner the popular political power he lacks as an out-of-touch monarch. Following King James's penchant for conflating secrecy and the divine rights of monarchs, the play showcases the Duke's and King James's desire to direct, manage, and orchestrate from behind a veil – in this instance, a religious one. The Duke's former soothing advice to Claudio can be seen as a devious way to make his political subject docile and submissive. By preparing him for death, the Duke not only asks Claudio to anticipate the afterlife, but he also demands that he subjugate himself to the rule of law, however unfairly it is being administered. This political appropriation of the role of a friar can be compared with Friar Thomas's frank appraisal of the Duke's absconcion of his responsibilities when the Duke asks him for advice on how to pass as a friar: "It rested in Your Grace / To unloose this tied-up justice when you pleased" (1.3.31-32). Friar Thomas sensibly exploits the word "Grace" to remind the duke of his divine authority to execute the law, especially in light of King James I's position on the Divine Right of monarchs to rule. Even when Shakespeare replaces the Duke's ultimate authority in Vienna with that of a friar, we still see his inability to rule judiciously as a God-like duke and his failure to act as a wise friar because of his Machiavellian inclinations.

We see further criticism of religious leaders with political posts and agendas (such as the Supreme Head of the Anglican Church, aka King James I) when Duke Vincentio convinces the Provost to exchange Claudio's head for that of Barnardine. One of the play's famous "problems" comes to fruition when the audience witnesses the Duke relish his role as a clandestine friar while simultaneously neglecting his duties as a ruler. Instead of revealing his true identity, confronting Angelo about his draconian measures of justice, and halting Claudio's unfair execution, he plays games with the lives of prisoners. Overstepping his boundaries as a "friar," an infuriated Duke Vincentio orders Abhorson and Pompey to send Barnardine to his execution: "Unfit to live or die. O gravel heart! / After him, fellows. Bring him to the block" (4.1.51-52). He is brought to his senses only by the entrance of the Provost when he switches to his performance of delivering a more caring assessment of Barnardine as "A creature unprepared to, unmeet for death; / And to transport him in the mind he is / Were damnable" (4.3.54-56). This change of sentencing conforms with long-held canonical law that prohibits clerics from participating in capital punishment. Because these life-or-death decisions were left for the state, we once again see Duke Vincentio blur the lines of distinction between a spiritual leader and political figure. Illustratively, Lucio's answer to Escalus's question about his knowledge of Friar Lodowick highlights the Duke's lackluster performance as a friar: "*Cucullus non facit monachum*; honest in nothing but in his clothes" (5.1.270). The Duke's performance has been panned, as has the ability of a ruler to serve as a spiritual leader.

Leggatt's excellent analysis on the series of substitutions in *Measure for Measure* allows me to borrow his argument that "the substitutions that are central to the plot are all, in various ways, unsatisfying" (344). Duke Vincentio's substitutions mark him as a failure. The Duke produces mixed results in his tenure as a friar, and since his abandonment of his true role as a Duke has resulted in so much chaos, we can only deduce that he is presented as a nearly catastrophic disappointment in all settings. Duke Vincentio directs many of the play's machinations and substitutions including Mariana for Isabel, Barnardine for Claudio, and Angelo for himself. All of these swaps could have been avoided were he to rule fairly and publicly instead of with a clandestine usage of the "seal of the Duke" (4.2.160) and other shady ploys. Instead of executing a path of lucid and fair justice, the Duke neglects his role as a leader and allows his people to be threatened by a megalomaniac. His substitutions always seek to ameliorate problematic situations that he has created.

Whether an audience member expects Isabella and the Duke's marriage to go through or not, there is little hope for the marriage to prove successful based on the Duke's inability to govern Vienna properly. Furthermore, the fact that Duke Vincentio acts as a friar when he first meets Isabella and then proposes marriage to her at the end of the play underscores and alludes to significant ethical problems that have plagued the Catholic Church for centuries. The scandalous relationships that sometimes, however rarely, developed between nuns and their male ecclesiastical superiors were a ripe subject for anti-Catholic fodder. Shakespeare leaves the subject "deliberately unexplored" despite the fact that it "recuperates the moral and sexual corruptions within the Medieval Church" (Cho 574).

In contrast to Shakespeare's positive depiction of Isabella's queer virginity, we see the Duke's performance as a fraudulent friar whose sexual queerness is seen as a negative. Although one cannot definitively argue that Shakespeare wanted audience members to imagine Duke Vincentio as gay, I feel compelled to take the opportunity to briefly examine this possibility given the other verifiable comparison between Duke Vincentio and King James I. If nothing else, something queer is afoot with the duke. Charles R. Forker cites various historical sources about King James I to conclude that "it was not uncommon for writers" to discuss the monarch's penchant for amorous affairs with men since it was "well known" that "James I frequently embarrassed contemporaries by making an open display of his physical attraction to male favorites" (88). Just as Shakespeare's contemporary Christopher Marlowe did not shy away from depicting Edward II's homosexuality, the Bard seems to hint as much about the Duke in two minor but telling instances that augment the argument about his inability to be a good Catholic husband to Isabella.

When disguised as Friar Lodowick, the Duke speaks with Lucio and asks him what he knows about the Duke. This cunning strategy to learn what his subjects genuinely think about him surprises Duke Vincentio when Lucio candidly proclaims the Duke's penchant for drinking and womanizing. In reference to whoring around, Lucio says that the duke "had some feeling of the sport; he knew the service"—i.e., prostitution (3.2.96-98). Readers of the play realize that Lucio should not be taken too seriously because of his listing in the Dramatis Personae as "a fantastic." The OED provides us with two contemporaneous definitions of the term that allow us to dismiss Lucio's talk as unsubstantial, idle, and uninformed gossip: "One who has fanciful ideas or indulges in wild notions" and "One given to fine or showy dress; a fop." Even if Lucio were more reputable, the bachelor Duke has little reason to hide this information from someone as inconsequential as Lucio. The Duke, as Friar Lodowick, replies that he "never heard the absent Duke much detected for women. He was not inclined that way" (3.2.99-100). The connotations of "detected" elicit images of secrets being divulged and the exposure of a clandestine act. The curious "not inclined that way" sounds like a subtle nudge-in-the-ribs allusion to the Duke not being attracted to women. The fact that a "friar" is delivering these lines on stage also evokes images and anti-Catholic stereotypes about all-male monasteries and their propensity for sodomy.

Secondly, the idea of a homosocial triangle comes to light in the Duke's marriage proposal to Isabella: "Give me your hand and say you will be mine; / He is my brother too" (5.1.491-92). Duke Vincentio's marriage proposal does not end with Isabella; in fact, the line does not end until Claudio is mentioned. The homosocial triangle's ability to strengthen social, political, and economic ties between two men over a woman is evident in this passage. Isabella's presence as a queer virgin further radicalizes this homosocial bond that these men are presumably about to begin. Furthermore, bringing attention to King James's amorous same-sex affinities highlights how the monarch's "male alliances, associated as they were with homoeroticism and sodomy, threatened the acceptability of male homosociality" (Crawford 367) in a patriarchal, all-male court.

Lastly, it places Isabella as a required but inferior part of this triangle, once again proving why her decision to leave the secular world is better for her as an individual. Even Michael Friedman, who argues for staging the play so that Isabella and the Duke's marriage is celebrated "as a form of recompense offered by the husband to his future wife to atone for sexual offenses committed against her" (454), agrees that the Duke's marriage proposal "springs not from erotic desire" (461).

Conclusion

Measure for Measure's setting in Catholic Vienna focuses our attention on the iconic figures of the nun to interrogate how religious vocations within Catholic nations allow individuals to function in their everyday lives. Following in the footsteps of Queen Elizabeth, Isabella embodies an early modern female protagonist usurping the power usually bestowed on the men in her life when she chooses the role she wishes to perform. Her ability to become a nun simultaneously distances her from her Christian relatives in England and celebrates her as the paragon of ideal womanhood that is more difficult to attain in Protestant nations. Just as this refusal to exchange her body in the heteronormative economy of sexuality marks her as a rebellious queer virgin, the Duke's brief performance as a friar elucidates not only the differences between real friars cognizant of their spiritual responsibility and politically motivated ones, but it also allows us to see Duke Vincentio as a failure who cannot rule effectively without problematizing his citizens' livelihoods. Audience members cannot imagine that Duke Vincentio's engagement to Isabella will end in any (re)productive manner if he is unable to function as a believable friar or an effective duke. The Catholic setting and Catholic characters of this play are integral elements in interrogating issues pertaining to women's agency, a ruler's effectiveness, and the possibilities of Catholicism as a lens through which these issues can be examined more clearly in a Protestant literary landscape.

Chapter Three

Convents as Feminist Utopias: Margaret Cavendish's *The Convent of Pleasure* and the Potential of Closeted Dramas and Communities

Margaret Cavendish was considered maddeningly eccentric and unconventional by her contemporaries. Only in the last twenty to thirty years has she been recognized by scholars of English literature as a trailblazer not only in the history of English women's writing but also in the development of science fiction (1666's *Blazing World*). As her works have become a staple of literary anthologies, the refreshingly provocative and brash manner in which she engaged in the centuries-old *querelle des femmes* is now entertaining a new generation of readers. Cavendish wrote in various genres and about diverse topics ranging from a biography of her husband, William Cavendish, Duke of Newcastle, to natural philosophy, and, more importantly for this study, women and their sexuality in seventeenth-century England.

Cavendish's 1668 *The Convent of Pleasure* utilizes the Catholic architecture and ideology of convents and nuns, respectively, within a Protestant historical landscape that figures such communities as antiquated and alien. Her ingenious employment of a dated English community springs from the same philosophical aims that inspired the utopian narratives that came into vogue at the end of the seventeenth century. She employs the utopian tropes of imagined communities to interrogate a woman's limited roles in Protestant society. Her text explores the intellectual, social, and erotic potential of all-female communities, as well as the secular, gendered power structures that surrounded them. This chapter's analysis of convents and nuns as literary tropes will demonstrate how Cavendish injects historical and contemporary socio-political realities into her creation of Lady Happy's convent so that the protagonist can fervently champion women's rights. Cavendish does so by initially employing the convent setting as a palatable backdrop for her philosophical musings and negotiations. After establishing the convent as an idealistic feminine community, Cavendish then subverts traditional views of the convent with characters who encloister themselves for erotic and intellectual intercourse.

This chapter's study of *The Convent of Pleasure* is sharpened by a traditional close reading of the dialogues, structures, and themes that Cavendish employs as well as by theoretical frameworks that deal with gender, feminism, historical contexts, and sexuality. Furthermore, in an attempt to gain some insight into what Cavendish's thought process might have entailed while writing the play, I utilize some of her quasi-autobiographical writings, most notably her 1664 epistolary collection *Sociable Letters*, to analyze her personal opinion on subjects addressed in the drama's content and thematic conceits.

The Convent of Pleasure was published in the playwright's second release of dramatic works, 1668's *Plays, Never Before Printed*. Like her other publications, this edition of Cavendish's writing was financed, approved, and enthusiastically supported by her husband. Circulated among aristocratic circles and the well-read, Cavendish's works received a small but significant amount of attention, mostly negative. Undeterred by critics who found it unbecoming of a woman to publish her writings, Cavendish sent copies of her works to colleges at Oxford and Cambridge. Her determination to be noticed by the cognoscenti and tastemakers of her day paid off posthumously; three years following her death a commemorative edition of poems and letters was published in her honor. These publications included laudatory letters from the Oxford and Cambridge libraries as well as works by Thomas Shadwell and Thomas Hobbes (Bennett 12).

Cavendish consistently attempted to appease those who perceived her as haughty by mimicking the rhetoric of a humility topos in her prefaces. Cavendish's imitation of such a trope is just that – an imitation. The indelible pride she has for her work seeps through despite any attempts she makes at acting humble. Illustratively, in the preface to 1668's *Plays, Never Before Printed*, Cavendish invites and repels hostile critics: "Having observ'd, that the most Worthy and most Meritorious Persons have the most envious Detractors, it would be a presumptuous opinion in me to imagine my self in danger to have any: but however, their malice cannot hinder me from Writing" (4). Besides the typical misogyny that Cavendish could expect from public responses to her writing, the duchess must have known that the socially progressive subjects she discussed and expanded on in her poems, letters, and plays would attract scorn. From Samuel Pepys to her female aristocratic peers, Cavendish's detractors found her noteworthy enough to discuss her and her works. Anticipating contemporary celebrityhood's adage that "any publicity is good publicity," Cavendish purposely banked her literary fame on engaging writing tropes and licentious subject matter (matriarchal kingdoms, all-female armies, lesbian nuns, etc.)[1].

For the scope of this chapter, *The Convent of Pleasure* is firm ground for sampling Cavendish's attention to feminist politics and theological debate in the context of this book's overall argument about depictions of nuns as representatives of early modern feminism. The ostensibly religious setting and characters of the drama are malleable tools with which Cavendish made politically prescient comments on the state of women in Interregnum and Restoration England as well as within the Catholic Church. The duchess did so by shrewdly employing Catholic iconography (the secluded, walled convent) and female professionals (nuns) to volley her attacks in the *querelle des femmes*. Readers may quickly understand the power convents possess to engender and support subversive communities. Cavendish's nostalgic use of the ideologies attached to such institutions highlights how Catholicism still contained the potential for female independence in a patriarchal world chafing at the idea that women could be respected as autonomous individuals.

Walking on Broken Glass: Cavendish's Religious Identity

Cavendish scholars have often reflected on her atypical religious beliefs. As Cavendish biographer Katie Whitaker puts it, "If she had any strong religious feeling, it was towards the natural world and its manifold wonders, rather than towards a distant, invisible God" (317). In one of her "Sociable Letters," Cavendish wades into controversial waters with her discussion of people who unexpectedly change their religion: "what Opinion a King or Chief Governour did Profess, the most part of their Subjects did the same . . . some for Honours, Offices, and Commands, others to Enjoy their Estates, and to save Fines, or Taxes, or the like . . . Thus some for Fear, and some for Favour, some through Covetousness, and some for Humor, changed their Opinions in Religion, but few for Conscience, and none for Reason" (181). England's potential to "slide back" into Catholicism was a topic that caused anxiety among many

---

[1] Danielle Dutton's *Margaret the First: A* Novel, New York: Catapult, 2016, captures many of Cavendish's notorious attributes in this lithesome and enjoyable work of historical fiction.

Protestant citizens throughout the early modern era. The end result of such angst was the deposition of King James II and the Glorious Revolution of 1688. Cavendish's ambiguous religious beliefs, her subtle literary associations with Catholicism, and her ruminations about an individual's motivation for changing religions serve as prime evidence of her love for engaging in debate about quasi-theological issues.

Cavendish's various references to nuns, female anchorets, life on the Catholic Continent, and same-sex communities engender discussion of her thoughts on England's most recent "Old Religion" and the roles available for women. In fact, given the difficult situation many English Catholics recusants faced, scholars of English Catholicism note that post-Reformation English women who chose to become nuns did so because "they had evolved a deeply held belief that they had a vocation for the religious life and were prepared to undergo considerable risk and difficulty to attain this state" (Stevenson 52). Consequently, English literature featuring convents and women who choose to enter such communities represents the strong will, religious conviction, and independent agency that such real-life women possess.

In fact, Cavendish also employs the personality and reputation of nuns as independent women to explore female autonomy in the philosophical short story "The She-Anchoret" - one of the lengthier pieces in her 1656 publication *Natures Pictures*. The anonymous anchoret's father has recently died, but not before advising her to "Live chast and holy, Serve the Gods above, / They will protect thee for thy zealous Love" (545). As in *The Convent of Pleasure*, Cavendish employs a pantheistic pagan reference to religious deities while simultaneously borrowing from Catholic theology as the woman resolves "to live like a kind of an Anchoret's Life, living encloistered by her self alone, vowing Chastity, and a Single-life, but gave leave for any to speak to her through a Grate" (547). The anchoret's wisdom hinges on her seclusion and ability to contemplate life's great matters without having to deal with a husband or children. Taking the form of something akin to an advice column, the story features dozens of characters from different professions and backgrounds who seek the anchoret to ask her for counsel on matters ranging from astronomy and biology to marriage and religion.

Just like Lady Happy, the anchoret rejects suitors early in her retirement. Unlike Lady Happy and her eventual marriage to the Prince, the anchoret decides to commit suicide by drinking poison when a king insists on marrying her, thereby sacrificing her life for her country and her "unspotted Chastity, holy Vows, and dutiful Obedience" in order "to quench the raging Lust of a wicked Tyrant" (705). Cavendish celebrates the independent woman's choice to live a secluded, chaste life by having the "State [set] up her Statue of Brass, for her Courage and Love to her Country" and the "Church Deif[y] her a Saint, for her Virtue and Piety" after her death (706). By amalgamating the state's and church's veneration of the anchoret, Cavendish creates a world where the profane and the sacred spheres of life lionize a woman's spiritual profession - one which stimulates the intellectual growth of a nun-like woman who aids society with her social, scientific, and theological advice.

Cavendish identifies herself with the hermit-like life of an anchoret in a musing from her 1656 autobiography *A True Relation of my Birth, Breeding, and Life*: "I could most willingly exclude my self, so as Never to see the face of any creature, but my Lord, as long as I live, inclosing my self like an Anchoret, wearing a Frize-gown, tied with a cord about my waste" (35). Indeed, the Jesuit priest Richard Flecknoe compares Cavendish to a hermit in a poem he wrote for a posthumous text her husband commissioned to celebrate her life and works:

> What place is this? Looks like some Sacred Cell
> Where holy Hermits anciently did dwell
> And never ceas'd Importunating Heav'n
> . . .
> No mirrour here in all the Room you find;
> Unless it be the mirror of the Mind,
> . . .
> Here she is Rapt, here falls in Extasy
> With studying high and deep *Philosophy*: (qtd. in Van Beneden and De Poorter 187)

Cavendish was childless and never expressed much desire for biological children. She considered her literary accomplishments as her offspring, much as nuns thought of their spiritual works and writings as their legacy to the world. This symbolic identification of her writing as her progeny surfaces in one of her "Sociable Letters" where she discusses the fear she experiences when her works must be transported by sea before being published:

> I should have been much Afflicted, and accounted the Loss of my Twenty Playes, as the Loss of Twenty Lives, for in my Mind I should have Died Twenty Deaths . . . but they are Destinated to Live, and I hope, I in them, when my Body is Dead, and Turned to Dust . . . I always keep the Copies of them safely with me, until they are Printed, and then I Commit the Originals to the Fire, like Parents which are willing to Die, wheanas they are sure of their Childrens Lives. (154)

This shift in changing what the signifier for one's legacy will be, from biological children to literary work, meshes well with Kate Lilly's study of seventeenth-century women writers who repudiate the obligations of marriage and child-rearing:

> If marriage is the institution of which these women most frequently write, in both positive and negative terms, that is because it is central to any analysis of the interactive, mutually constitutive relationship of the public and the private; and to any analysis of the political, legal, economic and sexual positioning of women according to marital status (married, unmarried, widowed). That none of them had children is also significant, giving them an actual and conceptual distance from the patriarchal confinement of female productivity within the maternal. (128)

Coming Out of the Dark: Cavendish's Closet Dramas

Cavendish's childlessness was not the only instrument that played a role in her works favoring environments and characters that allow women to be autonomous agents. The public theaters were closed while Cavendish wrote most of her dramas. Undeterred by a dearth of avenues where her work could be performed, Cavendish exploited the privileges of her rank and the freedom of not having a royal censor with which to contest or an audience to appease. She did so and transgressed patriarchal constructions of women by subverting gender stereotypes and exploring same-sex desire through the eschewing of traditional methods of producing plays in Renaissance England. Her aristocratic status, the closing of public theaters during the Interregnum, and her familiarity with Queen Henrietta Maria's Catholic court culture equipped Cavendish to ingeniously fictionalize realms rooted in the sociopolitical realities of her time. Through the literary setting of the convent, Cavendish destabilized heterocentric constructions of gender and helped pioneer the portrayal of lesbian relationships in the literature of early modern Europe.

Like other women who were literate and enjoyed the advancements of an intellectually open post-Reformation society, Cavendish "proposed extending education to women and restructuring domestic authority in order to improve the position of the female sex" (Boxer and Quataert 21). The Duchess of Newcastle achieves such argumentative feats in her philosophical letters, poems, and, most noticeably, in her closet dramas that flesh out her musings via character-driven plots that hinge on realistic scenarios and settings whose verisimilitude engages readers to imagine what the possibilities for women could be in all-female communities. Examples of such discourse include the Amazon-like retinue of soldiers in

1662's *Bell in Campo* and the quasi-religious convent in *The Convent of Pleasure*.

The shuttering of theaters in 1642 was a monumental and in some ways fortuitous change for English playwrights. The closure removed the need to appeal to socially mixed audiences and to deal with playing companies, actors, and financial demands. This new freedom, however dubious it may have been, enabled playwrights to subvert traditional dramatic structural forms and content. Karen Raber argues that since there were no public stages to perform plays, "every piece of dramatic writing produced in England during the civil war years was by necessity a closet drama" (188). Women, particularly elite women, had the most to gain from the emergence of closet drama as a more respected form of writing among the cultured classes, since they were no longer challenged to have their plays staged to establish their credibility. The semi-private nature of writing closet dramas mirrors early modern ideas about closets, or private rooms. Cavendish imagined her closet as a writing space that included "the limited circulation, particularly amongst family, friends and patronage networks, of her writings, providing a space to rehearse communication and creativity" (Knowles 186). Thus, Cavendish could feel secure that her writings would simultaneously be read, considered, and debated without entering an ostensibly wider realm of public circulation. Closet drama's divergence from the limited aspects of commercial theater gave writers an unprecedented amount of freedom to analyze gender relations in both the public and private spheres.

Cavendish's entrance into the world of writing is noticeable for its staunchly loyalist and elitist trappings. Forced into exile, albeit a pampered one in the court of Queen Henrietta Maria in France, Cavendish explored the upheaval that followed the death of the king and challenged all of the conventional notions about government with which she was raised. While the political themes of Cavendish's work were the traditional ones of a powerful monarchy and its courtly accoutrements ingrained in the sociopolitical structure of her narratives, her explorations of gender and sexuality were pioneering. Likewise, her malleable approaches to the religious environment of the convent – sometimes Catholic and at other times pagan – are influenced by both her open-minded view of religious beliefs, as witnessed in her autobiographical writing, and by her immersion in the exile court culture wherein the English Catholic queen was once asked if she could "abide" a Huguenot and she responded, "Why not? . . . Was not my father one?" (Hibbard 119). Another Marian influence on Cavendish's theatrical writing may have been the queen's insistence on not only participating, acting, and speaking in private plays put on before the court, some of which she wrote and directed, but also in her choice to sometimes "even dress[. . .] as a man" while on stage (Dolan 99).

If the birth of the closet drama as a necessary genre (although there are ancient-to-Renaissance-era antecedents for closet dramas) gave Cavendish free rein in terms of writing dramatic content, the reopening of the theaters in 1660 presented her with the ability to produce her plays for public consumption. Cavendish did not publish her dramatic texts until the Interregnum. Although Cavendish's chances to stage her own plays were limited because of the Interregnum and mainstream disapproval of female playwrights, the time seemed ripe for someone as confident as Cavendish to become a renowned playwright, particularly with the introduction of female actors on the English stage. However, there are no records of her plays being produced, and such an absence can be attributed to the very experimental content that she was allowed to generate with the closure of the theaters. According to Judith Peacock, Cavendish's subversive gender politics probably hindered the production of her plays after the reopening of theaters because her "utopian separatist scenarios" were "deeply disturbing to a society just emerging from a crisis concerning social position and changing sites of power" (87).

As one of the prefatory letters in 1662's *Playes* demonstrates, Cavendish was not interested in conforming to neoclassical ideas of play structure: "Likewise my Playes may be Condemned, because they follow not the Antient Custome, as the learned says, which is, that all Comedies should be so ordered and composed . . . but what may be naturally, or usually practiced or Acted in the World in the compass of one day" (11). Of course this naïve critique overlooks the fact that Shakespeare and his contemporaries had long done away with the classical unities of drama. As she goes on to attack Ben Jonson for the unnecessary length of *Volpone* (and rightly so, many twenty-first century readers still concur), Cavendish showcases her desire to flout rules (even antiquated ones) and rebel against the patriarchy by which she felt so oppressed and ridiculed. Like Virginia Woolf, Cavendish resented being denied a proper education because of her sex.

If Cavendish utilized her writing as a "refuge from exile's discomforts" to imagine a future she dreamed might happen, as Raber argues, then Cavendish can be seen as a firm believer in rejecting archaic, essentialist assumptions about gender and supporting the belief in gender as a construction of society. In one of the other prefatory letters to *Playes* Cavendish writes, "as for the niceties of Rules, Forms, and Terms, I renounce, and protest, that if I did understand and know them strictly, as I do not, I would not follow them: and if any dislike my writings for want of those Rules, Forms, and Terms, let them not read them..." (13). Although readers can continue to recognize Cavendish's insecurities about not being properly schooled, her subversion of the meek tone of the ubiquitous humility topos forewarns readers who may be shocked enough by the radical content of her plays to stop reading. Cavendish represents a transition in the content of dramatic prefatory materials that mark the emergence of "the contemplative reader" (Shaver 189). She encourages the active reader to abandon decorum and contemplate the liberties of transgressing gender boundaries in her plays. The duchess's suggestion in the preface to *Playes* that acting in theater can educate noble youth implies how she wanted readers to identify with her fictional characters, if not act like them in their lives, at least on the theatrical stage or the imaginary stage in their minds. Susan Wiseman argues that Cavendish's plays "act out scenarios in which women are on display, desired but also triumphant, and offer the reader, particularly the female reader, material for elaboration of fantasy" (99).

In another prefatory letter to *Playes*, Cavendish argues that acting in a play will instruct honorable youth "not only to know other men, but their own selves" (12). In yet another preface she underscores her insistence on pushing the envelope when it comes to depictions of gender: "I know no reason but that I may as well make them Hees for my use, as others did Shees, or Shees as others did Hees . . . we may as well understand the meaning or sense of a Speaker or Writer by the names of Love or Hate, as by the names of he or she, and better" (13). Cavendish makes her literary works and her explorations of gender constructions all the more personal through autobiographical self-fashioning. In a slightly contradicting rejoinder to the lines where she expresses antipathy for the allegedly mandatory classical unities of time, place, and action, Cavendish asks her readers to imagine her writings as mirrors to the real world: "I would have my Playes to be like the Natural course of all things in the World" (11). This bid for a reader's response to the verisimilitude she creates in her dramas highlights the importance of studying her provocative female protagonists, such as Lady Happy in *The Convent of Pleasure*. Whether or not readers can imagine themselves acting like the characters in Cavendish's plays, at least the author enjoys the traditionally cathartic experience of viewing a play (even if just in her mind), with some of her female characters being "intended as parodies of Cavendish's own exaggerated personality traits or humors," and others as Cavendish's dramatic projection of herself into a utopian fantasy world (Mendelson 205).

Sisters Are Doing It for Themselves:
The Ladies of Lady Happy's Convent

The Convent of Pleasure begins simply enough with three gentleman discussing their hopes to marry Lady Happy, whose wealthy father has recently died and left her his fortune. It could be a conversation heard in the drawing room among Portia's many suitors in Shakespeare's *The Merchant of Venice*. The subsequent scene continues the discussion of Lady Happy's marital future only to have the protagonist challenge marriage conventions in the first lines that she utters. She decides to follow Heaven's command for the rich to give to the poor by surmising that if her gifts are to be placed "rightly" she "must Marry one that's poor, old, ill-favoured, and debauch'd" (1.2.7-8). Readers' initial impression of Lady Happy is one of a charitable maiden whose description of herself as diametrical to an "old" and "debauch'd" man marks her as a young, ascetically-inclined woman. Lady Happy's employment of "Heaven" imbues the discussion with a religious ambience that soon appropriates Catholic imagery and ideology. Lady Happy's lady-in-waiting, Madame Mediator, incredulously counters, "But surely you will not incloyster your self, as you say" (1.2.14). Lady Happy's response to those who are shocked by her decision to retire is imbued with logically and theologically sound reasons for choosing to reject the secular world of courting, marrying, and reproducing. Mimicking Saint Paul's admonition in Corinthians that people should abstain from marriage to lead a life solely devoted to God – "For I would that all men were even as myself: but every one hath his proper gift from God; one after this manner, and another after that" (1 Corinthians 7:7) – Lady Happy argues, "Marriage to those that are virtuous is a greater restraint than a monastery" (1.2.19-20).

Cavendish's continual contrast between marriage and the monastery is echoed in one of her "Sociable Letters" when she expresses dismay over unhappy marriages: "it were better to be Barr'd up within the Gates of a Monastery, than to be Bound in the Bonds of Matrimony" (72). Lady Happy then rejects visitations and flirtations from would-be husbands by using antitheses that demonstrate how she has rationally evaluated her potential gains with possible losses:

> Or should I take delight in Admirers? . . . I should lose more of my Reputation by their Visits, then gain by their Praises. Or, should I quit Reputation and turn Courtizan, there would be more lost in my Health, then gained by my Lovers, I should find more pain then Pleasure . . . since there is so much folly, vanity and falshood in Men, why should Women

trouble and vex themselves for their sake; for retiredness bars the life from nothing else but Men. (1.2.20-30)

Unlike Lucio's outlining of the limited options for women in Shakespeare's *Measure for Measure*, "My lord, she may be a punk, for many of them are neither maid, widow, nor wife" (5.1.184-85), Lady Happy presents the broader lifestyle possibilities afforded to Catholic women: wife, whore, *or* nun. However, Cavendish does not set her play in a Catholic city like Vienna. Published, circulated, and read in England, the play would have been staged in the minds of most readers in their English homeland. At the same time, the use of the French titles "Monsieur" and "Madame" lends the play a Continental air. Like Shakespeare, Cavendish tries to have it both ways in a Protestant literary landscape. The play's lack of a named geographic setting demonstrates how her dismissal of classic conventions of playwriting gives her the freedom to create an unspecified state of possibilities for her female characters.

Lady Happy's reasons for making a quick departure to a convent dedicated to meditation and altruistic good works are elucidated when her attendants question her and label those women who sacrifice worldly pleasures when they enter a convent as "fools." Discreetly switching from a Christian idea of Heaven and the capitalized "God," Lady Happy talks about "gods" and "Nature." Careful not to offend those who lead an ascetic lifestyle in their devotion to God, Lady Happy laments the fact that people who wear uncomfortable hair-cloth, fast, and live in Spartan environments do so "not for the gods sake" (1.2.35), since "if it be neither pleasure, nor profit to the gods' neither do Men any thing for the gods but their own sake" (1.2.54-55). By having her protagonist engage in a theological debate, however superficial, Cavendish allows Lady Happy to enter an intellectual realm monopolized by men. The few women who were allowed to write about theological matters did so from a confessional perspective that highlighted their devotion and sacrifice to God. These women, usually nuns such as Saint Teresa of Ávila, did not typically publish on disputed matters of theology. Lady Happy's conclusion that "the gods are better pleased with Praises th[a]n Fasting" (1.2.58) allows Cavendish to enjoy the best of two worlds in her drama. She gives Lady Happy the authority of a prioress or respected nun-like figure to logically discuss matters of importance to the religious community, but has her reference pagan "gods" so as to not offend the mores of her Christian readers. Nonetheless, Lady Happy's sensible argument that "when the Senses are dull'd with abstinency, the Body weakned with fasting, the Spirits tir'd with watching, the Life made uneasie with pain, the Soul can have but little will to worship" (1.2.59-61), is possible because of her decision to join a convent where such behaviors are expected.

Unlike Isabella's desire for a "strict restraint" with the Order of St. Clare in *Measure for Measure*, Cavendish's Lady Happy does not share the Catholic calling that inspires Shakespeare's heroine. As a result, Cavendish uses the convent and the lifestyle of nuns as literary tools to make socio-political statements rather than strictly religious ones. After all, despite Cavendish's time in Queen Henrietta Maria's Catholic court, she never hinted at leaving the Anglican faith for Catholicism. Although English Catholic recusants suffered under the Interregnum and the hostile anti-Catholic culture leading to and following the Glorious Revolution of 1688, there was a steady increase of Catholic missionary priests in England during Cavendish's time. Because it is difficult to definitively ascertain the number of practicing Catholics in England at that time, if one assumes that an increase in the number of priests indicates a growing base of parishioners in need of them, then the increase of three hundred missionary priests from the death of Queen Elizabeth to 750 on the eve of the Civil War demonstrates that Catholicism did not fade from English culture as most Protestant-oriented providential histories of England tend to assume (Bossy 217). Consequently, there would have been ample opportunities for a privileged woman such as Cavendish to be a closet Catholic or even a public one, especially in exile. But she never was.

Despite her decision not to convert to Catholicism, Cavendish's early life was informed by sympathies with the Catholic recusant community. Her family's ties with King Charles I in the year preceding the Civil War led the Lucases to be grouped with Catholics, Laudian Anglicans, and the king's cliques. These associations subsequently set the scene for the Lucas family to become a "target for violence":

> On May 13, the day after the Earl of Strafford's execution, an organized crowd of about a hundred . . . tore down and burned the fences of the Lucases' new enclosures and destroyed their brick kilns. . . . Witnesses talked of . . . Lucas servants attacked, and of rioters who "wished heartily that Sir John Lucas had been there for they would have used him worse and would have burnt him or ended him." (Whitaker 37-38)

In one of her "Sociable Letters" Cavendish expresses discomfort with the amount of freedom the Anglican church provided parishioners to read, and, consequently, interpret the Bible on their own without the assistance of learned clergy: "The Church of England is the Purest, but yet it hath suffer'd the Scripture to be Read too Commonly, which hath caused much Disturbance, not only to Particular Persons, but in the Church it self, and hath lost much of the Dignity belonging to Church-men" (96). Such disregard for having the ability to read the Bible in one's tongue is an abhorrent thought to people of any Christian denomination in the twenty-first century, but during Cavendish's time it was still a matter of dispute. The majority of the Catholic Church hierarchy wanted to keep the Bible in the Latin Vulgate, rendering it unreadable to those literate only in their vernacular. Cavendish's tolerance for different religious beliefs would have been influenced by her time in the religiously tolerant Netherlands as well as by her husband's public defense of himself when he was attacked for allowing Catholics to serve in his army regiment. Regardless of what Cavendish's sympathies may have been for persecuted Catholics, this chapter asserts that the opportunities Catholicism could afford women were too much for Cavendish to pass up in her feminist approach to the *querelle des femmes*.

Because convents were the most recognizable all-female communities in mainstream European society, the ideology behind this same-sex utopia proved too irresistible for Cavendish to ignore. Cavendish improves upon Christine de Pizan's allegorical city of ladies by creating a fictive, physical community of women. However, the rebellious, separatist streak of Lady Happy and her peers does little to improve relations with men outside of the convent or achieve an equitable playing field between the sexes. Like real-world convents, Lady Happy's commune functions more as an *other within* than a truly marginal, outsider population, since it still deals with would-be suitors, disguised princes, and conniving gentlemen, similar to how abbesses and nuns dealt with the Catholic Church's male hierarchy and their intrusions into their community. Therefore, as noted by Anna Battigelli, Lady Happy represents a provocative amalgamation of Cavendish's two typical female protagonist types: the "active cavalier" and the "contemplative cavalier." Whereas the former is described as engaging "with her world, using language and action to change it," the latter "retreats from her world altogether" (Battigelli 26).

Provocatively enough, Lady Happy, like most nuns, represents aspects of both character types. The retreat of Lady Happy and her followers into the convent is not a silent or unnoticed action. The gentlemen and would-be suitors are up in arms about their loss of potential wives. Lady Happy's seclusion presents the threat of a scarcity of female goods and reproductive recession in the heteronormative marriage economy of early modern England. Battigelli is able to categorize Cavendish's "active cavaliers" through their actions of setting out to "reshape the unsatisfactory external world" by "cross-dressing, by taking on male roles, or, most significantly, by speaking eloquently" to "impose change on their world" (26). As such, by employing conventual culture and community as a means for creating a different world from the external one, Lady Happy and her peers achieve all of the same feats of the "active cavaliers" found in Cavendish's previously published dramas such as *Bell in Campo* and *Love's Adventures*.

Madame Mediator's report to the gentlemen about what occurs in the convent forces the external world to take notice of a matriarchal alternative. Likewise, since Cavendish is always intent on performing in what she imagines as the stage inside her readers' minds, the closet drama achieves its ideological goals via the text-dependent confines of the genre. Lilly's study on utopian writing by women demonstrates how Cavendish's quasi-utopian convent is a representative hallmark of how women approached such imagined communities in opposition to the way male writers constructed such lands: "Men's utopias have focused on political systems and laws; utopian writing by women has tended to focus strategically on the possibilities and problems of gendered social life and the weight of custom – micropolitical questions of sexuality, maternity, education, domesticity and self-government – while declining the burden of representing a fully articulated model of a new political order" (118). In a similar style, Cavendish's attention to how the convent will be ordered and how the women in them will go about their daily lives foreshadows Woolf's call for the literary world to respect women's writing that focuses on the domestic microcosms that affect life more profoundly than larger political narratives.

Despite the sociopolitical discourse involved in Cavendish's celebration of feminine power and authority, readers cannot dismiss the Catholic undertones of this community. Protestant polemicists constantly attacked the Catholic Church as monstrously feminine. Edmund Spenser often compares the church to the Whore of Babylon throughout *The Faerie Queene*. Catholic men are feminized in popular literature because of their involvement with Marian devotion. In stark contrast to such texts, Cavendish's drama exists in a continuum of literature that highlights the empowering function of the Catholic convent in order to respond to an attack on a Catholic "theology and an iconography in which women were understood as inappropriately visible, powerful, and esteemed" (Dolan 52). The women in *The Convent of Pleasure* are not invisible, powerless, or underappreciated in their quest to enjoy their bodies for their own sake.

Illustratively, Lady Happy's pleasure, as the play's title implies, will be sensual. Reversing the tradition of courtly love blazons that praise the exterior appearance of a woman's sensory parts in anatomic fashion, Lady

Happy employs octosyllabic rhyming lines to highlight how the convent will appeal to and be enjoyed by the women's senses:

Wee'l Cloth our selves with softest Silk,
And Linnen fine as white as milk.
Wee'l please our Sight with Pictures rare;
Our Nostrils with perfumed Air.
Our Ears with sweet melodious Sound,
Whose Substance can be no where found;
Our Tast with sweet delicious Meat,
. . .
This will in Pleasure's Convent *I*
Live with delight, and with it die. (1.2.108-14)

The emphasis on the women's enjoyment of clothing, paintings, perfume, music, and food asserts their agency in controlling their pleasures rather than on how their body will be used and enjoyed by others. Because nuns reject marriage and child bearing, the "nuns" of Lady Happy's convent have an excuse for circumventing patriarchal expectations of how their bodies will be exploited by their lovers, husbands, and children. Lady Happy's poetic description of the convent ends with an early modern erotic pun on "die" - to experience a sexual orgasm. The pun emphasizes not only her determination to live her entire life within the convent's walls, but it also invites the audience to guess what other forms of pleasure she and her cloistered comrades will enjoy.

The realistic requirements for having such a luxurious convent do not escape Cavendish, who populates the community with workers and servants much as real convents employed servants and, in the New World, slaves: "she hath a numerous Company of Female Servants, as there is no occasion for men" (2.1.65). At the same time, some of Cavendish's more egalitarian sympathies appear in Lady Happy's appropriation of convent culture's desire to support less financially endowed women by inviting them into their fold. She explains that she will sponsor women who cannot afford living single: "I will take so many Noble Persons of my own sex, as my Estate will plentifully maintain, such whose Births are greater then [sic] their Fortunes, and are resolv'd to live a single life, and vow Virginity" (1.2.110-13). As Harriette Andreadis has argued, Cavendish's commitment to transgressive sexual politics is the fortunate outcome of her privileged status: "Cavendish could afford to articulate such sentiments . . . from the safe vantage of her happy marriage to an approving spouse and her secure social status. Perhaps it is that very vantage that sharpened her understanding of women's status and allowed her to fantasize the paradoxical freedoms of female cloistered pleasures" (85). Despite the financial and political security she enjoyed because of her husband, Cavendish did not publish *The Convent of Pleasure*, *Bell in Campo*, or other avowedly gender-bending plays until after the Restoration, when she could be ensconced more firmly within her privileged state.

Historical, Political, and Religious Conventual Contexts: Both Foreign and Domestic

The occasionally luxuriant environs of convents had a place in pre-Reformation English aristocratic history. Sometimes functioning like women's clubs or retreats, convents were often visited by noblewomen who were granted permission to vacation in enclosed nunneries. These women would sponsor lavish entertainments and even secure papal indulgences "to allow guests from religious houses to eat meat" (Ward 191). When Madame Mediator reports to Lady Vertue that a Princess has arrived at the convent "to be one of Nature's Devotes" after hearing about the community (2.3.7), Cavendish follows the tradition of royal and aristocratic women visiting convents as a refuge from the testosterone-fueled extraconventual sphere.

Whether or not Cavendish was aware of the life of Mary Ward does not detract from the argument that Lady Happy and her posse are part of a seventeenth-century discourse that shows women attempting to find their own place in the religious landscape of England. Ward, a member of one of Yorkshire's and England's most well-known Catholic families, was a former nun with the Order of Poor Clares. Finding contemplative life unsuitable to her desires to be more active in the community and to have girls be as well-educated as boys, Ward founded the "English Ladies," who would work like the Jesuits but be governed by and responsible solely to the pope. William Harrison, Archpriest of England, led the opposition to the community of women in 1621 by attacking them for speaking "too freely on spiritual matters," which he claimed was "against the teaching of Saint Paul . . . that women should be silent in the churches" (Daly 63). The community of "English Ladies" was officially suppressed and Ward was imprisoned as a heretic and schismatic while in Munich in 1630. Pope Urban VIII eventually ordered her to be released, but did not give his approval for the continued existence of such a Jesuit-like community of women religious. Ward was opposed by Catholics and Protestants alike. Although Cavendish's community of women is not explicitly Catholic, or Christian for that matter, its threat to the male-dominated culture represented by the gentlemen and the intrusive prince finds a real-world parallel in Ward's entrepreneurial spirit and her oppression at the hands of the Catholic Church's patriarchy.

One of Cavendish's feminist literary descendants, Mary Astell, also used the enclosed community of the convent as an ideological foundation in her proposal for an all-female secular community of learning and empowerment in 1696's *A Serious Proposal to the Ladies*.

Indeed, Astell, whose mother was Catholic, carefully managed her proposition with an attempt to fend off Protestant critics who would see the community as too Catholic: "Now as to the Proposal it is to erect a *Monastery*, or if you will (to avoid giving offence to the scrupulous and injudicious, by names which tho' innocent in themselves, have been abus'd by superstitious Practices,) we will call it as *Religious Retirement*" (73). Despite her precautions Astell's proposals were vociferously attacked by the likes of Anglican Bishop Gilbert Burnet, who would counsel Queen Anne not to support Astell's recommendations.

Returning to Cavendish's fictional convent, we see the attacks Ward and Astell suffered mirrored in the male responses to Lady Happy and her ladies' decision to retire from the extra-conventual world. Cavendish imagines what men's responses would be to the all-female community by having Madame Mediator enter and exit the convent's supposedly grateless walls to facilitate discussion of its activities in the extraconventual world. Surely cognizant of the rich anti-clerical tradition of English literature, Cavendish has one of the gentlemen, Monsieur Facil, suggest that he and the other men should "fee the Clergy to perswade her out, for the good of the Commonwealth" (2.1.44-45). Both before and after the English Reformation, many authors satirized and exaggerated the cases of nuns who were sexually active with men. In such literature, male clerics are often portrayed as Pandarus-like pimps who whore their harem of bawdy nuns. Facil's suggestion not only echoes anti-clerical polemic but also mimics Protestant discourse regarding Catholicism's most exalted role for women. After all, Martin Luther wrote a letter to three nuns in the summer of 1524 that enjoined them to leave the convent for two reasons: if they were there under compulsion and because chastity is unnatural. Luther attests that "both Scripture and experience teach that among many thousands there is not one to whom God gives the grace to maintain pure chastity. A woman does not have the power [to do this] herself. God created her body to be with a man, bear children and raise them, as Scripture makes clear in Genesis 1" (141).

Additionally, Monsieur Facil's comment that the women should leave the convent "for the good of the Commonwealth" places the state before individual conscience by using Protestant-style rhetoric about women's roles. The capitalization of "Commonwealth" alludes to the republican form of government established in England during the Interregnum. This heavy-handed, Puritan-style administration was stridently anti-Catholic. Cavendish's royalist exile during the Interregnum placed her within a community of other refugees, such as Catholics, that received far less sympathy from England's government than under King James I. Knowingly or not, Cavendish shared the experience of so many Catholic Englishwomen who were forced by England's Reformation to join communities of women in "court," "print," and "across the seas" to gain access to "activism in an international arena" so as to defend their faith against anti-Catholic attacks stemming from their native soil (Dolan 10). In one of her "Sociable Letters," Cavendish mocks a Puritan lady for mindlessly regurgitating what she has learned from ministers who preach "such Non-sense in their Sermons, as God himself cannot turn to Sense" and for not confessing because she believes "Confession" to be "Popish" (27). This subtle jab at Puritans' vociferous anti-Catholicism is one of many instances in Cavendish's writing that betray her Catholic sympathies despite her adherence to Protestantism. Consequently, the idea that the "Commonwealth" and the body politic would benefit from the nun's uncloistering fuels the argument that women should be wedded and bedded in order to strengthen the Protestant nation-state.

Once again, nuns and women who want to circumvent marriage in order to fulfill other life goals are deemed abnormal and in need of patriarchal rehabilitation. Cavendish is timeless because she spoke the truth. Looking as far into the future (from the seventeenth century) as the themes found in Margaret Atwood's chilling 1986 dystopian novel, *The Handmaid's Tale*, the fears Cavendish expresses in Monsieur Facil's plan of attack continue to resonate with women who are forced to subjugate themselves to the molds set up for them by others. Cavendish has Madame Mediator stymie Monsieur Facil's proposal by reminding him that "she is not a Votress to the gods but to Nature" (2.1.46-47), thus placing her within a pagan realm that seems to be administered by a feminine deity rather than a masculine one. Lady Happy continues to expound on the convent's association with nature when she explains that its furnishings and accommodations will change "according to the four Seasons of the year, especially our Chambers" (2.2.12). This seasonal and natural flow mimics a woman's reproductive cycle and illustrates how the community works with nature rather than against it. The happiness of the convent's residents is foreshadowed to be short-lived when Madame Mediator says the ladies enjoy "so much Pleasure, as Nature never knew" (2.3.12). Cavendish realistically admits that this amalgamation of a controlled, separate space, however much it attempts to coexist with nature, is still otherworldly. Like Catholic convents idealistically devoted to God and contemplation of spiritual matters, the convent is too far removed from the realities of the mixed-sex secular world to serve as a model to be instituted in place of the status quo.

Such a realization of a convent's limitations, even quasi-pagan ones, inspires Monsieur Take-Pleasure's response to Madame Mediator's announcement about the convent's feminine deity when he argues that if Lady Happy is "a Votress to Nature, she must be a Mistress to Men" (2.1.69). Cavendish incorporates this line to provide a balanced discourse in the text. The gentleman's idea follows the natural order and biological precepts to which civilization subscribes. Because the species must procreate to survive, then females must have sex with males. Because the female must receive the male's seed, women were seen as the inferior member of the copulating pair. Once again, Madame Mediator defends the convent by reminding the men that the women have rejected men, since men are "Obstructers" who make women "Miserable" with "Pain" and "Trouble" (2.1.70-74). By focusing on the "variety of Pleasures, which are in Nature" (2.1.71), Lady Happy and her followers live in an artificial world buttressed by the appropriation of nature's gifts and the suppression of nature's dangers.

As readers find out, this controlled, separatist world cannot last forever. Nonetheless, its temporary existence within the walls of a quasi-religious convent offers hope to its residents as well as to English female readers who cannot experience any such community on English soil. Asserting her insistence on exploring both sides of an argument, Cavendish has Monsieur Adviser fervently protest the convent's rejection of the natural order: "Her Heretical Opinions ought not to be suffer'd, nor her Doctrine allow'd; and she ought to be examined by a Masculine Synod, and punish'd with a severe Husband, or tortured with a deboist [debauched] Husband" (2.1.76-78). Monsieur Adviser's reaction is a radical one, but it follows male-authored attacks on convents and fears that insecure men express about female autonomy. Using combative Protestant language that labels Catholicism as "Heretical," the suggestion of a male-controlled judicial body, "Masculine Synod," places the women's fate in the hands of male religious superiors. Such a group can be found in both the Protestant and Catholic churches, so Cavendish expresses dismay with the hierarchy of both realms of organized Christianity. It should come as no surprise, then, that Cavendish appropriates Catholic architecture and roles for women in favor of Nature, a feminine deity, rather than the masculine Christ. Monsieur Adviser's rant concludes with wishes for the women to be "punish'd" with abusive husbands, one of the very fears that motivated the escape of real and fictional early modern women to convents.

Although Cavendish does not imbue the nuns' dialogue with patently Catholic theological discourse, the heavily charged religious language employed to describe how Lady Happy gives "Indulgences and absolutions" (2.2.58) demonstrates how this politically feminist community improves upon the Catholic tradition of female monasteries by allowing its women to appropriate male clerical privilege. Cavendish precedes the news about Lady Happy's powers to offer the sacraments to her fellow encloistered women by having Lady Happy discuss her Epicurean philosophy that negates Catholicism's aesthetic expectations of the life religious:

> Can any Rational Creature think or believe, the gods take delight in the Creature's uneasie life? . . . for, What profit or pleasure can it be to the gods to have Men or Women wear coarse Linnen or rough Woollen, or to flea their skin with Hair-cloth . . . unless the gods and Nature were at variance, strife and wars; as if what is displeasing unto Nature, were pleasing to the gods, and to be enemies to her, were to be friends to them. (1.2.43-56)

Cavendish carefully distances the religious realm from a pagan one with the employment of "gods" instead of the monotheistic Christian God. The references to hair-cloth and other spartan, aesthetic environmental features of the life religious allude to the typical conventual lifestyle. Admittedly, Lady Happy's critique does not allow us to read the play as a subversive, recusant reclamation of the Old Faith. All the same, Lady Happy's insistence that the comfortable accommodations of her convent will allow the women religious to offer "prayers that are offer'd with ease and delight" (1.2.78) underscores the importance of configuring the community as a religious one so that its mission statement can serve as a bulwark against those who would seek to dissolve the convent.

One of the other conventual features highlighted by the ladies' retreat is the women's lack of children. In her "Sociable Letters," Cavendish intelligently writes about women's role as child-bearers in a marital economy instituted and maintained to perpetuate the patrilineal line:

> . . . a Woman hath no such Reason to desire Children for her Own Sake, for first her Name is Lost as to her Particular, in her Marrying, for she quits her Own, and is Named as her Husband . . . their Name only lives in Sons . . . whereas Daughters are but Branches which by Marriages are Broken off from the Root from whence they Sprang, & Ingrafted into the Stock of an other Family, so that Daughters are to be accounted but as Moveable Goods or Furniture that wear out; and though sometimes they

carry the Lands with them, for want of Heir-males, yet the Name is not Kept nor the Line Continued with them, for these are buried in the Graves of the Males. (101)

Despite Cavendish's critique of primogeniture and other sexist legal codes and social conventions that influence reproductive expectations, Protestant women could not as easily justify their desire to circumvent marriage and child bearing as Catholic women could[2]. As such, Protestant women who mimicked the eternal bachelor status of their male counterparts were socially ostracized and economically disadvantaged to a degree that men never were. Cavendish's use of the convent is both a nostalgic device and an exploration of the freedom women enjoyed, albeit however small, by choosing the secluded life available in Catholic nations.

Intriguingly enough, in a rebuttal to her husband's criticism of French clergymen as wasteful consumers of the nation's economy, Cavendish asserts that monks reduced the population through their celibacy, thus preventing civil wars wrought by the chaos of overpopulation (Whitaker 124). In her study of Medieval Catholic discourse about the gender identity of holy figures, Theodora Jankowski argues that just as single men, married fathers, and monks were more autonomous because of their lack of children, "the virgin nun or abbess was, for all intents and purposes, perceived as a 'man' who assumed powers usually reserved for bishops, abbots, and the clergy, as well as lords of the manor" (64). The would-be male suitors of the play express fear about the masculine power this enclosed community of women possesses when they seek to destroy it. Madame Mediator invokes the politically inspired English Reformation's dissolution of the monasteries when she tells the gentlemen that their only hope of disbanding the convent's residents is via the government: "The best way, Gentlemen, is to make your Complaints, and put up a Petition to the State, with your desires for a Redress" (2.1.80-81). Cavendish continues this sympathetic allusion to the mid-sixteenth century dissolution of England's religious houses when the anonymous gentlemen resolve to find other women to wed before they become cloistered since Lady Happy's convent "will never be dissolved, by reason it is ennobled with the company of great Princesses, and glorified with a great Fame" (3.10.39-40). Protestant culture valued the virginity of women, but it did so as a

---

[2] Michelle Dowd's *The Dynamics of Inheritance on the Shakespeare Stage* Cambridge: Cambridge University Press, 2015, provides a thorough history of the varying ways that English citizens, jurists, and artists negotiated laws regarding inheritance.

means to an end: heterosexual marriage and continuation of the patrilineal line. Beyond this emphasis on the ability of marriage to ensure proto-capitalist domestic security, Protestants also elevated the prestige of marriage "from its third-rate Catholic place in the moral hierarchy to the status of 'little church.' It was within this little church that children could be socialized to Protestant ideas of religion and society" (Jankowski 80). Again, Catholic nuns and Lady Happy's rebellious community reject marriage and children as burdens that distract them from their pursuits of corporal and spiritual pleasure, respectively.

In fact, the plans formulated by the anonymous gentlemen and those bestowed with satiric, allegorical names such as Monsieur Courtly, Monsieur Take-Pleasure, and Monsieur Adviser all hinge on their anxieties about a female community's agency. The group of men quickly bet on violent ends in order to gain access to the convent's women. After Monsieur Adviser proposes to set the convent on fire, Monsieur Take-Pleasure adds, "Yes, and smoak them out, as they do a Swarm of Bees" (2.4.4). Given that Lady Happy and her peers have proclaimed themselves to be votaresses of "Nature," the apiological language continues to explore the women's desire to act according to their subjective interpretation of the natural order. Although the true sex of the queen bee was not scientifically verified until the 1740s, there were Renaissance-era precedents for referring to bee culture as matriarchal. The Spaniard Luis Mendes de Torres is believed to be the first to record such thoughts as early as 1586; he was followed by the Englishman Charles Butler and his influential 1623 publication *The Feminine Monarchy*. Much as Cavendish's natural order is a second nature or artificial environment, Butler could not stomach the idea of humanity learning from the well-ordered matriarchy of bee culture: "Though he admitted that it went against the grain, Butler insisted that the fact of the queen bee was true. He was adamant, however, that that the sexual set-up of his hive was not to be mimicked by humans" (Wilson 91).

Given Cavendish's interest in natural philosophy and her advocacy for the humane treatment of animals in and out of scientific work, one could easily imagine Cavendish's proto-ecofeminist sensibilities[3] latching on to the political epistemologies inherent in references to the queen bee and the matriarchal society she cultivates. This cultivation begins in a slight allusion regarding the convent's own female-centric power structure, since

---

[3] See Bill Phillips's "The Rape of Mother Earth in Seventeenth-Century English Poetry: An Ecofeminist Interpretation" in *Atlantis* 26.1 (June 2004): 49-60.

"bees were regarded as sound economists and good husbandmen. They were of impeccable ethical character, being clean, chaste, pious and industrious. They were skilled geometers and exemplary architects" (Raylor 106). Furthermore, in the preface to her 1655 publication *Worlds Olio*, Cavendish continues the feminine appreciation of bee culture when discussing male and female attacks on her writing: "Men will seem to be against me, out of a Complement to Women, or at least for quiet and ease sake, who know Womens Tongues are like Stings of Bees; and what man would endure our effeminate Monarchy to swarm about their ears? For certainly he would be stung to death" (10).

Another plan the men hatch to infiltrate the convent requires their adoption of feminine clothing and behavior. Monsieur Adviser fears that they will betray themselves because of their inability to convincingly perform as women: "our Voices will discover us: or we are as untoward to make Courtsies in Petticoats, as Women are to make Legs in Breeches . . . We shall never frame our Eyes and Mouths to such coy, dissembling looks, and pritty simpering Mopes and Smiles, as they do" (2.4.42-45). The scene concludes with Monsieur Adviser stifling the men's attempts to pass as either feminine or butch women. Because the play's haphazard structure does not feature the subplot of the named gentlemen returning to the stage until Madame Mediator informs them of the Princess's true sex and his infiltration of the convent at the beginning of Act V, readers infer that the gentlemen abandon their hopes of passing. Even Monsieur Adviser's suggestion that the other men "be content to encloister" themselves with him "upon the same conditions, as those Ladies incloister themselves with her" (2.4.23-24) is ignored as the other men move onto other plans because they have little imagination for anything other than traditional heterosexual courting and marriage.

When it comes to the performance of gender and the possibility of abstaining from heterosexual intercourse, the men's limited visions are soundly rebutted in the following scene when the Princess arrives and asks Lady Happy to not only dress in a "Masculine" habit but to also act "Lovers-parts." The gender-bending involved in both Monsieur Adviser's inability to believe the success of such a ruse and in the convent's embrace of sexual fluidity finds precedent in Patristic texts about women's relationship with Christianity. Saint Jerome's writings even include a transcendent view about the fixities of sex: "As long as a woman is for birth and children, she is different from man as body is from soul. But when she wishes to serve Christ more than the world, then she will cease to be a woman and will be called man" (567). Saint Jerome opens the door for viewing gender as fluid when a woman commits to a life religious.

This commentary on women who serve Christ (arguably through professional routes) imbues Cavendish's convent residents with Patristic doctrine that validates the women's autonomy and their dismissal of gender expectations, albeit from an antediluvian perspective that values men as superior to women.

One of the unique creative freedoms that women of various backgrounds enjoyed in real-life convents was the ability to produce art from a female outlook. Lady Happy's peers follow suit. Unencumbered by the demands of a live commercial audience, much as Cavendish was in her writing, the women produce a series of dramatic performance art vignettes that detail the potential woes of women who choose to marry and have children. Like Medieval exempla or contemporary public service announcements, the performance pieces shed light on women who must deal with husbands who are adulterous, abusive, alcoholic, addicted to gambling, and/or employers of prostitutes. Women with children suffer similar tribulations when they either die while giving birth, have daughters that run off with lower-class men, get pregnant before they're married, or raise murderous sons sentenced to a public execution. Some of my undergraduate students have commented that the fast-paced succession of these vignettes has the potential to make them appear as comedically hyperbolic in their shallow depiction of such weighty issues. As other students have noted, however, the verisimilitude that women readers would have experienced in picturing fictional accounts that mirror real-life situations of their friends and family members, and possibly their own, would leave the showcase of woes as a serious warning about the dangers of being a woman in the seventeenth century.

The Princess dutifully notes after the performance, "though some few be unhappy in Marriage, yet there are many more that are so happy as they would not change their condition" (3.10.32-33). Lady Happy's peers have failed to offer a balanced view of married life. In one of her tracts in 1662's *Orations of Divers Sorts*, Cavendish's extreme anti-marriage rhetoric even goes so far as to say that death makes a better husband for women: "Death, is a cold bedfellow, but yet he makes a good husband, for he will never cross, oppose, nor anger her, nor give her cause of grief or sorrow" (166-67). Such hyperbolic language that rejects husbands as the cause of all wives' woes is echoed in the would-be nun Isabella's speech in *Measure for Measure* when she hears about Angelo's abandonment of Mariana: "What a merit were it in death to take this poor maid" (3.1.244). Given the fact that Cavendish and her feminist peers were working within the literary canon and responding to the misogynistic writings of the *querelle des femmes*, twenty-first century readers have to acknowledge how these women relished the freedom they had to enjoy such a rare opportunity. The artistic license they had to produce art from their own viewpoint could prove intoxicating and easy to exploit as a way to make a point that can be achieved with less extreme methods today.

The last vignette features a gentleman obnoxiously wooing a lady for his married master. Although he promises that the man will leave his wife for the lady, she uses religious language to protest the offer: "Heaven forbid I should be the cause of a Divorce between a Noble Pair" (3.10.12). This vehemence against the idea of divorce is buttressed by her solution to live in a world where she is courted in such an uncouth manner: "I must prevent my own ruin . . . by going into a Nunnery; wherefore, I'le put my self into one to night: / There will I live, and serve the Gods on high, / And leave this wicked World and Vanity" (3.10.18-21). Although Cavendish continues her careful use of the pagan "Gods" (provocatively capitalized in this instance), the escape to the convent mirrors the choice the audience of this play-within-the-play has already made. The intellectual, social, and even sexual pleasures the women in this convent, and real-world convents, enjoy are due to their rejection of all the potential barriers heterosexual copulation and marriage present women. Consequently, this female-dominated drama reinforces their ideology, beliefs, and actions to make the most of this enclosed space of creation. Much as the Spanish writer María de Zayas accomplishes in 1647's *Desengaños amorosos*, Cavendish's play has her female characters metatextually inform each other about the travails of married women in order to disenchant them about the promises, unrealistic dreams, and lies that they have heard about marriage. Similarly, despite Cavendish's writing from a Protestant literary landscape, she has her fictional characters as well as their creations in the performance piece choose to retreat to a convent, since "Marriage is a Curse we find, / Especially to Women kind" (3.10.22-23).

Whether a nun lives as a virgin her entire life or enters the convent after having raised her children, the absence of offspring engenders a fruitful abundance of time, energy, and resources for these women to follow other pursuits in life – particularly intellectual ones. In her discussion on the amount of free time with which women are provided, since they are not expected or allowed to enter the professional world of medicine, design, music, poetry, or painting, Cavendish argues that women should study in their "Closets" just as men study in "their Colleges." Thus, in a clear articulation and precursor to Woolf's a-room-of-one's-own sentiment, Cavendish's convent is the architectural promised land for intellectually curious women. Cavendish echoes Isabella's speech in *Measure for Measure* when the would-be nun argues that "Thoughts are no subjects, / Intents but merely thoughts" (5.1.448-49), as she imagines a female readership taking heed that "wherefore Women can have no excuse, or complaints of being subjects, as a hinderance from thinking; for Thoughts are free, those can never be inslaved, for we are not hindered from studying" (*Worlds Olio*, 12).

Such discourse about independent thinking represents the hope that Cavendish and other women held for the intellectual freedom that could be found in a convent. After all, some "nuns used literature, particularly drama, to express their ambivalent feelings and dreams of escape from the very convent life that gave them their opportunity for self-expression" (McNamara 538). In a nod similar to Cavendish's wishes for expanding the opportunity enjoyed by the privileged daughters of the European aristocracy educated by private tutors, convents engaged in "the practice of educating gentlewomen . . . throughout Europe and its colonies. Convents generally housed one or two dozen pupils" (McNamara 535). In many instances, particularly after the Counter-Reformation prodded the Catholic Church to engage in more areas of public assistance, nunneries "offered education and vocational training to youths" (Boxer and Queratea 31). Whether nuns were teaching novices or elite women who would return to the secular world, their role as educators implies their own status as learned women.

Constant Craving: Convents and Same-Sex Desire

When reading Cavendish's work, one must understand its historical context, especially when it comes to queer history. Although the word "homosexual," and the more sex-specific "lesbian," did not exist in the English vocabulary of the seventeenth century, equivalent terms were common in the vernacular. "Bugger" and "sodomite" were perhaps the two most familiar terms in general use for male homosexuals. The negative connotations of these words are evident in their vague meanings of either bestiality or homosexuality. "Tribade" was used to describe women who primarily engaged in sexual activity with other women. The "tribade" was the "active" partner who rubbed or penetrated the other woman (Jankowski 201). However, these terms for female homosexual activity were not commonly used in the legal language of the time. Although many scholars have asserted that sexualities did not constitute identities in the early modern era, newer research and common-sense thinking by academics such as Kenneth Borris and David M. Halperin suggests otherwise. Halperin prods intellectuals to question epistemological assumptions that separate "acts" from "identities." After all, if we seek to label the "Renaissance" and its flanking eras as "early modern" in order to highlight the time period's ties with our own conceptions of modernity, our understanding of sexuality as one of people's many ways of identifying themselves underscores the absurdity of imagining that our ancestors did not employ their sexual inclinations and, more importantly, amorous love for partners, to create their self-identification.

Cavendish's embrace of closet drama's freedoms allowed her to experiment with societal expectations in order to destabilize heterocentric assumptions about gender. For the duchess, gender, sexuality, class, the court, and public life were indelibly intertwined. Cavendish subverts the assumptions of heterosexuality found in Shakespeare's *As You Like It* and *Twelfth Night* by withholding the true sex of the Princess from readers. Valerie Traub argues that "the relationship between Lady Happy and the Princess is one of two femmes, [and] relies on the reader's (or auditor's) lack of knowledge of the cross-gender disguise" (179). To demonstrate that Cavendish was not ignorant of the rhetorical effects of dramatic irony, I will briefly discuss a play in which Cavendish informs her readers about a character's cross-dressing to serve as a contrast to the sexual possibilities engendered by a convent's special circumstances, which the duchess utilizes in *The Convent of Pleasure*.

In Cavendish's 1662 play *Loves Adventures*, which is closer to Shakespeare's comedic style than any other of Cavendish's works, Lady Orphant disguises herself as a man, Affectionata, to follow her betrothed husband, Lord Singularity, into battle. The pair bond, and Lord Singularity names Affectionata his heir in gratitude for everything "he" has taught him about love, women, and relationships. Lord Singularity's relationship with Affectionata is a palpably homoerotic one between two men for most of the play, since he does not discover that Affectionata is a female until Scene 36, the preantepenultimate scene. Cavendish emphasizes Lord Singularity's same-sex desire by italicizing the lines that contain Lord Singularity's profession of love for Affectionata in scene 19 of the second part of *Loves Adventures*: "And thus I do imbrace thee, and do wish our souls may twine / As our each bodyes thus together joyn" (87). Following Cavendish's usual political aims, she skillfully engages in a double discourse by not only promoting erotic same-sex relationships but by also employing the transient stage of cross-dressing only to reestablish Lady Orphant's true sex at the end. In this conclusion Lady Orphant is exalted in front of Lord Singularity (who promises to worship her as a "goddess") and all the other people in court as paragons of physical and intellectual female power.

When we consider the legal framework in which Cavendish was writing when it came to laws about same-sex relationships, we find English jurist Edward Coke's definition of buggery in 1644 as a sin committed "by mankind with mankind or with brute beast or by womankind with brute beast" (Bray 14). This definition makes Cavendish's exploration of lesbianism in *The Convent of Pleasure* all the more exceptional because Coke's definition does not acknowledge erotic woman-woman relationships. Bray believes that the history of lesbianism can "best be understood as part of the developing recognition of a specifically female sexuality" (Bray 17). The absence of legislation against intimate female same-sex relations underscores Cavendish's own argument in her "Sociable Letters" about the freedoms women should enjoy, since they are not truly citizens, hence subjects, within England's realm:

> as for the matter of Governments, we Women understand them not, yet if we did, we are excluded from intermeddling therewith, and almost from being subject thereto; we are not tied, nor bound to State or Crown; we are free, not Sworn to Allegiance, nor do we take the Oath of Supremacy; we are not made Citizens of the Commonwealth . . . and if we be not Citizens in the Commonwealth, I know no reason we should be Subjects to the Commonwealth: And the truth is, we are no Subjects, unless it be to our Husbands, and not always to them, for sometimes we usurp their Authority. (25)[4]

The humorous uxorious addition to Cavendish's opinion accentuates her discussion about a woman's limited freedom in a patriarchal society that does not deem women worthy of citizenship. This syllogistic argument about a woman's legal standing serves as an activist call to arms for women to engage in illegal behavior since they should not be considered "Subjects" of the Crown or Commonwealth.

Of course, as with the legal fate of many denigrated minorities throughout time, no parsing of legislation will condone such behavior until authority figures acknowledge the innate human rights of all individuals. Nonetheless, following Cavendish's logic, the women who engage in sexual lesbian relations are not rebelling against anti-sodomy laws. Simply

---

[4] Remarkably, nearly two hundred years later, Susan B. Anthony would use similar language to argue that women should be exempt from legal punishment since feminine pronouns were not used in the laws of the United States when she gave her speech "On a Woman's Right to Vote" after her 1872 arrest for attempting to vote in the presidential election.

put, because they are not subject to such legislation, they are neither citizens nor subject to laws that apply to citizens. But they are highlighting their absence from the English law books that ignore the possibilities of lesbian sexual activity. Thus, if women cannot be persecuted as lesbians engaging in sex, then their virginity remains intact, and the quasi-nuns in *The Convent of Pleasure* can continue to pay lip service to their expected vows of chastity.

Once again, Cavendish's life during the Interregnum undoubtedly engendered such progressive philosophies. The duration of Cavendish's sojourns in France and the Low Countries allowed her to absorb cultural movements uncensored by England's Puritan stronghold during the Interregnum. The social and political upheavals that spread throughout Europe in the mid-1600s were reflected in Cavendish's work, despite her royalist allegiances and nostalgia for pre-Civil War England. In fact, Cavendish's Bolsover Castle, built by William Cavendish and his father, Sir Charles Cavendish, features eroticized murals of the female virtues Justice and Prudence and Faith and Hope, respectively, amorously hugging and kissing (Traub 160). The murals offer the voyeuristic pleasure of not only seeing the female nude but also the homoerotic mingling of two women. While the classical allegory serves as an excuse for the titillating nudity, the lesbian representations of the Christian icons Faith and Hope make the deliberate homoerotic representation more provocative. Another potential source of conventual inspiration for Cavendish may have been the fact that William Cavendish built his mansion, Newcastle House, upon the lands formerly occupied by the Abbess of the black nuns of the Order of Saint Benedictine at St. Mary's convent in Clerkenwell, just north of the London city limits (Newton 88).

In rejecting the austere accommodations and lifestyle of the monastery that one expects in a nun's dedication to an ascetic lifestyle, Cavendish's characters queerly embrace heterosexual virginity but reject a sober, sexless lifestyle. They can be considered "queer" for defining themselves in "resistance to masculinist notions of pleasure, and masculinist notions of female subservience and economic dependence" (Jankowski 178) as well as for choosing "a life unscripted by the conventions of family, inheritance, and child rearing" (Halberstam 2). Lady Happy's promulgation that her convent will have no grate refers to a prevalent issue in the power accorded to nuns who lived in monasteries. The walled monastery represented the guarding of the nun's physical body: "the condition of her body was equated with the condition of her house's enclosure . . . if a monastery had a gate which was always open – or, worse yet, no wall at all – its nuns could be (and were) presumed to have vaginas (or hymens) that were equally open/broached" (Jankowski 69). Cavendish carefully protects her women from phallic penetration but does not deny them sexual liberty.

Madame Mediator's claim that Lady Happy "will suffer no grates about the Cloister" (2.1.53) belies how easy it can be to penetrate the convent. After all, Madame Mediator enters and exits the convent with ease. Likewise, the Princess's visit to the convent necessitates some physical entrance. Just as the convent's walls are not intact, the women's heterosexual virginity is threatened. When the Princess's true sex is revealed, the anticipated progression of the plot and the play's thematic concerns are unexpectedly subverted. Because the Princess is revealed to be a male only when Cavendish's husband pens the play's final scenes, we can still argue that Cavendish was attempting to create an all-female community that accepted lesbian relationships.

The Prince's presence showcases women's constant vulnerability to male deception and violence as well as the seemingly inescapable nature of heterocentric patriarchal hegemony. The construction of the ostensibly grate-free wall affords the convent's women the liberty to act as they wish before the walls figuratively tumble down on this radical retreat. This seclusion prevents a male audience from viewing the actions within the convent. Such isolation mirrors Cavendish's freedom in writing *The Convent of Pleasure* and her other dramatic texts during the Interregnum when no plays were performed on the public stage. Cavendish's separatist convent succeeds, temporarily, in its philosophical exploration of a woman's right to professional, intellectual, and sexual autonomy.

Cavendish's separatist utopian fantasy of an English all-female enclave skillfully plays with preconceived notions of the convent to allow characters free range in expressing themselves without limitations imposed by other institutions. The duchess was surely mindful of the rich literary tradition that focuses on men whose quest is to reach the desirous and seemingly unattainable virgin walled off by monastery- or castle-like structures. Such a narrative is most famously depicted in the thirteenth-century allegorical poem *Roman de la Rose*. Unsurprisingly, Cavendish uses her convent to challenge the traditional image of the mystical *hortus conclusus*. The literary enclosed garden of love is inspired by a verse from the *Song of Songs*, "My sister, my spouse, is a garden enclosed, a garden enclosed, a fountain sealed up" (4:12). The garden is at once a representative of the woman's guarded body, which is paradoxically unapproachable but also potentially penetrable. The garden of love can be more strikingly symbolic of "Ecclesia, the unconquerable Holy Church, embodied on earth as Mary, forever virginal and intact" (Kraman 139).

The latter interpretation of the *hortus conclusus's* religious possibilities underscores the significance of an all-female spiritual community. Although Cavendish never explicitly champions Catholicism in her writings, her appropriation of the convent as a heterosexually virginal community embraces tenets of Mariology.

Early in the fifth century, Saint Augustine warned his sister, who had just become a nun, that "The love which you bear one another ought not to be carnal, but spiritual: for those things which are practiced by immodest women, even with other females, in shameful jesting and playing, ought not be done . . . [by] chaste virgins dedicated by a holy vow to be handmaidens of Christ" (qtd. in Brown 8). Although early modern English heterosexist laws identified male same-sex relations as punishable, the law was mute when it came to sexual relations between women. This was not the case on the Continent. Nor was it a matter to which the Catholic Church was blind, as canons enacted during the council of Paris in 1212 required nuns "to sleep *singulæ . . . in lectis suis, non binæ*" and ordered lamps to "be left burning in dormitories during the night" (Bailey 132). The Catholic Church's creation of these rules proves that Protestant polemics denigrating Catholic institutions such as monasteries and convents as sites of sexual transgression were not created out of thin air. Cavendish's flirtations with the possibilities of intimate same-sex relationships find a conducive environment in her textual/philosophical laboratory: the Convent of Pleasure.

When the Princess enters the convent, her first lines underscore how her ideas about a convent mesh with Lady Happy's: "there are many, that have quit their Crowns and Power, for a Cloister of Restraint; then well may I quit a Court of troubles for a *Convent of Pleasure*" (3.1.3-5). The purposefully italicized contrast between "Cloister of Restraint" and *"Convent of Pleasure"* anticipates the erotic potential that exists within the male-free community of women. Pleasure as both a noun and a verb already contained highly charged connotations regarding the indulgence of sexual desires and appetites as early as the mid-1400s, according to the Oxford English Dictionary. Provocatively enough, the sexual energy comes not from heterosexual pairings, but same-sex ones.

The Princess asks Lady Happy to grant her one request that informs the audience about the erotic potential that has always lain beneath the surface in Lady Happy's naming of her all-female community: "I observing in your several Recreations, some of your Ladies do accouter Themselves in Masculine-Habits, and act Lovers-parts; I desire you will give me leave to be sometimes so accoutered and act the part of your loving Servant" (3.1.12-15). This trailblazing portrayal of lesbian relationships is startling in its clear depiction of women who take on what we now call the "femme" and "butch" roles. Of course, following the plot without regard for authorial intrusion and censorship, we find out at the end of the play that the Princess is a male and would naturally find himself more adroitly able to play the more masculine, butch role in a lesbian relationship. Unlike the dramatic irony we find in most Renaissance comedies that feature cross-dressed characters, such as Shakespeare's *Twelfth Night*, readers are never told about the gender-bending that occurs. The audience is led to believe that the Princess is a female – from her/his first entrance through her/his kissing scene with Lady Happy. Thus, Cavendish's careful employment of the phrase "Lovers-parts" allows us to see that this convent is exploited for all its latent sexual energy. Even if the Princess turns out to be a male and if readers delude themselves into believing that Lady Happy somehow knows about the Princess's true sex, we are still left with the Princess's report about other women acting like manly lovers with their female counterparts within the convent's walls. Furthermore, by continuing the matriarchal hierarchy existent within the convent and by having the Princess become Lady Happy's servant, Cavendish maintains the drama's thematic focus on the agency and desires of its female protagonist.

If we put aside the popularity of gratuitously erotic literary works that include nuns fornicating along with friars in homoerotic group scenes such as in Pietro Aretino's *Ragionamenti*, which was first published in England in 1585 by John Wolfe, we can also find historical records of lesbian relationships among nuns in early modern Europe. Judith Brown's 1986 monograph *Immodest Acts: The Life of a Lesbian Nun in Renaissance Italy* stands as a key, influential work in the study of both early modern lesbianism and the sexuality of nuns. Brown's study focuses on Benedetta Carlini, the abbess of the Convent of the Mother of God in early seventeenth-century Pescia, Italy. While Sister Benedetta was being investigated for her mystical visions, her fellow nun, Sister Bartolomea Crivelli, claimed she was forced to engage in sexual acts with her. When one considers Cavendish buying into the arguments of Protestant polemical works that view Catholic women, especially nuns, as only talking about the virtues of virginity rather than living them, *The Convent of Pleasure* continues to support a woman's resistance to heterosexual copulation, since only same-sex relations, regardless of gender performance, are explored under Cavendish's authorship.

Illustratively, the fourth act of the play begins with Lady Happy in an anxious state because she is in love with a woman: "why may not I love a Woman with the same affection I could a Man? No, no, Nature is Nature, and still will be / The same she was from all Eternity" (4.1.2-5). While Cavendish continues the careful distinction between the convent's pagan allegiances and those of a Catholic convent, she does so to showcase how the constructed nature of such separatist communities makes them fabricated pseudo-utopias that follow different laws, including those of "Nature." As a *hortus conclusus*, the convent's gardens are "kept curiously" (2.2.45), that is carefully, "so as not to have a Weed in it, and all the Groves, Wildernesses, Bowers and Arbours pruned, and kept free from dead Boughs Branches or Leaves" (2.2.47-49). Lady Happy's fastidious attention to the convent's maintenance as aesthetically pleasing distances it from reality. The convent's residents are opposing themselves to the natural biological order by creating a second nature; the universal understanding of the biological necessity of heterosexual copulation reinforces the incompatibility of homosexuality with nature. The artificiality of the environment is highlighted by having the garden and the pastoral landscape constructed by humans. These synthetic constructions of a natural environment derail the idea of nature and its heterocentric requirements to allow a "fluidity of gender roles and the playful pastoralism of female shepherds and shepherdesses" (Traub 291) that we find in Act IV after Lady Happy and the Princess embrace and kiss.

When the convent's garden is highlighted as artificial, the *hortus conclusus*, which is an allegorical representation of the female role models of all nuns, the Virgin Mary, subversively becomes the classical *locus amoenus* of Ovid's vision of unrestrained passion. Following the Renaissance comedic convention that expects unanticipated events and relationships to unfold in a topsy-turvy world, Cavendish appropriates the *locus amoenus* to safely explore lesbian desire since the world is anticipated to revert to heteronormativity by the conclusion. As far as the readers know throughout Act IV, when the Princess consoles the distraught Lady Happy by telling her they should "discourse, imbrace and kiss, so mingle souls together" (4.1.17-18), the promise of Platonic love is subsumed by the more fervent and corporal same-sex relationship between the two. The stage directions emphasize that "*They imbrace and kiss, and hold each other in their Arms*" (4.1.22). This passionate action, which if staged would shock, titillate, or inspire according to each audience member's prerogative, is preceded by a pastoral scene between the two lovers as Lady Happy plays a Shepherdess being wooed by the Princess, who is playing a Shepherd. Cavendish purposely chooses the pastoral landscape so that, unfettered by the strictures of society, it can allow for the continuation of the homoerotic desires to problematize "the familiar theme of friendship" (Andreadis 87).

Because the convent's strict membership rules permit only women, the pastoral scene does not follow the heterosexual formula for courting. Casting aside Petrarchan conceits about cruel mistresses and the flame of desire, the Shepherdess ignores the traditional, iambic pentameter-reciting shepherds who offer Lady Happy a life's worth of support. The Shepherdess chooses the Shepherd/Princess because he/she praises her intellectual acumen – "your Wit flies high" (4.1.53) – and her knowledge of astronomy, botany, meteorology, metaphysical poetry conceits, and Platonism.

This emphasis on Lady Happy's cerebral talents works well within the walls of a convent. Although social and educational hierarchies existed within convents, many nuns were expected to read and write. Even in post-Reformation England, recusant families who trained daughters for life in a Continental convent were sure to instruct them in Latin. By the seventeenth century most nuns needed to understand Latin for something as simple as singing. As opposed to sisters of the Middle Ages who uncomprehendingly sang in Latin, the English Benedictine nuns of Cambrai and Paris required "that the Divine Office and profession ceremonies were sung in Latin by quire nuns" (Stevenson 53). This Latin fluency also empowered nuns to read canonical legislation and rules, such as that which stipulated that the women could choose who their male superiors would be. The Rules for the nuns of the Order of Poor Clares discuss the responsibility of those who could read and those who could not wherein literate nuns were to read the Divine Office according to the custom of the Friars Minor and those who were illiterate would say Pater Nostres in lieu of the Divine Office. Cavendish gives the Princess these lines praising Lady Happy's intellect to underscore the verisimilitude between the fictional convent and real-life ones that emphasized the importance of educating its members well beyond what was expected of them in secular society.

Furthermore, Cavendish's nostalgic retreat to England's Catholic past as well as a realm ruled by a female authority figure may bespeak her desire for the Elizabethan era's promotion of educated women. Whereas "highborn ladies" during Queen Elizabeth's reign "were trained in classical and modern languages, logic, rhetoric, philosophy, and the sciences. . . . King James I hated learned ladies. They were ridiculed at his court, and soon the normal Stuart education for girls went little beyond the most basic skills of reading and writing, and the elementary arithmetic they would need in their household management" (Whitaker 15). Given Cavendish's frequent laments over being monolingual, her appreciation for the Catholic convent's culture of education must have been significant.

Once again playing with the all-female community's subversion of the natural order, the Princess concludes with the rhyming couplet, "Thus doth your Wit reveal / What Nature would conceal" (4.1.110-11). The transformed garden has become a place for non-normative forms of amorous expression. The Princess is rewarded for her flattery when Lady Happy exclaims that she can deny him neither her "Love nor Person" (4.1.135). The Princess hesitantly remarks that the courtship between the two is not in accordance with the heterosexual tradition: "In amorous Pastoral Verse we did not Woo. / As other Pastoral Lovers use to doo." Lady Happy replies, "Which doth express, we shall more constant be, / And in a Married life better agree" (4.1.137-40). While these lines reflect the grimly realistic representations of heterosexual marriage's negative aspects for women as dramatized by an all-female cast in Act III, it is more shocking for its explicit approval of same-sex marriage. The lovers' relationship reaches its climax within this convent-cum-church when their union is sanctified in a pagan May Day marriage ceremony. The pair is crowned king and queen of the shepherds after dancing around "the May-Pole" (4.1.143). The rebellious nature of this statement is clear. This same-sex ceremony, whether it is construed as a passionless friendship, sign of affection, or as a commitment ceremony falling short of actual marriage rites, is a daring precursor to the legalization of same-sex marriages that would come more than three hundred years later.

John Boswell's *Same-Sex Unions in Premodern Europe* has been mostly debunked since its 1995 publication. Nonetheless, numerous isolated reports of early modern same-sex marriages, albeit mostly when one member was disguised as the opposite sex, continue to crop up. For example, Michel Eyquem de Montaigne's "Journal de voyage," which follows his travels through Europe in 1580 and 1581, recounts hearing about a cross-dressed female who marries another woman: "still earning his living at the said trade, he fell in love with a woman, married her, and they lived together four or five months to her satisfaction, according to what is said. But, having been recognized by someone from Chaumont, and the matter brought to justice, she was condemned to be hung, which she said she'd rather suffer than return to a girl's state" (qtd. in Borris 91). Montaigne's unsubstantiated report can be considered hearsay and outright fiction, but that is exactly what readers deal with in Cavendish's play. Just as all myths and urban legends are popularly believed to contain a grain of truth in them, Montaigne's report speaks to the desire if not the surreptitious action of two women marrying one another. Furthermore, the fact that one woman cross-dressed in order to wed the other clearly parallels Cavendish's appropriation of the opposite-sex, marriage-less state of a Catholic convent to explore the possibilities of two *women* getting married, even if one were to label it a *mis*appropriation.

Cavendish's radical departure from the heterocentric norm could not have been lost on her or her husband. Within the same page that the Princess declares to Lady Happy "We shall agree, for we true Love inherit, / Join as one Body and Soul, or Heav'nly Spirit," Cavendish introduces her husband as the writer of the rest of the text: "Written by my Lord Duke" (4.1.141-42). Since no ending is provided to this intrusion of the Duke of Newcastle's writing, we assume that he completes the rest of the play. By the first scene of the next and final act, an "Embassador" from the Princess's kingdom reveals that the Princess is a Prince. The same-sex nature of the relationship becomes moot, and the two wed in the third and final scene. The quick conclusion reaffirms the drastically atypical nature of Cavendish's homosexual couple. Cavendish's reassertion of the necessity of marital alliance in society may be reflective of her aristocratic rank and loyalist allegiance – if she agreed to her husband's new version of the Princess/Prince.

Whatever the case may be regarding authorship, once the walls of the convent have been violated, the fantasy realm in which the queer virgins can be ignored because they are not part of the visible spectrum of society is obliterated. Moments before the Princess is revealed to be a male, the "Embassador" enters the convent – the first explicit instance of a male having penetrated the convent's walls – and the homoerotic bonds of the convent quickly unravel and are replaced by a powerful heterocentric patriarchy. Just like so many soon-to-be-wedded women in the plays of Shakespeare and his contemporaries, the usually loquacious Lady Happy is rendered silent. The Princess-turned-Prince tells the Embassador that his nation will have to accept his marriage to Lady Happy and proclaims, "otherwise, tell them I will have her by force of Arms" (5.1.21). A panicked Madame Mediator frets about the future of the convent's other women, and the Prince makes decisions about their future since as Lady Happy's husband he now controls her property. Readers are still unsure about Lady Happy's agency in this marriage.

In the following scene, Monsieur Adviser returns to report that "it is said, the Prince and she agreed to Marry; and the State is so willing, as they account it an honour, and hope shall reap much advantage by the Match" (5.2.47-48). In diametric opposition to everything that Lady Happy has espoused in the foundation of her convent, her marriage is not only approved by the patriarchal government, but her body is also appropriated as an "advantage" to a foreign state. Furthermore, the court jester, Mimick, suggests that the convent be turned over to "old decrepit and bed-rid Matrons" so that it may be called a *"Convent of Charity*, if it cannot possibly be named the *Convent of Chastity*" (5.3.24-26). Once again, the hetero-patriarchy has usurped Lady Happy's agency and her community by denying the erotic potential of the same-sex community they so eagerly wished for and briefly enjoyed.

The most important aspect of the Lady Happy's interactions with the Princess is that she believed the Princess was a female. In fact, so did Cavendish's original readers since the dramatis personae is listed at the end of the play. As such, the cast of characters accurately includes "The Prince," but Cavendish's original readers are blessed with entertaining ignorance by imagining the Princess is simply a masculine female. Given Cavendish's familiarity with Continental female actors during the Interregnum, she may have imagined a female actor playing the role of "the Prince." Likewise, British troupes of traveling actors on the Continent began including female actors in the 1650s. In one of her "Sociable Letters" Cavendish discusses "the Best Female Actor that ever I saw; and for Acting a Man's Part, she did it so Naturally as if she had been of that Sex" (206). Cavendish's appreciation for the gender fluidities of theater welcomes the female actors of the Restoration stage (some of whom played male roles), while paying homage to Shakespeare's repeated metadramatic references to his male actors playing the roles of women. In fact, throughout the play Cavendish has Lady Happy and other characters refer to the Princess with feminine pronouns and masculine adjectives. The most popular edition of the play, edited by Anne Shaver, lists the dramatis personae at the beginning of the play. By the time they have reached Act IV of the play, quick undergraduates notice the absence of "The Prince" they saw listed in the dramatis personae and begin to wonder how the plot will unravel to allow for a normative wedding. This situation might be ameliorated in future printings of the play that keep the list of characters in the original textual space after the conclusion of the play. The following image is a scan of the original printed edition of the play, which demonstrates the lack of the dramatis personae at the beginning of the closet drama:

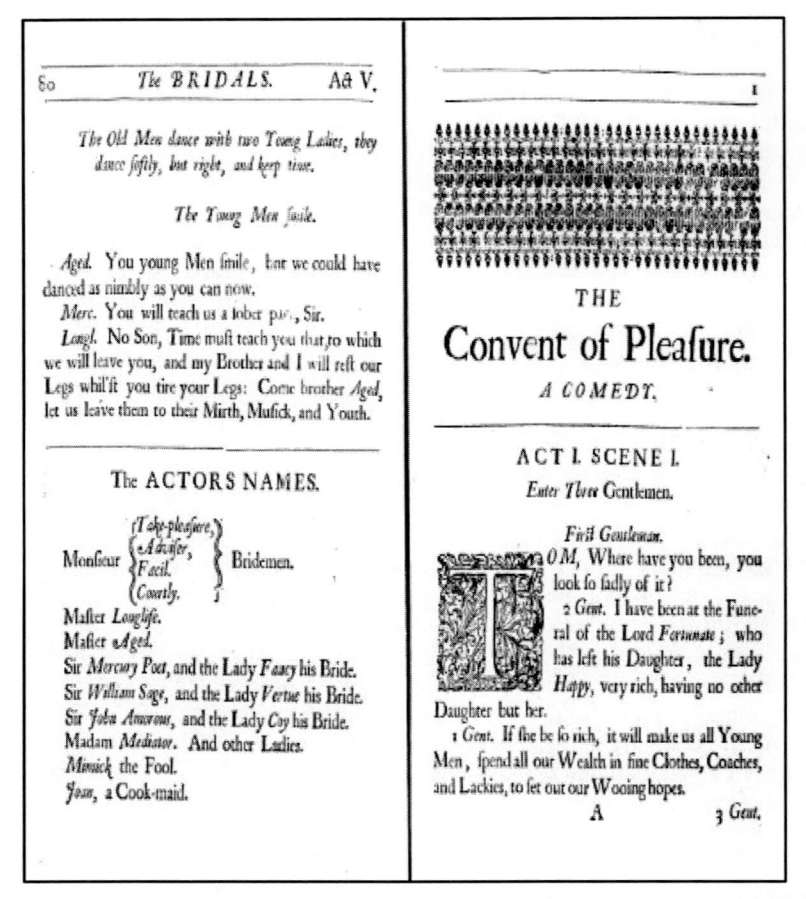

Figure 1. This image shows the last page of *The Bridals* and the first page of *The Convent of Pleasure* from *Plays, never before printed. Written by the thrice noble, illustrious, and excellent princess, the Duchess of Newcastle* (1668). As one can see, the dramatis personae section is listed at the end of each play, which removes the dramatic irony of the Princess's sex.

Conclusion

As long as Lady Happy believes that the Princess is a woman, then same-sex desire is embodied in the text. If the Princess asks to act like the other women who dress as men and perform the parts of lovers in the convent, then readers must assume that there are other women engaging in intimate same-sex relations. Regardless of who wrote the final scene of the play, Lady Happy's last line, which is spoken to Mimick, becomes chillingly poignant in lieu of everything that has occurred since her first public avowal to avoid the world of men and heteronormative marriage by entering the convent: "What you Rogue, do you call me a Fool?" (5.3.13). Indeed, the erstwhile queer virginal nun *has* been fooled. By what or by whom depends on the authorship of the last scene. If William penned this section, then he is mocking his wife and Lady Happy's delusions about their ability to create a world free of men and marriage. If Cavendish authored this final scene, she can be seen chastising not only Lady Happy for silently accepting her betrothal to the Prince but also the expectations of seventeenth-century comedy that necessitate heterosexual marriages and the restoration of order to the transient topsy-turvy world that most entertains audience members.

One can only speculate how much choice Cavendish had in allowing her husband to write the end of the play. Because Cavendish's right to authorship was endorsed by her husband, the amount of influence he was able to exert on Cavendish's work must have been considerable. Regardless of how *The Convent of Pleasure* ends, gender boundaries have been transgressed, with Lady Happy having expressed her lesbian desires and the Prince having happily engaged in his role as transgendered woman. By imbuing her characters with intersexual attributes, Cavendish not only "challenged contemporary assumptions about the nature of gender difference" but "destabilized the hierarchical worldview that defined the gender order" (Mendleson 208). Such challenges can be seen in her dismay over the plight of daughters who inherit land from their fathers only to have their name, heritage, and history "buried in the Grave of the Males." Given all of the rhetoric, logic, and argumentation that readers have received from Lady Happy, the ludicrous ending asks readers to question why comedies must typically end with heterosexual marriages. The Ovidian-like metamorphosis of the Princess's sex implies women's single life must end with a heterosexual pairing.

William's ambiguous authorship—after all, the little strips of text noting his authorship were later pasted onto the book rather than printed on them—showcases Cavendish's move to distance herself from such laughably pat theatrical resolutions. Cavendish brashly informs readers in an epistle preceding her 1668 *Playes, Never Before Printed* that her plays are not "suitable to ancient Rules" or "agreeable to the modern Humor." Then she dismisses the structure of her dramas and potpourri-like inclusion of sundry dramatic conventions in her plays as "Dialogues upon several Subjects" that she ordered into "*Acts* and *Scenes*" (5). In her various references to staging her plays in a theater, Cavendish dismisses the possibility of such an event because of the non-traditional nature of her plays. This dismissal has led most Cavendish scholars to agree with the statement that "the setting of the Duchess's plays was her own brain, where personified abstractions could argue or debate as long as pen and paper gave them leave" (Perry 213).

Cavendish's attempt to destabilize notions about gender and her startlingly bold declarations of amorous same-sex relationships in a positive light are trail-blazing. In order to make such thematic explorations more palatable, Cavendish began by appropriating her audience's notions about Catholicism, convents, and nuns to present the enclosed community of women as one with verisimilitude to its Continental counterparts. Although the women are initially seen as enjoying luxurious commodities, the development of Lady Happy and her interaction with her peers and the Princess showcase that the true luxuries are intellectual, social, and sexual. Cavendish morphs the *hortus conclusus* into the *locus amoenus* and takes advantage of a convent's potential to advance her unconventional ideas about life in the extra-conventual world. Following Aristotelian precepts about the cathartic elements of drama, Cavendish's audience can be purged of their anxieties about a virgin's role in Protestant England by briefly enjoying a woman's potential under Catholic rule.

Chapter Four

The *Sarao* as Conventual Rhetorical Space in María De Zayas's *Desengaños Amorosos*

María de Zayas y Sotomayor's novellas were provocative and prurient for her time period and have become timeless and timely in ours. The combination of Baroque grotesquerie, ingenious plot twists, and feminist themes in her 1647 masterpiece, *Desengaños amorosos* (*The Disenchantments of Love*), has enabled her to withstand the vagaries of time, censorship, and tastes to once again be part of the Spanish Golden Age literary canon. Zayas was one of Spain's most popular writers in the European marketplace alongside Miguel de Cervantes Saavedra, Francisco de Queveo, and Mateo Alemán. Though famously deemed "la dézima Musa de nuestro siglo" ["the tenth muse of our century"] by her contemporary Pérez de Montalbán, some publishers, incredulous that a woman could write such riveting stories with tight narrative structures, marketed Zayas's texts under Cervantes's name. Her work was later ignored by the prudish ethos of late nineteenth-century critics.

Zayas's oeuvre utilizes the malleable structure of the Italianate frame story and the psychological depth of the Spanish novel tradition (mastered by Giovanni Boccaccio and Cervantes, respectively) to inject a feminist narrative into a male-dominated discourse about a man's honor and a woman's role in defining this virtue in Golden Age Spain. The *Desenagaños* collection was preceded by Zayas's 1637 *Novelas amorosas y ejemplares* (*Amorous and Exemplary Novellas*), which revolves around five men and women who tell entertaining stories of love, friendship, and deceit while attending a *sarao* celebrating Lisis's engagement to Don Juan. Whereas this first opus follows the normative thematic tradition of Cervantes's novellas, the *Desengaños* limits the cast of storytellers to women. Consequently, compared to the first text, the *Desenagaños*'s narratorial structure exhibits a feminist pivot. Lisis, who has lost her first fiancé and is now engaged to Don Diego, orders the women to tell tales that will disenchant other women by revealing falsehoods that men concoct while courting them. The frame narrative structure of the novel creates a feminine community not unlike a convent, which is the most socially sanctioned location for a separatist female community – then and now. Nuns and convents are a repeated motif throughout Zayas's novellas. Of the ten tales in the collection, four feature protagonists who retire to a convent. The other six stories end with the female protagonist's death. To wit, four of the main characters in the frame narrative, including the two most important characters, Lisis and Zelima/Isabel[1], also reject the world of marriage and choose a convent as their preferred home.

As the introductory chapter of this book makes clear, the romanticizing of conventual life in literary fiction depicts convents as more ideal and utopian than they were in reality. Enforced claustration and bureaucratically imposed lifestyles of subjugated obedience and silence were not welcomed by all women. However, as more and more historians have demonstrated, nuns did not always faithfully follow these rules since many of them enjoyed more intellectual, artistic, and sexual freedom than their male superiors imagined they did. In a reflection of how early modern authors expressed their cognizance of such liberating possibilities, Zayas employs the convent as a signifier and metaphor for the potential power of female communities of discourse. As this chapter argues, the *sarao* setting of Zayas's novellas mirrors conventual society in that only women tell stories and they do so in order to educate other women. Like real-life choir nuns who were literate in Latin and taught novices the church's vehicular language, the storytellers of the frame narrative instruct the other women at the *sarao* (as well as readers) how to decipher men's language and actions for duplicity. These women do so in order to enlighten their female peers about men's attractive but deceptive wooing tactics. Furthermore, because the larger frame of the *Desengaños* features a removed, unidentified narrator, the women are granted ample freedom to share their stories and comment on them without the supervision of male authority figures. This system of communication mirrors the liberties of real-world convents when male clerics were not on the premises.

Similar to Cavendish's quasi-nuns offering a theatrical series of vignettes about the potential horrors of marriage, childbirth, and childrearing in

---

[1] The character name "Zelima/Isabel" refers to the young woman who narrates the *sarao*'s first tale. This autobiographical narrative reveals that the Muslim slave woman all the characters know as "Zelima" is actually the noble Catholic woman "Isabel." Because there are no other characters with either name, hereafter I refer to her based on the temporal narratorial moment when her Christian name is revealed and recognized.

1668's *The Convent of Pleasure*, Zayas's disenchantresses break the silence of women in Golden Age Spain's machista culture by freely discussing issues such as rape, domestic abuse, cross-dressing, adultery, lesbianism, uxoricide, and, more provocatively, what effect these practices have on women. Because the novella's surviving women take the veil and the frame narrative's protagonist breaks off her engagement in favor of life in a convent, the author's employment of the nun as a literary trope for interrogating gendered power structures and engaging in the *querelle des femmes* is an integral tool in Zayas's writing.

By fleshing out the lives of women who speak, sing, and share stories, Zayas achieves her most poignant political objective when she addresses the issue of the patriarchy's silencing of women. She challenges this customary silence by using her literary prowess to unmuffle the collective voices of women who have been oppressed, abused, battered, raped, and/or killed by men who attempt to bolster their sense of honor by controlling women's conduct.

In a culture where women were granted little say in legal matters, a woman's best antidote to oppression was conversing with other women and telling stories about the men that had wronged them. Scott K. Taylor's monograph *Honor and Violence in Golden Age Spain* has added to historical research that explores the power of women's words in the public negotiations surrounding the honor of both men and women: "[honor] was a tool, used equally by men and women to manage relations with their neighbors and maintain their place in the community" (7). Relatedly, Zayas elevates the female world of gossip by elucidating the power that women possess to construct community-based narratives about the men in their lives. Thus, it is conventual culture that Zayas has Lisis and her peers mimic in their three-night *sarao*. As in a convent, the women listen only to stories told by other women. These raconteuses continually support their sorority through valuable homosocial bonds that are strengthened by their shared resistance to the patriarchy, marriage, and violent sexism of Golden Age Spain's honor-obsessed, machista culture. Regardless of whether one of the story's protagonists ends her days as a murdered woman or as a nun, there are no happy marriages to speak of in either the desengaños or the frame narrative. Just as nuns choose a safe marriage to an incorporal, ethereal God, the wisest women in Zayas's world reject marriage to a mortal man.

What Lisis and her posse of imaginative female wordsmiths have to say in the *Desengaños* speaks volumes not only about the ten years of assumed silence we assign to Zayas's literary output between the publication of her *Novelas amorosas* and the former title, but also about the patriarchy's imposition of a culture of silence in which women were oppressed. Zayas negates the censorship that men attempted to enforce on women by bestowing each of her female characters with the rhetorical finesse and spell-binding greatness of a Baroque storyteller, enabling them to question the importance of a woman's role in a man's definition of his honor, expose the sexual hypocrisies of a heteropatriarchal society, and unleash the voices of those who are subjugated within their own home and social constructs. As such, Lisa Vollendorf's argument that Zayas's early modern feminism neither calls "for a complete reconceptualization of the patriarchal social structure" nor endorses "an alternative social organization" is only half correct ("No," 104). What my work highlights is how, ironically, the Catholic Church offers women a palatably alternative lifestyle choice within the constraints of a bureaucratic and sexist institution. Just as Zayas subverts the genre of love stories, the women of her narratives exploit the Catholic Church's alternative community for women – convents.

Despite the scarce, concrete information about Zayas's life, we know about her involvement in literary *academias*, a fact that strengthens this chapter's study of how the discursive freedoms the female disenchantresses enjoy in the frame narrative mirror the opportunities afforded to women in conventual culture. Spanish *academias*, like many European scholarly academies, met at a regularly scheduled time and place, followed specific protocols about suitable themes for discussion, decided who could be voted into the *academia*, and printed works that broadcast the merits of the organization and the intellectual productions of their members. Zayas's male peers welcomed her into their *academias* and celebrated her literary achievements.

Yet, the *sarao*, which the frame narrative employs as the setting for the telling of stories, can be formally contrasted with the *academias* in that *saraos* were parties that functioned both "to provide diversion rather than to display erudition or talents" and to "present diverse works, ranging from festive or amorous poetry that could be read (or more often sung), to erudite disquisitions, to prose tales read for the entertainment and enlightenment of the public in attendance" (García 41). As such, whereas *academias* are more geared toward establishing one's ethos as a learned scholar and thinker, the *saraos* serve a more utilitarian function: to entertain *and* enlighten. After a participant told a story or sang a song, the next orator would not begin until partygoers commented on the style and substance of the previous presenter's performance. This structure echoes that of the *academias* wherein other members would cheer, jeer, and/or debate a speaker's literary and scholarly skills, but because *saraos* are supposed to be more entertaining than educational, the literary performances mesh with their real-life social context. As such, relaxed partygoers can more easily respond to a story's reflections, references, and influences on their own lives. The storyteller of Zayas's third disenchantment anticipates as much when she prefaces her tale by saying, "Telling a true tale not only entertains but educates as well. Our intention is not simply to entertain but also to counsel women to be responsible for their honor and . . . to fear that what has happened to others they've heard about or will hear about may happen to them" (113)[2].

Because the power of authorship and explicit commentary has been restricted only to women in Zayas's novel, the *sarao* feels like a secularized convent wherein men have been invited to listen to women through grates or in the locutory. As readers find, the intellectual stimulation engendered by an *academia* comes alive in the matriarchal *sarao* as women create a liberating discourse that allows them to shoot their volleys in the *querelle des femmes*. In short, the *sarao* of Zayas's *Desengaños* functions as a profane version of the matriarchal convent.

Just as convents function more efficiently as a liberating community of women in their idealized, fictional form, *academias* did not treat female participants as equal to men. Most women writers did not attain the level of patronage of their male counterparts. Hence, we must attribute Zayas's literary fame to the accolades she received from her male peers. Zayas's own grand hopes for women and her belief in their innate intelligence are the impetus for the themes of her writings as one can see in this statement from the prefatory letter to the reader in 1637's *Novelas amorosas*: "The real reason why women are not learned is not a defect in intelligence but a lack of opportunity. When our parents bring us up if, instead of putting cambric on our sewing cushions and patterns in our embroidery frames, they gave us books and teachers, we would be as fit as men for any job or university professorship" (1).

---

[2] I employ H. Patsy Boyer's invaluable, learned, and widely used English-language translations of *Desengaños amorosos* throughout this chapter, except for when I disagree with her translations. In these cases I use my own translations by following the original Spanish with my English-language translations in brackets. In such cases, the original Spanish comes from Agustín G. De Amezúa y Mayo's definitive 1950 edition of Zayas's text.

Similar to the egalitarian beliefs many critics read in most of William Shakespeare's work[3], Zayas's text reflects her employment of writing to improve the condition of all women. Unlike oppressed minorities who come into power only to subjugate the original persecutors and those whom they were once like[4], Zayas understands that the vast majority of women do not have as much authorial power or authoritative recourse as she and other learned, higher-class women enjoyed. Thus, she offers the convent as a collective space wherein all women can find salvation: "I do this not for my own sake, because it doesn't affect me directly; you know me only by my writing and not by sight. I do this for all women because of the sorrow and the pain their bad name produces in me" (401). These metatextual lines showcase Zayas distorting the mutable narrative frame by having her double, Lisis, speak as a published author rather than an oral storyteller.

Fields of Gold: Baroque Tales and Female-Authored Narratives

Zayas's exceptional ability to write in the heightened and complex Baroque style mastered and propagated by elite and learned men solidifies her as a peer of the Golden Age masters such as Lope de Vega, Pedro Calderón de la Barca, and Francisco de Quevedo. This comparison becomes apparent when one considers the way Jeremy Robbins describes Baroque artists as seeking "to incite reaction on the level of both the senses and the mind" by using "complex imagery, difficult syntax, shocking and violent subject matter, and striking juxtapositions of antithetical concepts" (15). Zayas's disenchantments are so replete with these elements that one would be hard-pressed not to view her as a Baroque master. By amalgamating the gossipy, telling-it-like-it-is style expected from women with the masculine narrative concern for Golden Age themes, rhetoric, and aesthetics, Zayas constructs a paradoxically sexually neutral and dichotomous narrative framework that attracts attention from male and female readers alike.

---

[3] See Alfred Harbage's *As They Liked It: A Study of Shakespeare's Moral Artistry* (New York: Harper Torchbooks, 1961) for an eloquent reading of the English Bard's dutiful regard for the masses and the public audience of his dramas.

[4] See Paulo Freire's seminal 1968 text *Pedagogy of the Oppressed* for a Marxist interpretation of the cycle of oppression that so many societies find difficult to break.

Zayas's intricate plot structures begin to subtly work toward their final goal even in the *Desengaños*'s initial setting. The gathering of disenchantresses, ostensibly a *sarao* celebrating Lisis's impending marriage to Diego, is set during the three days preceding Lent. Lisis has recovered from her previous fiancé, Don Juan, leaving her for her cousin. Lisis now plans to marry Diego on the day before Lent. The particular day of this wedding, Mardi Gras (known in Spain as Carnaval), foreshadows Lisis's later dissolution of the engagement. As the last day before Lent, Mardi Gras is usually marked by festive celebrations in anticipation of the somberness of Lent. Thus, Lisis plans for her first full day as a married woman to occur on Ash Wednesday. This solemn day when Catholics mark their foreheads with ash to remind us of our mortality begins the forty days of Lent in which many husbands and wives refrained from engaging in sexual relations on most days. Lisis does not want to consummate her marriage with Diego, so she picks the one time of the year to marry him when she can abstain from her duties as a wife for religiously sanctioned reasons. Her subtle rejection of marital bliss is a tell-tale sign that the following evenings will not unfold like the audience anticipates they will since "in order to legally fulfill the requirements of legitimate wife . . . the marriage must be already consummated" (Dopico-Black 25). Even if she were forced to marry Diego, Lisis attempts to avoid or at least delay the transition from maiden to wife.

Zayas's rebellious goal to silence men and allow women to share their stories is revealed to readers when Lisis lays out the rules for her *sarao*: "only ladies were to tell stories (this accorded with the men's belief that women have always been storytellers); second, the stories they told should be true cases, and they should be called 'disenchantments' (in this I'm not sure she pleased the men; since men are always trying to deceive women, they don't want women to be undeceived)" (37). Zayas's utilization of the parenthesis allows us to see the defiant nature of the former part of these rules as the narrator agrees with men's stereotype about women as gossiping "storytellers" in order to place the female-only narrative within a frame that is palatable to men. By wryly agreeing that women are innate storytellers, the narrator tempers some of the men's fears about allowing this form of sexism to exist through Lisis's proscription of their ability to tell stories. The provocative nature of this prohibition leads to a disclaimer vouching that the ten tales "should be true cases" and then labeling them "disenchantments" that will displease men because they will elucidate the obfuscation of their own tales. By affirming the authenticity of the "disenchantments," the narrator exposes the stories that men tell about themselves as facetious enchantments. Lisis's command that the women tell true tales to disenchant women about men presents a problematic situation for the men in attendance since there were significant repercussions for being known as a dishonorable man during the time period.

The men are certainly out of the loop regarding this end of Lisis's intentions, but various references throughout the frame narrative hint that Lisis and some of her other female confidants know of her ultimate plan: to enter a convent. The most telling clue appears during the frame story that introduces the third night of story-telling. Lisis has rejected the dress and jewels that Diego sent her. She wears "pearls," "aigrette plumes whiter than the untrodden snow," and a "profusion of lilies" on the sleeves of her gown (306-7). The virginal white that Lisis embellishes herself with signal to the reader that she has snubbed Diego's sensual clothing for a more symbolically pure ensemble that will serve as a luxuriant antecedent to her departure for the convent.

The premeditated nature of these apologues becomes apparent when the narrator peppers the frame narrative with clues about Lisis's role as the mastermind of the *sarao* while the storytellers orchestrate how their stories will unfold in the context of Lisis's plan. For example, the narrator parenthetically informs us that Zelima has "already instructed the musicians as to what they were to do" regarding her long ballad in order to set the audience's mood (39). Likewise, when Lisis ends her disenchantment readers learn that Isabel is collaborating with Lisis regarding some mysterious conclusion: "aware of her intention because Lisis had told her earlier what she planned, [Isabel] wanted to let her rest before she made her closing comments" (396). Readers may realize that the stories serve as highly entertaining subplots that comment and reflect the encompassing diegetic frame that plots Lisis's agency as she moves from betrothed to single. Furthermore, the frame narrative stands out as a creative one in the genre of novels that includes a gathering of people telling tales (e.g., Boccaccio's 14th century *The Decameron*, Geoffrey Chaucer's 14th century *The Canterbury Tales*, and Marguerite de Navarre's 16th century *The Heptameron*) because the manner in which the plot advances within the frame serves as an immediate, contemporary reflection of the disenchantments' themes. Taken together, these disenchantments can be considered a collective digressive apologue since each intercalated narrative offers Lisis a didactic story that engenders the context for her dynamic change from fiancée to nun in the frame narrative.

Because all the active participants in the frame narrative of the *Desengaños* are women, the collection appropriates woman's gossip to challenge conventions about its negative consequences and to assert a woman's agency in the creation of a reality-based discourse of community. The powers of women's gossip in shaping the past and constructing the future are evident in Chris Wickham's study of this form of talk:

> Gossip—and *fama*—establishes common versions of the relevant past inside the talking group (which can be as small as two, and as many as a whole community), and common versions of a set of moral attitudes to that past. It creates and polices group identity. But it is also transactional: one can contest it, directly, by another version of the past, or strategically, with another framing or interpretation of the past. (26)

Although the legal distinction of *fama* is separate from the *mala fama* propagated by the spread of negative gossip, Wickham's study of the close relationship between the two terms allows us to see the women of the frame narrative trying to assert authority in a society where those in power deemed their voices inconsequential in the legal sphere. Except in the case of some dowries and some widows,[5] men ran the legislative and judicial world of law which caused women to construct a person's reputation by way of talk in the marketplaces, on street corners, and in private, neighborhood homes. These two spheres are distinct in their official jurisdiction, but the spatial implications become more ambiguous when issues of honor and its conjoined twin, reputation, enter the court room.

Some readers might argue that the tales do not constitute women's gossip because men are present in the *sarao*. On the contrary, if women's gossip needs to find its way back to the discursive communities of the privileged men who legislate, prosecute, and judge, then a man must eventually be at the receiving end of these tales. The communal context of the *sarao* facilitates the process by showing women that they can and must speak in front of men with authority if they hope to wield any power. However, Zayas posits that women cannot rest once they share their stories with men. They must facilitate a co-ed discussion, as was more common in *saraos* than *academias*, in order to help men learn how to correctly perform an exegesis. As Anne Cruz has noted in her study of the differences between Cervantes's and Zayas's novellas, Zayas's novellas are "metonymic" and "carefully juxtaposed to each other and all are subsumed under the frame tale's master plot" wherein the individual narrators as well as the readers are aware "that the messages conveyed by their tales simultaneously affect and are affected by the amorous relations

---

[5] See Stephanie Fink De Backer, *Widowhood in Early Modern Spain: Protectors, Proprietors, and Patrons,* Leiden: Brill, 2010.

of the aristocratic young men and women" (97). For example, the discussion that follows the second disenchantment, "His Wife's Executioner," finds the men excusing the husband's violent actions and the women (correctly reading the story according to the narrator) damning Don Pedro's response. Without the women cleaning up the men's sexist interpretation of how Don Pedro was wrongly influenced by the honor code, the cycle of excuses would only repeat itself. Thus, the women's gossip requires the presence of men to assert how integral their storytelling is in rectifying the culture of sexist violence. Zayas proffers the idea that storytelling and literature can have real-world effects and that the aims of the *sarao* are not naïve pipe dreams by having Don Juan, Lisis's erstwhile lover, admit that men are guilty as charged:

> In the name of all these gentlemen and in my own name, I must say that these disenchantresses have made and proven their point; with just cause they have taken up the defense of women. We acknowledge that this is true, we admit our defeat and confess that there are men who through their deception and cruelty, stand condemned, thus vindicating women.
>
> When the gentleman heard what Don Juan said, they agreed that he was right. (270)

The fact that gossip can be transactional underscores the importance of these tales' point of view. The stories are recounted by narrators who attest to repeating the tale accurately: "[t]hey told me this story exactly as I have related it" (237). Without linking the *sarao*'s female-authored discourse to that available in a convent, Marina S. Brownlee also appreciates the powers of gossip in Zayas's novellas: "The pleasure of reading gossip . . . ranges from titillation, on the one hand, to power that turns the customarily powerless victim of surveillance into the powerful manipulator of surveillance, on the other, to even a third possibility, as a source of constructive self-analysis" (4). Brownlee recognizes the powers of recovering the powers of gossip for women narrators by discussing its "self-analytical and healing dimension" (6). In turn, this recovery serves as a "cultural indictment" of the "brutal repression and hypocrisy of the zealously cultivated code of honor" and "calls for a rethinking of society's collective values, gesturing toward an improved model, while also serving as a form of consolation for wives who do not suffer an equally repressive domestic environment" (6). The therapeutic nature of Zayas's collection is anticipated by the first frame story when Lisis "convalesced" and "got well and the sun of her beauty gained new brilliance" (37) in anticipation of hearing Zelima's story. In fact, Lisis recuperates only through this homosocial bond with Zelima, positioning same-sex relations as healthier than Lisis's desire for Don Diego.

The analytic, therapeutic, and call-to-action elements of gossip are vividly fleshed out via the characters in the frame narrative. The nun Estefanía's modeling of behavior is mimicked by her cousin Lisis after she reflects on all the gossip (stories) she has heard. The individual narrators actively take the side of the tale's female protagonists, especially during their closing remarks following each tale's conclusion, to elucidate how men have wronged these tragic heroines. In contrast, one can easily imagine that a male-authored version of Laurela's tragic end in "Love for the Sake of Conquest" would have focused on her unchaste behavior and glossed over both Esteban's duplicity and her father and uncle's immoral actions. Such a narrow view of relationships can be found in the omniscient narrator's commentary at the end of Cervantes's "The Jealous Extremaduran" from his *Exemplary Novels* collection. The dark novella revolves around a jealous man who does not allow his wife to leave their home because he fears that she will cuckold him. The narrator faults youth, free will, and "these duennas in their black habits and their long, white head-dresses" (180) instead of blaming the old man's demise on the jealous husband's warped sense of owning his wife. Thus, Matilde, like the other female storytellers in the frame narrative recuperates the life and story of the real-life woman she discusses in "Love for the Sake of Conquest."

The producers of Baroque culture insisted on appealing to the senses and the mind of the audience. Such a style finds its expressions in the way Zayas involves her readers in the frame narrative. The frame narrative's inclusion of discussions amongst members of the *sarao* invites the reader to reflect on the tales. In contrast to the solitary narrator of Cervantes's *Novelas ejemplares*, who comments on each story, the narrator of the *Disenchantments* describes the conversations that the gathering of men and women have after each story and offers us glimpses into the discrete interpretations different *sarao* attendees have about a certain tale. This reflective atmosphere invites the reader to imagine what their comment would be were they a member of the *sarao*. Because Lisis is the host and celebrant of the festivities, one would not want to cross her; if Zayas's graphic depictions of the barbarous actions of men against women were not enough to force readers to sympathize with the plight of these women, then their imagined participation in the discussion may make them more compassionate.

In several instances the narrator, ostensibly a stand-in for Zayas who concludes the volume with her personal signature, directly addresses and forces the reader to enter the *sarao*. At the beginning of the second night of disenchantments, the narrator locates the reader in the room during the night the tales are told: "Who doesn't realize that there must be some people here tonight who aren't altogether well-intentioned?" (168). The connection between the participants of Lisis's party and the reader becomes further cemented because the audience is mixed – both men and women attend the *sarao* and both sexes read the collection of novellas. The heterogeneous audience influences the reader to consider the stories in a more universal and multidimensional manner.

Asignatura Pendiente: Honor and *Fama* in Golden Age Spain

King Alfonso X of Castile's *Siete Partidas*, an effusive, mid-thirteenth century volume of laws that influenced Spanish legal and cultural epistemological thinking well into the seventeenth century, covers such topics as kingship, sacraments, government, property, marriage, testaments, and ecclesiastical offices. King Phillip II updated this set of laws when he published the *Nueva Recopilación* in 1567. The influence of the *Siete Partidas* could still be felt in the way its all-encompassing jurisdiction gathered "administration, morality and adjudication" in a manner "which [left] little room for that separation between public and private space characteristic of a modern society" (Casey 166). One can interpret the *Siete Partidas* and its descendants as a catalogue of the way early modern Spanish society valued certain morals, individuals, minorities, and objects.

Two titles of this seventh *partida* enumerate "the loss of privileges and legal rights that accompanied a devaluation in one's reputation" (Bowman 103). The legislators articulated clear distinctions between a bad reputation (*mala fama*) and infamy (*infamia*). Although to contemporary ears the two terms sound synonymous, the lawmakers wanted people to understand that whereas a bad reputation was a "social condition," infamy was a legal condition (Bowman 105). Infamy could be repealed because it was a legal status, but a person's bad reputation was harder to ameliorate. The lengthy discourse found in these legal codes indexes the various ways someone could be deemed infamous either through public self-incrimination (such as retracting an earlier statement made in court) or by another person defaming them. Events that a man's wife was involved in could also impugn his honor regardless of the woman's agency in the situation – for example, rape. One need read only a brief excerpt from Cervantes's seminal *Don Quixote* to recognize how early modern Spanish society judged a man's character by the actions of his wife: "since the flesh of the wife is one with the flesh of the husband, any stain that besmirches her, or any defect that appear in her, redounds to the flesh of the husband" (282). In Shakespeare's work one need think only of the actions of Othello, Leontes, and Claudio to see the same anxieties played out on the English Renaissance stage.

The most practical reason why men would be vigilant about their wife's sexuality lies in the issue of primogeniture and ensuring that the children for whom the husband invests and to whom he leaves his estate, fortune, and name are biologically his own. This vigilance often entered paranoid territory because men no longer had a signifier of their wife's chastity, the hymen, after they had broken it when consummating their marriage (Black 25). As such, scurrilous talk about their wife's infidelity could be taken as evidence, however circumstantial, to convict their wife as an adulteress. The Spanish Augustinian friar, poet, and humanist Fray Luis de León reified such sentiments in his influential conduct book *La perfecta casada* (1583), which was given as a wedding present to new wives in Spain as late as the twentieth century during Dictator Francisco Franco's authoritarian regime (Cowans 117): "aquella sola es casta en quien ni la fama mintiendo osa poner" ["only she is chaste who infamy, even based on lies, cannot stain with a bad remark"] (278). Zayas explodes these ridiculously high standards through her gothic and hyperbolic stories that illuminate how women should not be judged based on the cruelty forced on them by male culprits. She does so by contrasting the public masculine discourse of honor with the domestic feminine discourse of truth within the *sarao*-as-convent-like matriarchal community.

The outcome of being labeled an infamous man was serious: "*Infames* could no longer obtain the same dignities or honors that those of good reputation could claim. They could no longer serve as councilors to kings or occupy important ecclesiastical posts. They could neither make wills nor offer testimony" (Bowman 103). Based on such historical evidence, one can recognize why certain members of society would want to silence their detractors, opponents, and victims. Defaming someone was such a significant act that a separate title was written to warn kings about being "especially careful not to defame others, to injure their reputations and thereby render them *enfamados*" (Bowman 104). This medieval and early modern mentality regarding a person's reputation shares clear ties with Spanish society's preoccupation with a man's honor. Zayas was cognizant of Alfonso the Wise's impact on Spanish law as well as its machista culture as she alludes to him in the tale "Innocence Punished": "As King Alfonso the Wise said, man's heart is a deep and trackless jungle where cruelty, a wild and savage beast, has its home and its hearth" (197). Aware of how antiquated ideas about men's honor were, Zayas rebuts the construction of honor that seventeenth-century male writers propagated based on figuratively antediluvian principles. As Elizabeth Lehfeldt asserts, seventeenth-century "[c]ontributors to the [discourse of masculinity] could only imagine solutions rooted in late medieval and (occasionally) sixteenth-century exemplars, and failed to envision a new model of masculinity better suited to the circumstances of the seventeenth century" ("Masculinity," 47). Such a problematic discourse was a ripe target for Zayas's refreshing take on epistemologies of honor.

Simplifying Golden Age Spain's obsession with honor into a neat summary belies its complex makeup, but one can define Spanish society's conception of this value as dealing with a man's worth as determined by his birth, rank in society, ability to repay debts and maintain good credit, actions, and reputation. Marcelin Defourneaux describes it well by saying that honor was "an expression of a man's personal worth, and his social standing which could easily be destroyed by others" (32), while Laura Gorfkle adds that honor is "more a public virtue than a matter of personal integrity and individual conscience" (75). The facile manner in which someone's reputation could be tarnished by public discussions is reflected in the hair-splitting language employed by the authors of the *Siete Partidas*. The fact that a man's honor could be sullied by idle talk created an atmosphere of surveillance when it came to conversations held at court and in public, not to mention in private as women's gossip could circulate its way to the jurisdiction of men. Hence, Zayas's tales not only offer readers the voyeuristic pleasure of eavesdropping on the conversations of an aristocratic *sarao*, but they also subversively expose the power of women to avenge men for the wrongs they have committed by constructing a man's *mala fama*, which could lead to the man being labeled an *infame*.

Zayas is subversive because she vitiates the importance of the most common form a man was thought to be dishonored – a fiancé's, wife's, sister's, mother's, daughter's, or niece's infidelity. She highlights the power inherent in a woman's ability to dishonor a man by publicly revealing his sins and shortcomings through talk and story-telling. Guido Ruggiero has argued as much about the authority women were able to wield over a man's *fama*: "women's gossip in a patriarchal society should not be underrated. For what was often labeled idle words, in an environment so finely attuned to reputation, actually was a potent form of power" (60). Zayas underscores the dangerous effects of gossip by making not only men but also women victims of its power, as in the disenchantment "Too Late Undeceived" when one woman's lies about another leads to the slandered woman's murder. Because woman-on-woman malice is constantly rejected by Zayas, the narrator interrupts the story of "Innocence Punished" to indict the actions of a woman who has let down a member of her oppressed sex: "What surprises me most is the cruelty of the treacherous sister-in-law, who, being a woman, should have taken pity on her" (192).

Zayas enlivens her novellas and the audience's understanding of women's powers to create destructive discourses. The narrator of the frame narrative reveals the author's appreciation for the attraction everyone has for gossip regardless of one's sex: "eso tienen las novedades, que aunque no sea muy sabrosa, todos gustan de comerlas" ["that is what novelties [gossip] possess, for even though they are not very savory, everyone likes eating them"] (102). The careful diction of the food metaphor invokes the environment of Golden Age Spain's culture of consumption, a double-edged societal milieu wherein wealth from the New World stayed in the hands of a few while the countryside was famished, and formerly rich noblemen maintained their reputation and fended off malicious "novedades" about their devalued financial state.

Another component of Alfonso the Wise's *Siete Partidas* that is significant in this discussion of Zayas's recuperation of women's voices is the section that approves of a father murdering his married daughter and her lover if he catches the two of them in an adulterous act: "he has a right to kill her and the man whom he finds committing this wickedness with her" (1417). Zayas reflects on this law in "Love for the Sake of Conquest," when Laurela's father conspires with his uncle to murder her after she has engaged in premarital sex. Although the unmarried Laurela did not cheat on her husband, her father had already betrothed her to Don Enrique. In Golden Age Spain, even before a woman was married or betrothed, her male family members were custodians of her chastity so that they could assure her future husband that he could honorably exercise his right to the sole possession and enjoyment of her body and sexuality. The roots of this law that allow a father to murder his adulterous daughter are not only due to sexism since it makes no mention of adulterous sons, but also due to its relationship to the *Siete Partidas*'s concept of why marriage exists: for men to avoid lust, for men to be better fathers to the children he is certain to be father of, and "to avoid quarrels, homicides, insolence, violence and many other very wrongful acts which would take place on account of women if marriage did not exist" (886). Mariló Vigil's study of women's role in sixteenth- and seventeenth-century Spanish society demonstrates that the *Siete Partida*'s approval of a father murdering his adulterous daughter was extended to condoning husbands who murdered their cheating wives with the revision and reification of older Spanish laws, such as the *Fuero Juzgo*, *Fuero Real*, and the *Siete Partidas*, in 1567's *Nueva Recopilación* under King Phillip II (148). Vigil's analysis explains that while this approbation of uxoricide was on the books, it was only officially executed five times in two hundred years. Taylor's study of adultery and violence in seventeenth-century Spain implies that the number might be larger by studying Good Friday Pardons, which demonstrate that "some actual husbands clearly did murder their wives over adultery" (196). Nevertheless, it would be no stretch of the imagination to hypothesize that not all of these murders were officially reported and/or recorded.

In an intriguing anecdote, Vigil recounts the historical tale of a man named Cosme from the Catalonia province of Spain who called for the execution of his adulterous wife in 1629. Church friars attempted to convince Cosme to forgo his vengeance and allow his wife to live. Cosme disagreed and so the friars intervened by taking the wife to a convent before her husband could stop them (151). A popular verse in Sevilla was inspired by Cosme's hysterical screaming and gestures when he found out that he was robbed of his justice: "Todos le ruegan a Cosme / que perdone a su mujer; / y él responde con el dedo: / señores, no puede ser" ["Everyone begs Cosme / to forgive his wife / and he responds with the finger: / gentlemen, it will not suffice"] (qtd. in Vigil 151). This historical example of the convent acting as an earthly salvation for women whose agency has been usurped by patriarchal law and by their male masters is a motif that Zayas employs repeatedly in her disenchantments. Again, the fact that the previously mentioned uxoricidic law granted men the right to *private* justice leads one to imagine that it produced a chilling effect on the *public* report of such acts.

Given the lax concern for the plight of women in this patriarchal society, one can easily understand why Zayas would seek to inject some anti-matrimonial invectives into the mainstream discourse. The unrecorded, private nature of these acts of uxoricide is fleshed out by Zayas in tales such as "The Ravages of Vice" and "Innocence Punished." The horrific nature of such draconian punishments is exaggerated by the fact that Zayas's protagonists are innocent of consensual adultery. Despite both characters' innocence, their respective husbands still choose to mortally wound them. "Innocence Punished" offers readers an example of art imitating life in that the protagonist, Ines, miraculously does not meet death despite being walled up for several years without light or fresh air. She is rescued when a woman hears her moans and sends for help. Ines eventually enters a convent. Following the salvific path of Cosme's wife,

Ines eschews her role as a pawn in the violent sexual economy of patriarchal Golden Age Spain by entering a convent. Recent studies of the confessional literature written by nuns in the early modern era has illustrated how "childhood traumas . . . attracted women to the claustral ideal" (McNamara 492). Such traumas were usually sexual in nature and perpetrated by men. Thus, although the majority of women in Zayas's tales are post-pubescent if not full-fledged adults, the attraction to the convent as a utopian haven reveals itself in women who discuss the traumas they have endured in the context of their heterosexual relationships.

The success of Zayas's endeavor to criticize the honor code and offer an alternative model of life is showcased by Lisis's decision to renounce her engagement and enter a convent. Lisis explains her decision by referencing the didactic nature of these narratives and attesting that she cannot even "trust in my good fortune" because she feels "no more loyal than the beautiful doña Isabel whose many trials did her no good, as she told us in her own disenchantment. That's when all my fears began" (402). Lisis's lesson exemplifies how female-authored courtship novels like the *Desengaños* usurp the traditional gendering of the "ideal courtier as male" in courtesy manuals by using the plots of these novellas to "fulfill an instructive function, demonstrating how to project an effective public mask through ritual displays of courtesy" (Armon 109). Zayas, of course, does so in her uniquely Baroque fashion. As various clues are dropped to inform the reader that Lisis has an ultimate goal to achieve at the end of the *sarao*, it soon becomes apparent that Lisis's genteel speeches and the luxuriant nature of the *sarao* is a contrived setting for breaking her engagement with Diego. As such, Lisis is careful to cite Isabel's tale, "Slave to Her Own Lover," because Isabel fleshes out the first story by being its real-life protagonist. If Zayas had not included the character of Isabel, then the partygoers, especially the men, might not have believed the authenticity of these tales. By placing Isabel's narrative first in the collection, each succeeding story hinges its verisimilitude on the fact that Isabel's presence testifies to the authenticity of each tale. Lisis uses the stories as a justification for her broken engagement, which allows her to fashion herself as a woman of learning who cannot acquiesce to exposing herself to the dangers that marriage could pose in Golden Age Spain's honor-obsessed social milieu.

By citing the educational function of these courtship novels, Lisis highlights how the *Desengaños* employ exempla to help readers. This rhetorical strategy flourished during the Baroque period because it explicitly proclaimed itself with "a particular pedagogical function, let the reader beware," so that the very idea of "the exemplum as a metacritical tool to comment on the deceptive nature of language itself" could be exploited (Brownlee 28). Hence, these stories can be interpreted as didactic exempla. This Golden Age interest in the subjectivity of fictional characters lends itself to Lisis's goal of disenchanting women by interrogating and challenging the courtly wooing of men like Esteban with an Inquisitorial zeal that exposes the deceitful words that such men use to fool women to act against their own best interest. The power of such men's discourse is rendered mute in its authenticity or believability by the more credible words of the quasi-omniscient narrators who vouch for the accuracy of their tales. The fact that these tales are told within the architecture of courtship novels augments the seditious style in which Zayas appropriates a masculine domain to her advantage. Shifra Armon groups Zayas along with Spanish Golden Age writers Mariana de Carvajal and Leonor de Meneses to assert that "[f]emale novelists after Cervantes unlock a doctrinally unassailable discursive site, that of courtship narratives, to rearticulate power relations between women and men" (xii). Even within the formulaic borders of the courtship novel, Zayas uses the transactional powers of women's gossip to challenge the power structure that subsumes women to the will of men by imbuing each of the female narrators with a lucid narrative voice that exposes the truth behind many a pretentious courtly wooing.

The final element we must mention before embarking on closer readings of these novellas is one that is missing in these narratives: children. The standard concern with a woman's sexuality and her submission to men is repudiated by the absence of progeny. Despite the frequency of rape episodes in the disenchantments, it is important to note that none of the protagonists are pregnant women. A horrifically gothic image of a pregnant woman appears in the second disenchantment, "Most Infamous Revenge." Juan rapes Camila, Carlos's wife, in order to avenge him for refusing to marry his beautiful but poor sister, Octavia. Camila escapes Carlos's anger by living in a convent for a year. Carlos is unable to avenge his wife's rape by murdering Juan because he has fled town and none of his spies can find Juan. Upon her return, Carlos refuses to eat or sleep with her, and after a year of being reunited he goes mad and poisons her. The poison does not initially kill her and so her whole body "swell[s] monstrously" and her stomach is "distended at least a rod from her waistline" as if pregnant (108). Of course there is no child and Camila dies after six months of suffering "great martyrdom" (108).

There is no talk of child-bearing because Zayas wants to erase such a possibility to focus on men's appropriation of women's bodies as well as on men's infallible insistence that their honor is wrapped up in their woman's sexuality. Additionally, because the tales' narrators do not usually comment upon the prospect of a raped woman becoming pregnant, Zayas's stories render these men as impotent ruffians and negate their ability to propagate. In effect, Zayas's women narrators abort the future of these men. They silence their lineage and extinguish their legacy. These women reassert their place in the primeval scheme of things by preventing their bodies from being exploited as vessels of reproduction for a violent patriarchal society. This negation of a next generation hews closely to Lee Edeleman's nihilistic take on reproductive futurity, the ideology that enforces the necessity and goodness of reproducing, because it "impose[s] an ideological limit on political discourse . . . preserving in the process the absolute privilege of heteronormativity" (2). Were it not for the vast cultural differences between Zayas's seventeenth-century Spain and Edeleman's fiery twenty-first century polemic, Edeleman's misanthropic treatise could prove fruitful for those who wish to examine the absence of children in these narratives through the lens of a queer misandry that questions the value of bringing children into a violent, patriarchal world. All the same, Zayas's careful choice not to include children in her writings further underscores the *sarao*'s verisimilitude to real-life convents filled mostly with women who have rejected birthing and raising children so that they may follow their own paths in life unencumbered by the needs of others, with the exception of widows who took the veil.

Domestic Violence Ends in Silence:
A Case Study of the *Desengaños*

"Domestic violence" is not only a heated term in today's debates about the physical violence enacted on women, children, and, sometimes, husbands, but it also presents an anachronistic quandary in our discussion of seventeenth-century life. The domestic world as we understand it was not as clearly defined and recognized as separate from non-domestic spheres of influences such as church, law, and society in the early modern era. These permeable spheres regularly interacted in an intertwined but conflicting relationship with one another. Home life in seventeenth-century Spain, like much of Europe, was not a homogenous institution. Class, race, and economic status rendered each individual's home life unique. James Casey asserts that home life was usually nuclear in early modern Spain according to the official census, but because the extended family "cooperated very closely," the realities of domestic living arrangements led to mutable architectural possibilities wherein, in one Andalusian example, "[p]arty walls are run up and torn down, new doors opened into the patio or street, windows blocked off, according to the needs of each generation" (211). Domestic life was not always stable as families grew and shrank according to mortality rates as well as economic status that supported slaves or servants. As manuals by the likes of Juan Luis Vives and Fray Luis de León written for the education of wives as domestic caretakers indicate, the relatively private life of the home was supposed to be a woman's workplace and sanctuary. Zayas constantly demonstrates that the latter was far from a reality in many cases as women were neglected, degraded, abused, and sometimes raped and murdered within their own home.

The Ravages of Vice

My examination of Zayas's portrayal of domestic violence will begin at the end, with a brief examination of the tenth and final novella in the collection – a horrific story narrated by Lisis entitled "The Ravages of Vice." In this novella Dionisis marries Magdalena and is then informed by her step-sister, Florentina, that she is in love with him. The two have an affair, and, on the advice of a maidservant, Florentina arranges for Dionisis to walk in on what appears to be Magdalena having her own affair with a male servant. Underscoring the wantonness and excess associated with his namesake, Dionisis flies into a violent rage and murders everyone he encounters save for Florentina, who is saved by the maidservant.

As he stabs his wife to death in their bed, we see the walls of domestic life figuratively coming down on Magdalena as she is mortally silenced without being allowed to utter a single word in her defense; much as the husband in Calderón's 1629 drama *El medico de su honra* murders his loyal wife simply for suspecting that she has cheated on him. Zayas rectifies the misogyny in her narrative by laying the blame on the husband and figuring Florentina as the figure of revelation and repentance. In contrast to Dionisis's unmediated rage, Florentina regretfully describes Magdalena's death scene with spiritual-like veneration: "She couldn't even utter alas! Before her saintly soul abandoned the most beautiful and chaste body" (392). The recuperation of Magdalena comments upon her namesake, Mary Magdalen. This Biblical and cultural allusion allows us to see Zayas reflecting on a long history of misogyny stretching back millennia, since most Westerners incorrectly believe Mary Magdalen to have been a prostitute despite a lack of Biblical support for such a claim.

Zayas rewards Florentina by having her retreat to a luxurious convent that allows her to continue communicating with the outside world, especially the man who helped her retreat to a convent, Don Gaspar, thanks to the rich dowry she possesses from all of her estates: "At last she achieved her desire and became a nun in one of the most sumptuous convents in Lisbon. . . . Today she still lives a saintly and devout life. She writes to Don Gaspar, never forgetting her gratitude to him. She sends him many gifts in acknowledgement of the debt she feels. . . . It was from him that I heard this disenchantment that you've just heard" (396). Lisis's relation of this story is indebted to the comforts of Florentina's convent and her ability to communicate her personal narrative beyond its walls. Patsy Boyer posits that Zayas identifies with the "other woman," Florentina, because the author herself took such "delight in her transgressive creativity" (22). Just as Zayas is rumored to have entered a convent later in life, Florentina is rewarded rather than punished for her non-normative desires. To solidify such a progressive outlook on women's sexual autonomy, Zayas has the disenchantress Laura criticize and recuperate women with a more liberal attitude towards sex before beginning her story: "I blame them all and I excuse them all" (172).

Because Magdalena is stabbed to death in her bedroom just as many other women in the *Desengaños* are murdered in the alleged safety of their own homes, much academic work on Zayas has focused on the spatial relationship between women in the novels and their homes. The home, a woman's sphere, is paradoxically heralded by the patriarchy as the location in which women can maintain their honor (virginity) and safety as well as the one place in which women can be legally beaten and killed by their male superiors. Ironically, humanist philosophers often aped the Church's rule of enclosure for nuns when advising women on how best to maintain their honor and chastity. The walls of a house serve to silence women from expressing their pain to the outside world. As noted in the case of Cosme, society's belief in moral behavior could sometimes rescue a woman in public places or within the confines of a Catholic Church that decries the death penalty.

Triumph Over Persecution

In another improvement or subversive *imitatio* of her male predecessors' work, this time Cervantes's *Novelas ejemplares*, Zayas repudiates the acceptance of a woman taking back the man who physically abuses her. In Cervantes's "Rinconete and Cortadillo," the two picaresque boys that the novel is named after observe a community of organized criminals consisting of pickpockets, murderers, and prostitutes. One of the prostitutes, Cariharta, refuses to take back her abusive boyfriend, Repolido, until another bawdy woman, Gananciosa, and the community's leader, Monipodio, convince her that it is the proper thing to do. Gananciosa tells Cariharta that when men "attack and beat and kick us, then they adore us" (Cervantes 107). Cariharata begins to buy into this perverse reasoning and interprets Repolido's weeping as a sign of his love for her, even though he beat her. After a bout of public quarreling between the couple, Repolido hyperbolically pledges to degrade himself in order to win over Cariharta: "if it's because Cariharta wishes it, I won't just kneel, but I'll be a slave and put a nail in my forehead for her sake" (110). The couple soon make amends and are last seen "embrac[ing] each other again" (118).

Lenore Walker's watershed studies on battered women detail the common cycle of domestic abuse that many women face in violent relationships with men. The first period begins with a man's frustration and rising tensions, the second period includes physical violence, and the third period features the man's contrite behavior as he "attempts to make amends for the painful battering by behaving in an especially loving manner" (Walker 54). Cervantes's depiction of the groveling Repolido clearly falls within the period of contrite behavior. Unlike the feminist narratorial intrusions one anticipates when reading the *Desengaños*, no one steps in to reprimand or comment on Repolido's and Cariharta's ludicrous behavior. Such conduct never needs to be excused under pretenses of irony or "just comedy and entertainment." After all, even in Cervantes's non-picaresque novella "La fuerza de la sangre" ("The Power of Blood"), a woman who is raped in her sleep seeks to regain her and her family's honor by marrying her rapist seven years later when she learns of his identity. One need not be a seventeenth-century woman or a twenty-first century feminist to be disgusted with Rodolfo's unapologetic rape of Leocadia in Cervantes's tale. When Thomas Middleton and William Rowley adapted Cervantes's novella for their Jacobean play *The Spanish Gipsy*, their Rodolfo, Roderigo, eventually admits his guilt and does so with genuine regret as he seeks to repent for his sins. Hence, "because some of Cervantes's contemporaries clearly . . . felt the need to 'correct' the lack of remorse shown by Rodolfo," Cervantes's tale presents "readers with a series of deafening silences and asks them to interpret those silences" (Ife and Darby 180). Silence is a form of oppression, and one cannot count on readers in a violently patriarchal society to explore such absences of explication in a non-sexist, anti-violent, edifying manner. Given that domestic abuse did not come into the forefront of mainstream American consciousness until the 1970s, and given that it is still a topic Spain is still wrestling with in the early twenty-first century, we should not expect Cervantes, who is penning a picaresque novella, to separate this tale of domestic abuse from the other grotesque behavior exhibited by the gang of thugs featured in the novella. That is, until we read Zayas.

Fittingly, Lisis's cousin, the nun Estefanía, tells this most hagiographic of the tales in the penultimate disenchantment of the collection, "Triumph Over Persecution," which is based on the popular medieval tale "The Empress of Rome." Zayas's novella focuses on the travails of Beatriz, the wife of King Ladislao of Hungary. When her husband leaves to participate in a military battle, his brother, Federico, begins to woo Beatriz despite her protests. She eventually has him imprisoned, albeit luxuriously, until her husband returns. However, Federico reaches Ladislao before Beatriz does and convinces him that Beatriz was seducing *him*. Upon reuniting with Beatriz, Ladislao "elude[s] her embrace" and flies into a violent rage: "[h]e raised his hand and struck her with such force and cruelty that she fell at his feet, bathed in her innocent blood. Without hesitating, without letting her speak, he called his four huntsmen" (328). Beatriz is abandoned in a forest to fend for herself against wild beasts. After miraculous interventions by the Virgin Mary, Beatriz is saved, and Ladislao learns of her innocence by way of her donning a masculine disguise and convincing Federico to publicly confess to his crimes. The narrator is careful to note that Ladislao silences Beatriz when he returns from battle by not allowing her to clear her reputation from Federico's accusations. The audience is also informed that the king has ordered Beatriz's eyes to be pricked out because they "had brought about his dishonor through their immoral glance" (329). In an attempt to combat Ladislao's ridiculous obsession with his wife's agency, the narrator redeems Beatriz and allows her to be the last important character to speak when she reminds him of the pain she has endured because of his rash decision to banish her: "I am the very one for whom your eyes shed those tears, the one who has suffered such dishonor and misfortune" (363). Beatriz has usurped Ladislao's claim to honor by making herself the signifier of honor, since she was the one who lost it.

Ignoring the ideology that constructed a husband's honor based on the sexuality of his wife, the narrator allows Beatriz to enjoy her renewed sense of honor by denying Ladislao any more words. Readers witness Ladislao suffer from want of his wife as he yearns "to enjoy again *the loving embrace* of his wife and *the glories* he had missed in her absence," only to be told by Beatriz that "she would not consent," since for her "there could be no husband, no kingdom in this world, for she aspired only to her divine spouse and the kingdom of Heaven" (emphasis mine, 364). The narrator empowers Beatriz by shifting the dynamics of power in her favor. Beatriz rejects Ladislao by rebuffing the very embrace he once denied her. She refuses to "consent" to Ladislao's desire for her "glories" even though they are legally married. She rejects her role as a wife subject to her husband's desires. Furthermore, she informs him of her new reality – one in which there can be no husband except for God. This rejection also entails a refutation of the patriarchal system in her snubbing of any earthly monarchy, which takes on masculine linguistic connotations both in the original Spanish, "reino," and in the English translation, "kingdom." Rendered figuratively impotent, Ladislao takes the habit as a follower of Saint Benedict. Before the narrative ends we are told that Ladislao dies "many years before Beatriz" (364), which once again accentuates her dominance over him. In contrast to Cariharta's pathetic acceptance of her abusive boyfriend, Beatriz silences her husband's desires and rejects his period of contriteness, consequently breaking her silence and ending the cycle of domestic abuse.

Beatriz foreshadows Lisis and her friend's departure for the convent in the frame narrative when she takes "all her ladies" with her as "they [take] the habit" accompanying Beatriz, who is to live "a holy life until she was very old" (364). The transformative, cathartic elements of professing the life religious can even be read psychoanalytically as a rejection of the Oedipal complex as Zayas's characters proceed "from the house of the father to the house of God, which, in terms of psychic attachment, is a conditional return to the house of the mother" (Greer 110). The domestic home is robbed of its matriarchal potential by Spanish laws that allow men to murder women within their homes. Thus, women must escape these secular spatial constraints for the paradoxically physically-constraining but spiritually-liberating walls of the enclosed convent, with its metaphorically feminine and virginal qualities.

In yet another nod to the intellectual potential that permeates conventual life, Estefanía learns of Beatriz's tale by having read it. Rather than having heard her tale in the oral story-telling tradition, Estefanía has learned from reading just as the readers of Zaya's novellas are supposed to. This metatextual reference invigorates the idea of a public female readership that can learn from female writers in the *querelle des femmes*.

The narrative's constant veneration of the convent, nunhood, and religious figures such as Jesus Christ and the Virgin Mary may be a major reason why the Inquisition, rather than censoring Zayas's stories, "considered them highly edifying" (Boyer 14). Fray Pío Vives, Prior of Santa Catalina Mártir in Barcelona, praises the book in his official approbation of its 1648 publication in the city: "en él veo un asilo Donde puede acogerese la femenil flaqueza más acosada de importunidades lisonjeras, y un espejo de lo que más necesita el hombre para la buen dirección de sus acciones" ["in this book I see an asylum where feminine weaknesses can take refuge from being harassed by flattering importunities as well as a much-needed mirror for men to better direct their actions"] (5). After all, the narrators continually contrast religious women with the women who contribute to their sex's bad reputation: "You will find [good women] if you visit the sanctuaries in Madrid . . . for you'll find good women taking the sacraments every day, unlike the kind who seek you out in parks and along the riverside" (401).

Although Beatriz's sexuality is muted after she has been miraculously saved, the tale's narrator hints that women can exploit their sexuality as nuns by coquettishly teasing men. Before Estefanía tells her tale she informs her audience that, shockingly, nuns learn how to tease men: "la hacienda que primero aprendemos el engañar, como se ve en tantos ignorantes, como asidos a las rexas de los conventos, sin poderse apartar de ellas, bebiendo como Ulises, los engaños de Circe . . . sin considerar que los engañamos con las dulces palabras, y que no han de llegar a conseguirs las obras" ["The first task we learn is how to deceive, as can be seen in all the ignorant men who grasp the rails of the convents unable to free themselves, drinking like Ulysses, from Circe's deceptions . . . without realizing that we deceive them with our sweet words and that they will never obtain their rewards"] (339). Estefanía empowers herself and her fellow nuns by highlighting the sexual agency they possess in constructing themselves as the ultimate object of courtly love. They are literally walled in, forbidden, and married to the most imposing and powerful of men: God. These coquettish nuns enjoy their role as cockteases by perversely exploiting their vow of chastity as an aphrodisiac. As Estefanía sees it, men view nuns as the ultimate conquest and proof of how well they can deceive women: "the deceptions of nuns are sought after precisely because of their impossibility. The more men think about them and covet them, the more entangled they get" (310). Provocatively enough, historical studies of amorous relationships between nuns and secular men prove that Zayas's fiction was rooted in reality. According to Mariló Vigil, throughout the sixteenth and seventeenth century, the locutories of Spanish convents were frequented by Don Juan-like courtiers who would present themselves as poets or as pious men who wanted to assist in Mass. Vigil finds that these courtiers had access to these permeable spaces either with the accompaniment of a nun's family members or sometimes by themselves (241).

Estefanía then proffers nuns as role models for the women attending the *sarao* by explaining that they should be as equally alluring and unavailable as nuns. She next positions sexual relations as a game that women can master: "The same thing would happen with secular women if they didn't sell their favors so cheap" (310). Casting herself as an avenger and a "master of deception," Estefanía circulates nontraditional ideas about nuns and their queer sexual power as virginal temptresses. After all, in Spanish Golden Age culture the religious and the secular were not always discrete entities. Vigil argues that in this culture "el galanteo y el erotismo eran beatíficamente sublimados mediante unas supuestas inquietudes espirtuales de los jóvenes galanes, y unos supuestos afanes redentores de las esposas de Cristo" ["gallantry and eroticism were beatifically sublimated by means of the supposed spiritual anxieties of the young gallants and the supposed redeeming eagerness of the brides of Christ"] (246). Zayas's intoxicatingly rich characterization of this nun concludes with one last zinger before Estefanía shares her story and anticipates its effect on listeners: "If the gentlemen aren't properly castigated by my disenchantment, they will be when they seek me at home in my convent, because I'll turn them over to a dozen of my sisters, which would be like throwing them to the lions" (310). This violent imagery disrupts the assumptions of an audience that has already come so far as to accept that a nun such as Estefanía can straddle the line between being a pious woman and one who pretends to be a conquerable object of affection, since the two personality characteristics are not mutually exclusive. Having pushed the envelope to condone violence in this hyperbolic image of women proudly, defiantly, and aggressively tearing a man to shreds, Zayas invokes male castration anxieties and fears about women's dominance.

Estefanía's brief but audacious preface to her story serves as a rich foreshadowing of the domestic violence that her female protagonist will repudiate, thanks to her intelligence and an intercession by the ultimate female divine, the Virgin Mary. Julia Kristeva touches upon the metaphoric relationship between reclamations of the feminine divine via nuns and the Virgin Mary: "a concrete woman, worthy of the feminine ideal embodied by the Virgin as an inaccessible goal, could only be a nun, a martyr, or, if she is married, one who leads a life that would remove her from that 'earthly' condition and dedicate her to the highest sublimation alien to her body" (256). The women in Zayas's tale usually take one or two of these forms, as we see innocent wives murdered in martyr-like fashion and widows taking the veil after the welcome death of their husbands. Whatever route these protagonists take, Zayas makes certain that their lives are recorded and circulated by her female storytellers. Intriguingly enough, none of the young women have fathers and some of their mothers are present. Hence, even in this secular realm the female authors are relatively free from the patriarchy just as nuns would be, with the exception of transiently meddling extraconventual male authorities. This fairy tale-esque motif of a young protagonists having only one parent embellishes the liberties of the ruling matriarchal culture present in Zayas's *sarao*.

Another legendary element of this story is that Zayas surely named this novella's protagonist after Beatriz de Silva who in 1484 founded the Order of the Immaculate Conception, the same order to which Estefanía belongs and the one that Lisis, Isabel, and their mothers join at the end of the frame narrative (O'Brien 233). Lisis, as is noted in the conclusion of the *Desengaños*, will still receive visitors in the convent. If such an open invitation to extraconventual visitors implies that she will not take the veil, we see her decision to enjoy some modicum of sexuality or affectional relationships. For if a fully professed nun marries God she marries a male figure, even if he is incorporal. However, a woman residing in a convent who decides to follow less stringent religious professions strikes a bolder path in respect to non-heteronormative behavior. Whether she may have hetero- or homo-affectional desires, she is not tied down in the same way that a veiled sister is. She is queerly independent.

Love for the Sake of Conquest

The sixth disenchantment, "Love for the Sake of Conquest," often attracts attention because of the way it deals with gender roles and sexuality. I augment such a reading by also examining the story through the lens of domestic violence and silence to showcase how Zayas infuses each tale with a startling display of how women are oppressed by cleverly deceitful men. The narrative begins by following Esteban, who is madly in love with Laurela, as he contemplates how he can woo his love interest. Esteban decides to cross-dress so he can become a maid to the aristocratic Laurela, who is barely a teenager. As "Estefanía" he audaciously proclaims his love for Laurela and laments the fact that "she" is a woman and cannot marry Laurela. After revealing the truth about his sex to Laurela, Esteban convinces her to elope and have sex with him. In another allusion to Cervantes, Zayas has Esteban convince Laurela that the home where they go to consummate their love is his own when it is actually his friend's. This clear reversal of Cervantes's "El casamiento engañoso" ("The Deceitful Marriage"), which features the woman tricking the man into believing the luxurious house in which she is a servant is hers, asserts the dangers that women always face without a home, room, or conventual cell of their own. After they have consummated their passion, Esteban tells

Laurela that he is poor and already married. Abandoned at a church, Laurela is taken in by her stern uncle and aunt, who inform her father of the situation. Because the family cannot catch Esteban and exact their retribution on him, they decide to restore Laurela's honor by killing her with a false wall they construct and push on top of her. Because this murder happens within the alleged safety of the home, Laurela's sisters and mother are inspired to opt out of the secular domestic life for the security of the walls that they choose to protect themselves within, inside the convent's feminine community.

Although Esteban passes as Estefanía throughout the story, the narrator showcases masculine duplicity as a characteristic that Esteban cannot just discard along with his man's clothing. In one of his many songs to Laurela, Esteban demonstrates his desire to dominate Laurela. The theme of feminine silence versus masculine vocalization appears in the third song Estefanía sings in the story. Consumed by jealousy over a rival for Laurela, Esteban compares the young maid to the lovelorn Echo and casts the rival, Don Enrique, in the role of Narcissus:

> Thus may you be heard
> by your Narcissus, unfortunate nymph,
> and your own love turned into Echo,
> your own beauty into misfortune;
> and if perhaps the cause
> of the love that burns me speaks with you
> may its accents tell you
> my tender and loving sentiments. (221)

The Renaissance reawakened interest in the classical myth of Narcissus most memorably recounted in Ovid's *Metamorphoses*. Proud Narcissus rejects the advances of men and women who desire him and is enraptured by his own image when he observes his reflection in the Stygian pond. The nymph Echo is described in Book III of *Metamorphoses* as possessing two contradictory and stereotypical qualities of women: she cannot speak first (obedient) and she cannot stop speaking once she is spoken to (shrewish) – "quae nec reticere loquenti / nec prior ipsa loqui didicit, resonabilis Echo" (lines 357-58). Described as mindlessly talkative, Echo is an inferior being whose agency depends on that of another, in this instance Narcissus. By wishing that Laurela be transformed into Echo, Esteban desires to silence Laurela into a parrot-like woman who can only regurgitate the words of rejection uttered by her love interest. In *Metamorphoses* Narcissus repudiates Echo's signs of affection by slowly beating himself to death uttering "vale" [farewell] (501) as Echo repeats his words. Echo is left repeating the sounds of woes she hears from the naiads who surround the pond when Narcissus dies. Thus, Esteban reveals the misogyny of his true sex in his insistence that Laurela become a woman who cannot vocalize any of her own thoughts or desires unless they are sanctioned by a man. Even so he wishes her eternal woe if he cannot possess her and be the domineering man who will control her speech.

Esteban continues his campaign of silencing Laurela during their confrontation about his sex. Esteban launches into a lengthy tirade meant to win over Laurela by erasing any thoughts she might have had about forming an intimate same-sex relationship with Estefanía: "Who's ever seen a woman fall in love with another woman? Because this is the way things are, find it in your heart to become mine and give me your hand in marriage" (227). Although Laurela eventually runs away and has sex with Esteban, there are some hints that she has been considering the possibility of a relationship with Estefanía. After the mature discussion about Neo-Platonic love that Estefanía, Laurela, and the other maids and sisters engage in, Laurela begins to recognize the possibility of true love between two members of the same sex, since Estefanía has so well argued that "[s]ouls aren't male or female and true love dwells in the soul, not in the body" (224). A maid offers a retort to Estefanía's arguments by saying that a woman loving another woman is "amor sin provecho" ["a love without advantage," from the Latin "profectus"] (236). I employ my translation of the line because I think Boyer's translation, "a fruitless love" (224), glosses over the more cynical connotations of the word "provecho," deriving its roots from the Latin "profectus," the past participle of "proficere," which means "to go forward, make progress, be advantageous" according to the Elsevier's Concise Spanish Etymological Dictionary.

Estefanía replies to the maid by saying that "es el verdadero amor, pues amar sin premio es mayor fineza" ["it's true love, for loving without reward is the greater and purer kind"] (236). The roots of the Spanish word for "reward," "premio," derives from the Latin word "praemium," whose underlying meaning is "taken before others." The Latin roots of these words are important to this discussion because they offer us a better understanding of the conversation's implications. When Estefanía repudiates the maid's desire for an advantageous love, one sees her employ the Neo-Platonic discussion to describe love as one between equals where one does not take advantage of another. The "premio" also implies that a man should not love a woman simply so he can take her out of circulation and away from other wooers, reaping either the rewards of taking her virginity or bartering her to another man to gain further "provecho" in a homosocial triangle that would by default categorize the woman as simple chattel. In the end, Laurela is a prize, one which Esteban diligently worked for, but a prize nonetheless. Claudio Cifuentes-Aludnate astutely notes that the Greek origins of Esteban's name, *stephanós*, means crown, which can be easily imagined as a laurel wreath with which he will coronate himself by taking possession and then abandoning *Laurel*a (57). Hence, Laurela is nothing more than an object or notch on the belt with which a man chooses to decorate himself.

Zayas flirts with the more liberating possibilities of amorous same-sex desires when Laurela's maids and family members jovially respond to Estefanía's love-struck speeches with laughter. Even Laurela's father, Bernardo, makes a quip regarding his daughter's relationship with Estefanía: "That's splendid . . . and we can expect lovely grandchildren from such a chaste love" (216). This tongue-in-cheek comment has a twofold purpose. Firstly, it laughs off the fear Laurela's parents have about her becoming pregnant out of wedlock; this anxiety is expressed through how closely they guard her: "Whenever she left the house she was accompanied by her mother and her sisters" (206). Secondly, it continues the discourse of silencing women's agency. Every time the maids "all laugh at the notion that [Estefanía] had fallen in love with Laurela" (214), they erase the possibility of a serious romantic relationship between the two. Although it eschews the seriousness of the situation, it does so by ambiguously accepting it as a frivolous love affair. The nonchalant disavowal of a lesbian relationship can be attributed to the fact that a same-sex relationship between two women was not prosecuted as commonly as male same-sex relationships were. This dismissive comment also underscores that the real fear circles around a man's honor as reflected in the women in his life. Because Estefanía and Laurela's love cannot result in an out-of-wedlock or illegitimate birth, then there is nothing of concern. Lesbian relationships are so unthreatening that Bernardo has no problem with a maid that loves and adores his daughter seeing her naked as she undresses and clothes herself.

This feminist discourse which seeks to balance the respect accorded to amorous relationships between members of the same sex with those between men and women to the benefit of both is muted when Esteban's sex is revealed. Esteban's attempts to silence Laurela's desire for an idealistic, Neo-Platonic love once again demonstrates Zayas showcasing the ways in which some men enchant women to act contrary to their best interest. This silencing occurs in a mixed-sex community, but what about in a same-sex community? Laurela's sisters flee to a convent a few months after her death because her demise "disenchanted them about what they could expect from men" (237), which raises the prospects that the Neo-Platonic love that so intrigued them may achieve its true potential in a same-sex community that does not censor their voices or desires. Reflecting a culture where truly independent and autonomous women were ridiculed and considered outcasts, sometimes even if they cloaked their independence in religious terms, Zayas assures the safety and agency of her female characters by placing them in a communal space where they could be more readily guarded and respected, since the "model of [female] sanctity was inside convents" (Saint-Saëns 60). Because women had to retire in groups, communication and story-telling were default activities of such social communitarian lifestyles. The need for this discourse privileges Zayas's disenchantresses and their quest to engage in debate.

The women's exile into a convent might suggest that the rest of their lives will be enveloped by spiritual silence, chastity, and obedience. But these novels propose that complete isolation is not the only possible conclusion. Despite the minuscule amount of information we receive about characters such as Beatriz and Florentina after they are encloistered, the presence of Lisis's cousin Estefanía and the frame narrator's invitation to the interlocutor, Fabio, to visit Lisis in her retreat imply that life is not over when one enters a convent. Estefanía has returned home from her convent in order to recover from an illness. The permeability of her convent implies that some nuns were able to enter and leave more fluidly than one would expect after the Council of Trent (1545-63) imposed a rule of enclosure on nuns. In Italy, and one would imagine in most other nations, "families did not easily relinquish the daughters they had thought be free to visit with them and whom they had planned to see at will" (Weaver 73).

Theodoroa Jankowski's study of the Catholic discourse on virginity and nuns would lead one to view Estefanía's exit from the convent as a sign that not only is she transgressive, but also that her entire convent is teetering on the edge of infamy: "The walled monastery, representing the walled garden (body), ensured the virginity of the women inside it, especially if the wall (hymen) had not been broached. . . . If a monastery had a gate which was always open . . . its nuns could be (and were) presumed to have vaginas (or hymens) that were equally open/broached" (69). Zayas decides to add more irony to Estefanía's transgressive condition by stating that she is a "nun of the Immaculate Conception" (306). The celebration of the Virgin Mary's non-penetrative pregnancy is reflected in Estefanía's saintly "white habit with a blue scapular" (306). The color of purity is juxtaposed with the fact that she cockily wears a laurel over her veil even though she has not told of her disenchantment because she "felt confident of being as spirited as her companions" (306). Zayas surrounds Estefanía with the innocent and submissive raiment of her calling. Yet she imbues her with a brash confidence and the ability to freely leave her convent and engage in a lively discussion about women's rights and the treachery of men in a secular, mixed-sex audience. Again, we see Zayas give a voice to those who would normally be silenced.

Conventual Pedagogy

In a vein similar to Estefanía's insistence on remaining involved in the extraconventual world, readers learn that when Lisis ends the *sarao* by announcing her intentions to enter a convent alongside Laura, Estefanía, Isabel, and Isabel's mother, she "remained secular" (404) – or a lay sister. The familial living arrangements that Zayas's characters take on in the convent reflect the demographics of convents in Golden Age Spain, according to Elizbaeth Lehfeldt's research: "Convents brought female relatives together in a sort of home away from home. Even if there was a push to send unmarriageable daughters to the convent, they were frequently joining other female relatives there" (43). Lisis's decision not to take complete vows allows Zayas to extend Lisis's social life by inviting the "illustrious Fabio" to "seek her with chaste intent" and "find her at your service, with loyal and honorable good will" (405). As Sherry Velasco notes on her study of lesbian desire in Zayas, Lisis's decision to break her engagement with Don Diego and "live instead among women disrupts the heterosexual plot resolution that traditionally has been believed to neutralize the temporary yet potentially transgressive same-sex flirtation scenes involving the *mujer vestida de hombre* (cross-dressed woman) motif that was so popular, especially on the early modern stage" (34).

Furthermore, lay nuns existed as a hybrid group in conventual life. Professed sisters were known as "religiosas clérigas para el oficio divino," whereas "Donadas" were women who were able to enter and exit the enclosed convent in order to communicate with and bring things in from the outside world (Lehfeldt 151). In comparison, lay sisters usually were expected to wear the religious habit of the community and remain enclosed, but were allowed to conduct business with the extraconventual world. The narrator's claim that Lisis will continue to chastely flirt with men once again informs our understanding of how early modern convents existed. Because female monasteries were neglected compared to their male counterparts when it came to financial support and intellectual attention from the church hierarchy, convents had to rely on donors, usually wealthy female widows, to a larger extent than male monasteries did. When these donors decided to move into the convent, they were reluctant to part with their lavish home environment and would recreate it inside their new spatial arrangements: "Nuns who could afford to do so also often created elaborate living quarters for themselves within the cloister precinct. In 1637, for example, a nun at Santa María de las Huelgas paid the convent 17,340 mrs. for expenses related to her cell. Designed as separate parlors or even apartments, these living quarters often functioned as mini-households" (Lehfeldt 184).

Zayas's goal to create a community where women's voices are heard reaches its zenith in the frame narrative's conclusion. By this point, Lisis has heard enchantments and disenchantments about love. Her dissolution of her engagement with Diego demonstrates that she will not be deaf to the Cassandra-like warnings of the other disenchantresses. Zayas is careful to have Lisis tersely summarize the tragic fates of the ten disenchantments' protagonists before she affirms that she has not been "disenchanted from personal experience" but through "ciencia" ["knowledge"] (403). Lisis's declaration that her conclusion was reached through inductive reasoning informed by the experiences and experiments of these women's real-life stories reveals the emerging feminist consciousness of a society that allows women to speak freely. Although Golden Age Spain was far from such a utopian society, Lisis's convent offers a brighter prospect for her ability to engage in intellectual intercourse within a same-sex community. Before she tells her tale, Lisis mimics the language of the scientific method that a budding feminist scientist such as Margaret Cavendish would be proud of: ". . . let [men] not speak ill of the science they teach. Here I shall speak without deception, and I myself shall put to the test the greatest disenchantment, which is to die in deception without having learned from all the warnings, and while disenchanting others, letting myself be deceived" (368). This call-to-action instructs listeners and readers to approach the novellas as a pedagogical tool for modeling their lives. Lisis does as much when she breaks her engagement since it emerges as the logical conclusion for any female attendee of the *sarao* who has listened to the ten tales.

The frame narrative constantly foreshadows that Lisis has something up her sleeve for the end of the *sarao*. For example, she ominously wears black for the *sarao* when she enters on the first night. Early on, the narrator hints about Lisis's mysterious intentions when she says that during her illness, she "never let on to anyone . . . the revelation of her new desire until the right moment" (36). Likewise, we can see how in Lisis's discussions with Isabel, "the lovely doña Isabel, aware of her intention because Lisis had told her earlier what she planned, wanted to let her rest before she made her closing comments" (396). The matriarch of the party is presented as a clever schemer who will control her own life rather than let her husband do so. In fact, Lisis's words allude to Juan Luis Vives's 1528 treatise *De officio mariti*, which perversely uses Cicero's praise of the eloquent Cornelia to justify the denial of a proper education for a woman so that she may remain archaically pure in her speech:

> Tampoco cuadra en una mujer la elocuencia aunque la antigüedad admiró la palabra de muchas, como Cornelia . . . pero no tanto porque pronunciaran muchos discursos elocuentes como porque hablaron poco y esto, pura y no corrompidamente; . . . Tu emperor incluye entre las ciencias de tu mujer el silencio, gran adorno de su sexo. [Neither does it become a woman to be eloquent even though antiquity admired the words of many women, such as Cornelia . . . but not because they engaged in many eloquent discourses as much as that they spoke little, purely, and incorruptibly; . . . amongst other forms of knowledge you teach your wife, your rule includes instructing her on silence, the grand adornment of her sex.] (qtd. in Bergmann 127)

Lisis's use of the word "ciencia" repudiates Vives's mocking reference to the education of silence with which a husband is supposed to instruct his wife. Rather, Lisis lists the protagonists of each of the disenchantments by name to further humanize their tales and to footnote her argument.

Accordingly, once more we find Zayas challenge the status quo of palatable endings that offer a heteronormative resolution to the author's flirtations with same-sex relationships. The author accomplishes this rejection of rote conclusions when she refuses to marry off Lisis and allow her to be silenced as Vives would have instructed Diego to do. Instead, the frame narrative's denouement ends with the potential for a loquacious community of like-minded women – a stark alternative to the inequitable power structure entailed by a marriage during the Renaissance.

Even at the highest levels of Spanish society Margaret of Austria, Queen of Spain, was "forced to find female companionship in convents" because close female friendships were denied at the male-dominated court where political advisors to the king, such as the influential Duke of Lerma, could select which women would join the queen's coterie of ladies-in-waiting (Sánchez 141). Convents were often the last and only unhindered spaces of female solidarity. Lisis expresses as much when she announces her retirement: "I shall take refuge in a sanctuary. I plan to retire to a convent from where, as from behind a safety barricade, I intend to observe what happens to everyone else. With my beloved doña Isabel, whom I intend to accompany as long as I live, I'm going to save myself from the deceptions of men" (403). Because Lisis chooses to accompany her erstwhile slave, she accentuates the idealistic vision of the convent as an egalitarian home wherein master and servant are equal, even if in reality egalitarianism was not the norm in the vast majority of real-world convents.

Likewise, Lisis's employment of "ciencia" further justifies Zayas's endeavor to elevate the *querelle des femmes* percolating through Europe's literary circles. The frame narrative's sole professed nun, Estefanía, also learns from reading and listening to other women rather than through experience: "I do not speak from my own experience but from knowledge. At a very young age I dedicated myself to a spouse who has never deceived me and never will" (310). Estefanía's statement posits her as a representative of the real-world nuns who Lisis and her peers shall follow after enjoying the experience of listening to no-holds-barred tales from other women and desiring to enjoy the opportunities afforded by a same-sex community. Because Zayas's early modern feminist ideology can be described as advocating "safety, education, and justice for women" and guaranteeing "women's autonomy over their bodies and minds" (Vollendorf, "No" 112), Zayas mobilizes Lisis to exemplify the kind of female readership she seeks to educate and influence through her writing. Lisis's broken engagement would not have been justifiable without the recounting of ten tales of graphic violence perpetrated against women at the hands of the men they are supposed to trust. The efficiency of these tales in educating and disenchanting women is so profound that *sarao* attendees leave "admirados de su determinación" ["admirers of her determination"] (460). In contrast to Boyer's more languid translation that "everyone else was amazed by Lisis's decision" (404), I believe that my version is more faithful to Lisis's bold agency in the matter. Her valor in leaving Diego and breaking her engagement is implied in the Latin root of "determinación," "determinare," which is a compounding of the prefix "de" (off, from) and "terminare" (to terminate, limit). Thus, Lisis's audacity is noted for its ability to succinctly end any thought of her marrying Diego.

The effectiveness of the disenchantments also exhibits itself when the partygoers congratulate Laura "on her daughter's divine intelligence" (404). Although some attendees are described as spreading malicious gossip about the *sarao*, Zayas characterizes them as "vermin" and prods the reader to feel as if they should agree with the audience members who laud Lisis's decision and hence her education. This drive for educating her readers puts Zayas in line with other writers of the Baroque period who sought to provoke readers with original, shocking subject matter that would "force the individual to question his or her assumptions and priorities and realign them if necessary" (Robbins 15). The pedagogical function with which Zayas imbues the *Desengaños* resembles Queen Isabel of Castile's support and work towards ensuring that nuns were literate in Latin. Just as some of the women in the tales are older when they enter the convent, the queen learned Latin at a mature age and wanted other Spanish women to follow her lead by ensuring that the religious reforms Cardinal Cisneros was undertaking would include nuns (Surtz 4). This historical antecedent buoys a reading of the tale's communal learning environment as a mirror for the convent's educational community.

During the reign of King Phillip III, the monarch and his entourage would normally attend Mass in convents both in Madrid and other cities. When the king left town, the queen and her children would stay in a convent of the Discalced Carmelites in Madrid. Historians assert that although the politically outspoken queen was unhappy to be left behind so often, she found solace with the "network of women whom she could trust" and with whom she could discuss "her problems and concerns" (Sánchez 29). The queen's well-known piety (she was alleged to have set her heart on professing as a nun before she was betrothed to the Spanish king) made the convent a comfortable home for her when the king was abroad. However, conventual life did not only appeal to the queen and other early modern Spanish women because of its religious underpinnings. The enclosed convent, despite how permeable the walls truly were, allowed women to practice and engender a level of spiritual devotion that could render them desirable spiritual leaders with political influence. King Phillip III was criticized for befriending and trusting religious figures such as confessors and nuns because of the "special influence" it imbued them with since they had the "opportunity to speak . . . and voice their opinions on given matters" with the king (Sánchez 25). For example, powerful nuns such as Sor María de Agreda (a member of the Conceptionist order) counseled the subsequent king, Phillip IV, on matters of policy and war. Although such instances were rare, they were not unheard of.

Because of women like Agreda and Queen Margaret, one can see how the convent offered women a chance to pursue cultural and intellectual interests that were unavailable to them in the extraconventual world. Such opportunities allowed them to assert their social and political clout in the secular realm. The pedagogical promises of convent life are what Zayas places the hopes of her characters on since it was the only available alternative for non-aristocratic women who craved an education and the ability to engage in the literary and social *querelle des femmes*. In establishing her ethos as a learned writer, Zayas rebuts Boccaccio's backhanded compliments to women in his work *De mulieribus claris* (1362). Zayas's counterargument is successful by focusing on a plethora of contemporary, intelligent, and powerful women including queens, princesses, ladies-in-waiting, nuns, and authors such as Ana Caro "rather than using examples from the past" (140) to make the debate immediate and lively at the beginning of the fourth disenchantment.

Zayas's reference to the role of men in propagating the culture's sexual divide helps us see her as an early modern feminist. Expanding on the various references to truly noble gentlemen who defend women, such as Don Enrique in "Love for the Sake of Conquest," who still wants to marry Laurela despite her affair with Esteban, Zayas has Lisis express women's wishes about the expectations authentic *caballeros* should fulfill: "I swear if you did love and cherish women as was the way in former times, you'd volunteer not just to go to war and fight but to die, exposing your throat to the knife to keep them from falling into the hands of the enemy. This is the way it was in earlier days, particularly under King Fernando the Catholic" (400). Because Lisis's declaration comes at the end of the collection of disenchantments, she offers a stark reversal to the pile of deceased female bodies that has accumulated throughout the ten stories by asking men to volunteer their lives and bodies ("your throat") in defense of the women they swear they love. Zayas employs Lisis to continue the discourse that decreases men's voices in order to make it an equitable dialogue between the sexes by suggesting that the men jeopardize their vocalizing body part. Furthermore, by contextualizing the valor of men in a temporal framework that posits genuine chivalry in the memory of fifteenth-century Spain, Zayas returns to the nostalgic settings of her *Novelas amorosas* to describe the contemporary state as a postlapsarian one in which men must change in order to "keep their women from being captured, taken prisoner or, worst of all, being dishonored" (400).

Time and again we see women choosing the convent as an alternative to the secular world. But, as Margaret Greer has noted in her expansive study of Zayas's work, "women who have actively desired and pursued their lovers are more likely to become nuns, while those who have been more passive victims of male desire more often choose secular convent life" (417). This distinction is key to solidifying my focus on convents as a literary tool for exploring gendered discourse systems. Although Lisis has already had her heart broken by Don Juan in the first novella collection, she cites "ciencia" rather than experience in her decision to retire. The novella's final paragraph makes it clear that not only does she not take the veil in the convent, but she also awaits male visitors. Like Florentina, Lisis will speak with men and continue to narrate her story and engage in intellectual discourse with men. As such, Lisis exploits the convent's safety to her advantage with little regard for the duties and responsibilities of a professed nun.

Other women, however, such as Beatriz, have banished all mortal men from their lives. We hear little about such women communicating with others from behind the veil other than to God. After all, although convents grant women the opportunity to tell stories, gossip, and share information, not all women take advantage of the freedom. Rather, they take their right to remain silent as a form of silent protest, which can be, ironically, interpreted as a more subversive action than those who continue to talk with one another. By refusing to engage with the secular world, these nuns reserve their mental faculties for the life that awaits them after death and the perfect husband they choose to spiritually commune with on a daily basis. Furthermore, many nuns used the popular bride of Christ identity to not only legitimize "the immediacy of their relation with God, but, more pertinently, their authorial voice" (Black 169). Zayas relishes the possibilities of this authorial voice, with its semantic link to authority, by enveloping these disenchantresses with the convent-like setting of the *sarao* so they can present credible arguments using their stories as evidence to substantiate their claims about men's duplicitousness. Thus, the women of the frame narrative who choose the convent over heterosexual marriage - Lisis, Isabel (who takes the habit), Isabel's mother, and Estefanía - acquire acceptance from mainstream society because of their spiritual proximity to God, regardless of whether they lead their lives as professed nuns or lay nuns. Isabel's decision to become a nun demonstrates how liberating the vocation could be since she already lived for years as a slave, and yet she still chooses the convent's restraints over those of a single woman and of a wife.

If members of Zayas's audience are predisposed to categorizing and dismissing the women who flee to the convent as social rejects because of their failures to have successful heteronormative romantic relationships, Zayas has the narrator model audience reaction in the novel's ultimate paragraph. She does this when the narrator addresses her interlocutor, Fabio: "The end is not tragic but rather the happiest one you can imagine for, although courted and desired by many, [Lisis] did not subject herself to anyone" (405). The narrator's careful diction thrusts Lisis's agency into the forefront, since she employs the highly charged verb "subject" to emphasize the character's insistence on maintaining her body and being autonomous from any mortal. Just as powerfully, the narrator notes that Lisis is "courted and desired by many." She could be romantically successful in mainstream, normative terms. But she knows how her individuality, agency, and autonomy will be exponentially vitiated by marrying a mortal man in the society portrayed in the disenchantments. By reclaiming Lisis's virginity, rejection of marriage, and acceptance of the convent as a positive choice, Zayas attempts to mold her audience's reaction.

In effect, the convent serves as the promised land for these secular women who mimic the opportunities of a secluded, same-sex community with a *sarao*. Just as these women righted wrongs through storytelling and shared information about alternative lifestyle options through their semi-private gossiping, Zayas's printed discourse engages in the *querelle des femmes* and paradoxically posits a millennia-old institution as a progressive safe haven for women. Armon notes in her discussion of women's courtship novels that in many of these tales, even before some of the female characters enter a convent, they appeal to church authorities to aid them in their quest for justice: "The Church is depicted as an ally of women on many occasions . . . We have already seen how, in Zayas's 'La inocencia castigada,' two women leverage their complaint to civil authorities by first gaining the support of their archbishop" (85). Zayas repeatedly eschews the traditional ending of comedic romance narratives that feature heterosexual marriages by having the female characters who live until the end of the tales instead choose an incorporeal husband - Jesus Christ.

The prolific tribe of female storytellers that Zayas gathers in the *Desengaños* expresses her Baroque sensibilities and political aims. By barring men from telling stories and recuperating the role of women's gossip in Spanish Golden Age society, Zayas employs bold characters and a reversal of power between the sexes to entice a courtly and popular audience intrigued by the unique nature of the narrative frame. Once readers are engaged by Lisis and her alluring assembly of siren-like storytellers, they are riveted by the captivating disenchantments of courtship, love, sex, and violence, all of which are stylized by prophetic poetry and vivid prose. Then the aura of gritty realism that permeates each story envelops audience members so that they learn while they are entertained. These attractive narratives offer the context for Zayas's goals of removing the tape that has been placed over the mouths of countless women who need to tell their stories and of introducing a feminist strain of dialogue into the literary discourse of Golden Age Spain.

Chapter Five

Straddling the Secular and Spiritual Divide: Sor Juana Inés de la Cruz's Life and Literature

With a room of her own; an intellect that astounded the New World's most learned men; a *telenovela*-worthy biography replete with enigmatic lovers, envious peers, and ecclesiastical enemies who spanned the rural countryside, the pretentious court, and the enclosed convent; and a literary finesse that amazes to this day, Sor Juana was the real-world embodiment of Shakespeare's Isabella, Cavendish's Lady Happy, and Zayas's soiree of secular nuns. In the Hispanic world, Sor Juana Inés de la Cruz's literary works have been studied, lauded, canonized, and marketed for centuries as some of the greatest examples of Baroque poetry. As Sor Juana's literary prowess has begun to receive formal recognition in the English-speaking world over the past few decades, many English-language scholars have come to understand how the unlikely figure of a cloistered Mexican nun came to stand alongside formally educated, privileged, elite male writers such as Francisco de Quevedo and Luis de Góngora, her Spanish Golden Age contemporaries, in the pantheon of Western literature.

This chapter focuses on how Sor Juana balanced her secular interests with her duties as a nun who took a vow of poverty, chastity, obedience, and enclosure but refused to stop writing for the extraconventual world. Fleshing out the desires of Zayas's secular and lay nuns, Sor Juana took the veil but did not abandon the viceregal patronage she enjoyed at court. By using the safeguards to which she was professionally entitled, Mexico's "Phoenix" rose from the obscurity of the convent to combat misogyny, to argue for a woman's right to education, and to write poems and dramas that astound and delight readers to the present day. Sor Juana accomplished such feats by using her faith to support her intellectual abilities and activities.

By focusing on one representative piece from each of the three genres that Sor Juana mastered, "Hombres necios" ("Foolish Men"), poetry; "La respuesta" ("The Answer"), prose; and *Los empeños de una casa* (*The Trials of a Noble House*), drama, I elucidate the manner in which she syncretically expresses disillusionment with the patriarchy yet manages to meet the expectations of her religious profession. Sor Juana's literature positions her as a hybrid figure – pious nun *and* worldly feminist – who is able to fuse the secular and the spiritual in *belles lettres* poetry that articulates both the traditional teachings of Christ and feminist rhetoric in laymen's terms. "Hombres necios"'s engagement in the *querelle des femmes* repudiates misogyny by attacking men's constructions of women as pliable objects prone to manipulation. Sor Juana accomplishes this feat by utilizing her status as a nun to defend herself against the criticism that she faces for being both a writing-woman and writing-nun. The way in which Sor Juana amalgamates the rhetoric of Christian humility with a secular defense of respect for the individual makes her a Renaissance icon.

By focusing on Sor Juana and her literature, this chapter offers a transatlantic approach to the study of nuns to complement my contextualization of women's issues in the early modern world. I avoid adding to the intelligent research already done on Santa Teresa of Ávila and her works because her oeuvre is much more religious-minded than Sor Juana's, despite the potent erotic themes it reflects. Because of Sor Juana's more secular and political literary interests, her work embodies the hopes and potential inherent in the fictional depictions of nuns discussed in previous chapters. Sor Juana's works were printed and widely disseminated in Spain, hence she is part and parcel of Golden Age Spain's literary culture just as much as she was part of colonial Mexico's cultural production. Her first printed collection, 1689's *Inundación castálida*, was republished nine times. Writing from the epicenter of New Spain, Sor Juana imbued her work with creole tropes and diction unknown in the Old World.

The incorporation of Sor Juana's poetry, prose, and drama into the English classroom necessitates a discussion introducing Hispanic culture into an Anglo-Saxon cultural framework. As the field of Early American literature continues to expand its geopolitical borders to include texts written outside of colonial New England and the Middle-Atlantic states, Sor Juana's written work should become useful in the increasingly multicultural classroom, particularly in the American West and Southwest, where Mexican Americans and other students of Latin American descent enroll in Early American literature courses. If we remember that Spain's and Mexico's erstwhile possession of what is now the United States encompassed gigantic swaths of the American West and South, it becomes imperative to think about Sor Juana's cultural milieu, centered around New Spain's viceregal capital of Mexico City, as an influential component of early American life.

Likewise, teachers must be cognizant of the hermeneutics involved in the translation of her texts from Spanish to English. A translator's task is made doubly difficult by the fact that Sor Juana was not only well-versed in the rich literature of Golden Age Spain, but also adept at writing in the florid, topsy-turvy, wit-obsessed, wordplay-loving style of the Spanish Baroque. Excitingly enough for contemporary readers, her vocabulary and language were further enriched by her status as a New World-born *criolla* immersed in the colonial language of her ancestors and the innovative linguistic creations of her multi-ethnic and multi-racial Mexican peers. Sor Juana's sparkling language makes her texts doubly rich and complex because it combines Góngora's style of Baroqueness, *culteranismo*, which is preoccupied with verbal dexterity and showmanship, with Quevedo's *conceptismo*, which is more concerned with examining existential crises.

Sor Juana's epistolary masterpiece of Baroque ingenuity and theological syllogism, "La respuesta," which was her response to a letter from a clergyman who admonished her for her secular literature, offers us a vision of the nun as a women's rights advocate, as a rhetorical mastermind, and as an intellectual heavyweight. By employing the clichéd humility topos in a tongue-in-cheek manner that underscores the literary staple's tiredness, Sor Juana safely takes shelter in her role as an obedient nun while she simultaneously promotes progressive ideas about the role of women in society and their ability to engage in theological debates. Finally, this chapter's examination of her Golden Age secular drama *Los empeños de una casa* closely aligns with the sociocultural literary exegesis of this book's previous chapters by illuminating how the characters, storyline, and spatial arrangements of this *comedia* offer viewers an example of what a woman-as-nun could accomplish given time and space to create art. I also highlight how Sor Juana's sympathies for convent life energize the play's female protagonists and question masculine and feminine gender roles within a closely-knit society of nobles structured not unlike a convent.

Sor Juana is an ideal representative for showcasing the potential of real-world early modern nuns who created art – visual or textual – and who recognized the convent as their own university replete with a women's studies department and tenure-track stability for excelling at their craft. Reality will of course intervene, and, as this chapter demonstrates through its discussion of Sor Juana's "La respuesta," I discuss how nuns were also keenly aware of the male authority figures whom they had to obey. Nonetheless, the spatial, temporal, and financial freedom most nuns enjoyed thanks to benefactors (dowries from family members or sponsors) allowed them to write spiritual and secular works in a feminine community.

Sor Juana's life story and literary work have been so valorized by her native country that her likeness is exchanged every day by countless Mexicans by way of the country's 200 peso bank note. Her name graces schools throughout Mexico and the popular Mexican singer and actress Susana Zabaleta wore a dress with the opening line of "Hombres necios" emblazoned on it to a red carpet event in 2004. From Irving A. Leonard's thoughtful chapter on Sor Juana in his seminal monograph, *Baroque Times in Old Mexico*, to Nobel Prize-winner Octavio Paz's unrivaled biography on his homeland's most famous nun and Samuel Beckett's English-language translation of Sor Juana's poetry, the New World's most respected nun has been afforded a high-level caliber of literary and historical respect, even from male scholars, that has escaped many early modern and even contemporary female writers to this day. Such unarguably deserved scholarly attention can be attributed to Sor Juana's neutralized gender, rendered so by her status as a virginal nun, which made her more palatable to masculine literary analysis in the decades before second-wave feminism shook up academia.

Figure 1.1: Obverse side of the Mexican $200 peso note featuring Sor Juana's image.

Although we would be dealing in generalized speculation, we can attribute a similar reasoning behind the scholarly attention received by other nuns such as Santa Teresa of Ávila, Hildegard of Bingen, and Julia of Norwich. Sor Juana was acutely aware of the paradoxical nature of her ambiguous gender since she, like other nuns, was to be revered for a purity based on the negation of the sexual activity of the very body part that categorized her as a woman. She expresses as much in a poem she writes to a man who suggests that she would be more acceptable as the opposite sex:

> So in my case, it is not seemly
> that I be viewed as feminine,
> as I will never be a woman
> who may as woman serve a man.
>   I know only that my body,
> not to either state inclined,
> is neuter, abstract, guardian
> of only what my Soul consigns. ("Respondiendo," 141)[1]

Her profession as a nun allows her to repudiate a sexuality that is described and limited by a male-dominated heteronormative discourse by using spiritual language that focuses on the sexless soul as the arbiter of a person's identity. Surprisingly, Sor Juana does not directly cite Galatians 3:28, "There is neither Jew nor Greek: there is neither bond nor free: there is neither male nor female. For you are all one in Christ Jesus," despite her direct combat with Saint Paul's admonition for women to stay silent in the church. Sor Juana's third gender discourse works not only in the early modern era but also within our own contemporary society as her unmarried and childless life circumvents biographies that view her as a "wife of" or "mother of."

Joan Gibson, in her study of "the logic of chastity" in the early modern period, attests that Sor Juana responds by positing "if her work was not appropriate for a woman, and if she could not or would not be a man, she would attempt to go through the middle. Virginal chastity and an unsexed

---

[1] Although new translations of Sor Juana's work are being published on a nearly yearly basis, this chapter employs the most widely read and cited version in American academia, Margaret Sayers Peden's 1997 translation. Unless otherwise stated, all translations are by Peden. My translations will be noted in brackets versus parenthesis for Peden's translations. The original Spanish text is featured on the page immediately to the left of the English translation in Peden's edition.

mind, she argued, allowed her to elude altogether the logical dilemma of how a woman could have 'manly' powers and provided a linguistic escape from the sexual double blind, through recourse to grammar" (8). As such, her work has gained more attention on its own merit than that of other female authors whose personal lives, especially their relationships with men, are closely examined through autobiographical, psychosexual readings that are rarely forced on male authors. I propose that the sense of respect and empowerment that fictional nuns such as Shakespeare's Isabella and Cavendish's Lady Happy enjoy because of their heterosexual chastity is palpable in Sor Juana's life and writings. Whatever the case may be, Sor Juana's intellectual prowess and artistic accomplishments highlight how the hopes of Shakespeare's, Cavendish's, and Zayas's characters are realized in Sor Juana's independent streak, celebrity, and masterly and eclectic oeuvre of prose, poetry, drama, philosophy, and theology.

A Life Uncommon: The Sacred and Subversive Nun

I offer only a brief foray into the key characters and events in Sor Juana's life that allow us to better appreciate and contextualize the texts under discussion. Paz's biography of Sor Juana and the dozens of well-written introductions to English-language translations of her work reveal the complex worlds of the court and the convent within which Sor Juana worked. Further pertinent discussions of people integral to the discussion of a certain text are woven into the respective sections of this chapter. Despite leading a cloistered life that called for silence, Sor Juana was too important and public a figure for the church to vanquish when she transgressed the behavioral boundaries promulgated for nuns. Sor Juana's rise from a bastard *criolla* to a celebrity nun who could count on powerful members of the oligarchy to support her is novel unto itself.

Sor Juana was born in either 1648 or 1651 as Juana Ramírez de Asbaje on a hacienda in San Miguel Nepantla, a town near the volcano Popocatépetl in what was then the outskirts of Mexico City. Mexico, then known as New Spain, had a population of six million inhabitants from various racial, ethnic, and religious backgrounds. Pigmentocracy and place of birth determined one's social status and professional prospects in a stereotypically colonized New World fashion wherein Spaniards, although small in number, were at the top while the indigenous and the African slave populations (and mixes thereof), although vastly larger in number, suffered at the bottom (Stavans xxv). Sor Juana was exposed to this multicultural society's kaleidoscopic milieu at an early age because of her proximity to servants and slaves of different backgrounds. Her early exposure to these individuals would be reflected in the polyglot sounds with which she infused her writings.

Fittingly enough, Sor Juana's hybrid literary identity is prefigured in her natal hometown's name: Nepantla is a Nahuatl (Aztec) word denoting a space in the middle or in between two objects, places, or times. Born to a *criolla* (Mexican-born) mother, Isabel Ramírez, and her unmarried Basque partner, the Spanish-born Pedro Manuel de Asbaje, the young Juana could not expect to be respectably married off to a man with a more elite background. Several biographers trace many of Sor Juana's themes to the absence of her biological father and the number of illegitimate children to which her mother gave birth. However, in one of Sor Juana's rare references to secular father figures, in Epigram 95 "Que dan el Colirio merecido a un Soberbio," she seems to have coped well with her status as a "bastard." The speaker argues that "Más piadosa fue tu Madre / que hizo que a muchos sucedas: / para que, entre tantos, puedas tomar el que más te cuadre" ("Far more generous was your mother / when she arranged your ancestry, / offering many a likely father / among whom to choose your pedigree") (157). Sor Juana audaciously supports her mother's and other women's license to enjoy multiple sexual partners by highlighting the freedom it gives mothers and children to choose the most beneficial of fathers to claim as their own. Given the complete absence of her father in the autobiographical "La respuesta," Sor Juana did not publicly agonize over not having a patriarchal figure in the family. Rather, she chose the ultimate masculine deity as both father and husband when she took her vows as a nun and Bride of Christ.

An autodidact out of necessity and desire, Sor Juana attempted to receive formal schooling as often and wherever she could. When she was around three years old, she snuck into her older sister's classroom to learn how to read, and at around seven years of age she begged her mother to dress her as a boy so she could attend schools and the university in Mexico City. Sor Juana reluctantly understood that she would have to teach herself all the things she wanted to learn. The precocious scholar disciplined herself with a cheese-free diet because she "heard that [cheese] made one slow of wits" ("La respuesta" 15). She pored over the books on sundry topics in her grandfather's library and punished herself by cutting her hair to an unfashionably short length if she had not learned what she set herself out to master. Such endearing accounts of her early education foreshadow how comfortable Sor Juana must have felt within the mental and physical strictures of the Catholic convent. Her will and discipline anticipated the self-mortification and self-denial common among nuns, and the security and intellectual serenity she found in her maternal grandfather's library boded well for years of scholarly study in her cloister. Patience and private space were important to Sor Juana as a youth and would prove conducive to her vocation as a nun.

Sor Juana's mother eventually sent her precocious thirteen-year-old daughter to live with relatives in the viceregal capital. The family introduced her to courtly life, where she soon became a favorite of aristocrats and nobles alike. Although Sor Juana's beauty did not hinder her success at court, amid a throng of equally beautiful women, her intellect and extroversion stood out. In 1664, Sor Juana struck gold when the new vicereine, Doña Leonora Carreto, Marques de Mancera, requested that Sor Juana enter her service. As a lady in the viceregal court, Sor Juana augmented her autodidacticism while writing poetry and other works for her patrons. Her years at court, which Sor Juana neglects in her autobiographical writings, proved fertile ground for years to come when she wrote lyric poetry about amorous relationships that followed Petrarchan and courtly conceits of love as a game of attracting and repelling potential love interests. The most valuable lesson Sor Juana learned from her time at court was currying favor and support with the well-connected. As the Spanish empire switched viceregal administrations in and out of New Spain, Sor Juana was consistently able to find support for her work even after she entered the convent. Her most important patron, the vicereina María Luisa de Lara y Gonzaga, Countess of Paredes and Marquesa de la Laguna, who reigned with her viceroy husband from 1680 to 1686, ensured the publications of the first two volumes of Sor Juana's works in Spain. Because her literary identity was forged by writing in colonial Mexico and being published in Spain, Sor Juana can be seen either as a hybrid figure or an exemplar and prototype of a writer at the heart of the world's first great trans-oceanic Empire.[2]

Sor Juana began her life as a nun in 1667. Initially she entered the venerated mendicant order of the Discalced Carmelites, made famous by its founder, Saint Teresa of Ávila. However, she left the strict order after three months. Following a brief return to the courtly milieu that connected her with the men who would pay for her dowry to enter a convent, Sor

---

[2] Unless otherwise noted, this paragraph and others that offer glimpses into Sor Juana's life and sociohistorical context are amalgamative summaries based on these sources cited elsewhere in this chapter: Octavio Paz's *Sor Juana or, The Traps of Faith*, Stephanie Kirk's *Convent Life in Colonial Mexico: A Tale of Two Communities*, Pamela Kirk's *Sor Juana Inés de la Cruz: Religion, Art, and Feminism*, and Kristine Ibsen's *Women's Spiritual Autobiography in Colonial Spanish America*.

Juana finally decided upon the Convent of Saint Paula in 1669, a Hieronymite order conveniently located a kilometer from the viceregal palace. Her former convent must have chafed at Sor Juana not only because of its more rigorous practices but also because of its elitism. While the Discalced Carmelites usually attracted women born in Spain, Saint Paula's convent was founded with the intention of being solely for *criollas*. As a New World-born woman without a legitimate father, Sor Juana probably felt more at home with her creole peers. Sor Juana must have felt that this comparably more lenient convent would afford her the time and space for continuing her intellectual pursuits. Despite all nuns' vow of poverty, luxury was of the essence for Sor Juana and her peers. Her "cell" was more like what we would term a townhouse: two floors, a private a bedroom, a private kitchen, and an area to keep her collection of books and musical and scientific instruments. Following a New World tradition anathema to our contemporary sensibilities and our conceptions of what a Christian life should entail, Sor Juana had a slave gifted to her by her mother.

Recent studies of conventual life in the New World demonstrate that the majority of internal affairs were managed by nuns without the assistance of ecclesiastical superiors. While most facets of monastic life were hierarchical, conventual administrative positions consisted of three-year terms earned through elections, with evidence suggesting "that intelligent women often advanced rapidly through the ranks to high levels of convent administration" (Ibsen 8). Such democratic means of governing a community must have appealed to Sor Juana and other women who were appalled by the sexist, seemingly Byzantine way that monarchical and oligarchical early modern societies were structured and run. Although in some of her writings Sor Juana complained about sisters who interrupted her studies, she was seemingly allowed to miss all but the most important prayers and rituals of conventual life. Furthermore, her sisters elected her to to the office of *contadora*. In this position she recorded the names of professed nuns as they entered, took vows, and died.[3] My examination of the original manuscript's detailed notes in the margins allowed me to see firsthand the pulse she had on the lives of her sisters. Sor Juana's marginalia includes remarks on those who were there before her, which

---

[3] *Prophessiones que hazen las Religiosas de el Monasterio de sancta/Paula de la Orden del gloriosso Padre Nuestero Santo Geronimo. De esta ciudad de Mexico.* MS-1.35-214, [12] 18 x 33 cm. Benson Latin American Collection at the University of Texas-Austin.

denotes her eye for history. In 1680 she was even commissioned by the government to write a poem, the complex "Allegorical Neptune," describing the triumphal cathedral arch that was constructed to mark the onset of a new viceregal reign, that of the Marqués de Laguna.

With her own room and an ever-growing library, Sor Juana understood the convent offered "the least unsuitable and the most honorable" lifestyle she could choose to "insure" her salvation, given "the total antipathy" she felt toward marriage ("La respuesta" 17). Although she takes care to couch her explanation within a religious discourse that articulates her hopes for her spiritual salvation, a close reading of "La respuesta" demonstrates that while Sor Juana was a faithful Catholic, she was far from being a mystic or fanatic. In fact, she had a Mexican predecessor to emulate had she wanted to take the route of the more ecclesiastically palatable Santa Teresa of Ávila: Sor Maria Magdalena (1576-1636), New Spain's first mystic. Sor Juana did not report any visions, and her most oft-cited self-admission of a heavenly gift was her God-given need to study. Nonetheless, she was acutely aware, like the fictional characters discussed in previous chapters, that conventual life offered the best remedy for treating her intellectual "inclination," which she could not decide was either "a gift or a punishment from Heaven" ("La respuesta" 17). If nothing else, Sor Juana's decision to become a nun was utilitarian and pragmatic for a dutiful Catholic woman enamored of the intellectual life. The convent's locutory was often the site of intellectual intercourse between Sor Juana and Don Carlos Sigüenza y Góngora, a professor of math and astronomy at the University of Mexico, and Father Eusebio Francisco Kino, a famed mission-founder of the American Southwest. Sor Juana's networking skills proved invaluable in her battles with ecclesiastical enemies who sought to squelch her secular writings. Nobles, aristocrats, and learned men from the universities often visited Sor Juana and spoke to her through barred windows in the convent's locutory, which she managed to turn into an early modern intellectually minded salon.

Sor Juana correctly described her love for intellectual, philosophical, and theological inquiry as a double-edged sword. Although she was commissioned by both church and state to write in various genres for sundry occasions, the combination of her celebrity, courage, and content soon attracted powerful, misogynist detractors within the church hierarchy. The beauty and passion of her inclusive religious works, which have been heralded for their linguistic dexterity and "genuine feeling for popular religion in a multi-racial society" by ingeniously combining "dog Latin, the defective Spanish of Basque and Portuguese speakers, Negro *patois* and – most original of all – whole sequences in Nahuatl" (Terry 246), were always overshadowed by her equally successful forays into profane literary production.

Again, without going into details about all of Sor Juana's various altercations with her male superiors throughout her time as a nun, I want to highlight the most significant confrontation she encountered with ecclesiastical authorities due to her writings since it served as the catalyst for "La respuesta," her most autobiographical work. A Portuguese Jesuit, Antonio de Vieira, delivered a sermon in 1650 describing the meaning of one of Jesus Christ's *finezas* – a divine act of love for humanity. The *fineza* under consideration was Jesus washing the feet of his disciples. Whereas Vieira argued that "Christ had washed his disciples' feet for love's own sake; Sor Juana, on the other hand, viewed the act as evidence of Christ's love for humanity" (Stavans xiii). The rhetorical minutiae involved in discriminating the values of the differences between both interpretations were firm and popular ground for the theological debates of the early modern period. Sor Juana's well-argued response to this forty-year-old sermon carefully followed the precepts of Scholasticism still popular in the Hispanic world of the late seventeenth century.

Sor Juana wrote her response in the form of what came to be known as the "Athenagoric Letter" at the request of the Bishop of Puebla, Don Manuel Fernández de Santa Cruz y Sahagún. While Sor Juana probably could have expected her treatise to be circulated in manuscript form, she did not anticipate that Fernández would print the letter for wider circulation in November 1690.

Fernández was considered a foil to the misogynist Archbishop of New Spain, Francisco Aguiar y Seijas. After previously sending a copy of the printed edition with a personal dedication to Sor Juana (Stavans xiv), Fernández sent her a sternly worded letter under the guise of "Sor Filotea de la Cruz." In this letter he tells her that it would better suit her sex if she wrote about devotional matters rather than philosophical and scientific topics. Ironically, this letter responds to Sor Juana's astute theological treatise that Fernández himself requested. The wisdom Sor Juana expresses in her tract causes alarm within the ecclesiastical community. Sor Juana knew that the Sor Filotea pseudonym, meaning "lover of God," was the Bishop of Puebla's and that it was not another nun chastising her. Perhaps Sor Juana imagined that the Bishop's initial request was a trap. Whatever the case may have been, Sor Juana's feminist energy was ignited in March 1691 when she wrote the first feminist text written by someone born in the New World: the lively and rhetorically adept "La respuesta." In it, she refuses to cease writing on secular subjects, a point made clear by the length of her response to the bishop and the eloquent letter's profane subject matter. As Frederick Luciani has asserted in his valuable work on Sor Juana's literary self-fashioning, in "La respuesta," every "anecdote is, in a sense, a reiterative, miniature version of the whole story . . . Sor Juana's *inclinación a las letras* is God-given and God-directed, and therefore ineluctable, orthodox, benefic" (85).

The years following the initial circulation of "La respuesta" were times of turmoil for Sor Juana and ones marked by an opaqueness of facts that vexes historians to this day. While "La respuesta"'s arguments for a woman's education and her right to engage in theological studies permeated ecclesiastical circles, Sor Juana enjoyed two more successes as a writer. Her *villancico*s to Saint Catherine of Alexandria, a celebration of female intelligence embedded in palatable spiritual rhetoric, were published in 1691, and her second volume of works was printed in Sevilla, Spain, in 1692. This latter work's inclusion of Sor Juana's rebuttal to Vieira's sermon may have precipitated the tribulations of her last years. According to historian Elias Trabulse, Sor Juana was under an Inquistorial investigation in 1693 "that accused her of heresy, disrespect for authority, and activities incompatible with her monastic state" (Wray 67).

The church's scrutiny of the allegedly *sor*did Sor Juana coincided with an epic spate of floods, famine, and plague that ravaged Mexico City between 1691 and 1693. Bread was in short supply, natives rioted, royals took refuge in religious homes, and mass prayers and sacrifices were made in the public plazas. Officials looked for scapegoats, and after the inundated city dried, retributive hangings and punishments were carried out. Sor Juana lost two close friends during the crisis, Juan de Guevara and Diego de Ribera, and witnessed the death of ten nuns in her convent within fourteen months. After researching Sor Juana's final letters to superiors as well as those of her peers in context of the religious culture of early modern Mexico, historian Dorothy Schons concluded that "it is not unlikely that she blamed herself somewhat for the sad state of affairs in Mexico. . . . not one cause, but many, working toward a common end, gradually broke the strong spirit and made her accept the martyr's role" (55-57). Although one can argue about the authenticity of Sor Juana's agency in signing documents of abjuration and the selling of the majority (but not all) of her books and musical and scientific instruments in 1694, her genuine appreciation for conventual life and her duties as a Catholic and nun came to light in her final days. According to Sor Juana's contemporary biographer Father Diego Calleja, when the plague breached the walls of the Saint Paula convent, she dedicated days and nights on end nursing her spiritual sisters (Stavans xlii). Eventually, Sor Juana became ill and died on April 17, 1695.The tragic end of such a brilliant, young mind is ameliorated by knowing her life was filled with creativity and rebellion. Sor Juana's works, as we shall see, mark her as a hybrid in many ways: temporally, spatially, sexually, and literarily.

By expanding the borders of the early modern world transatlantically to include Europe's New World colonies, the culture of New Spain-cum-Mexico highlights the Spanish Golden Age's long reach. Whereas most literary scholars and historians mark the end of Spain's cultural apogee with the death of the dramatist Pedro Calderón de la Barca in 1681, Sor Juana's 1695 death might be a more appropriate (and equally arbitrary) bookend to this period. Coupling her employment of elite, Old World cultural tropes, stylistics, and lexicons with creole, New World sensibilities, language, and imagery, Sor Juana's literary output marks her as the New World's first progenitor of cultural ingenuity. None of her accomplishments could have been achieved, however, without her profession as a nun. Besides the spatial and temporal liberties this career afforded her in a misogynist world that could only grant her the *rara avis* status of the "Phoenix" or the clichéd feminine "Tenth Muse," Sor Juana's socially approved chastity rendered her a sexually neutral being that allowed male peers and historians to seriously evaluate her life and work.[4]

Precious Illusions: "Hombres necios" and Feminist Poetics

"Hombres necios" ("Foolish men") is arguably Sor Juana's most popular text; the poem is taught at the college level and memorized by high school students throughout Latin America. In order to appreciate the poem's popularity, we must first examine its well-crafted structure and manipulation of language. The poem's stanzas are composed in the form of redondillas, which are four octosyllabic lines that end in consonant rhymes with the scheme of ABBA. The surface-level modesty of the poem's structure belies its need for the well-honed craft of a poet attuned to the delicate balance of quick rhyme schemes and terse line lengths. Sor Juana showcases her poetic agility by confronting disparate but related strains of the poem's subject within each stanza.

The speaker reveals her quick wit through the use of contrasts that point out the fallacy of "Hombres necios" in nearly every stanza. The poem's opening lines unleash the polemical floodgates that saturate this

---

[4] As previously mentioned, unless otherwise noted, I am indebted to Paz's masterful biography of Sor Juana, *Sor Juana, or The Traps of Faith*, for information about her life and its controversies.

poem with a clever feminist rhetoric and impassioned tone: "Hombres necios que acusáis / a la mujer sin razón, / sin ver que sois la occasion / de lo mismo que culpáis" ("Misguided men, who will chastise / a woman when no blame is due, / oblivious that it is you / who prompted what you criticize") (1-4)[5]. The first two words engage in an ad-hominem attack against the speaker's adversaries. Although Peden's translation of "necios" works metrically, she misses the insulting tone that would be felt were she to use a close synonym of "necio" – foolish or stubborn. Granted, either of these choices sacrifices the octosyllabic measure of the lines. Nevertheless, the poem's speaker has already launched a personal invective against a group of men that vex women with their deceitful flirting and wooing.

Hence, Sor Juana's choice of the quick, light rhythm of the redondilla begins to pan out. The elegant trappings of the sonnet or the lofty expectations of the romance would be out of place for the bold, direct, and argumentative tone of the poem. Additionally, the redondilla's eponym, *redondo* (round), adds to the speaker's womanly authority by utilizing the blueprints of a circular narrative structure that many literary critics usually conceive of as a hallmark of female authors. Furthermore, the musical quality of the regular measure of each line and the swift turn-around of the ABBA rhyme scheme allow the reader or listener to more quickly memorize the lines.

Sor Juana's engagement with the discourse of the *querelle des femmes* positions her in a circumatlantic intellectual sphere linking her with other female authors she probably never read: Spain's Zayas (1590-1661), New England's Anne Bradstreet (1612-1672), and England's Cavendish (1623-1673). Despite each woman's assumed ignorance of the others, their status as seventeenth-century women writers partaking in the *querelle des femmes* unites their texts in a feminist struggle with global connections. It would be fun to hypothesize about a transnational collective unconscious informing each of these author's writings, but simply reading their texts affirms that the similarities between their lives and experiences were more analogous than incongruent when it comes to their status as learned women whose texts were widely read. Because of their shared pan-Hispanic culture, Zayas and Sor Juana offer the most concrete example of

---

[5] Although I use Peden's translation, I prefer to translate the poem's title as "Foolish men" instead of her "Misguided men" to better capture the poem's overall mockery of puerile men who cannot see past their own sexism and the double standards they propagate in their condemnation of women.

how women from different spectrums of similar Western societies were combating the same sexist impediments. Although Zayas's 1664 collection of novellas, *Desengaños amorosos* (*The Disenchantments of Love*), offers the convent as a safe haven for women attempting to escape a heteronormative sexual economy that renders them chattel, her texts were not written in or constrained by the expectations of a nun writing in a convent.

By the same token, Sor Juana's writing from the Convent of San Jerónimo in Mexico City was far removed from the cultural milieu of the Hispanic metropolis, Madrid. She used her previous experience at court and her conversations with the vicereines who sponsored her as fodder for invectives against the patriarchy's employment of the double standard. The argument put forward by the frame narrative's protagonist, Lisis, who has just heard the tale "Love for the Sake of Conquest" in Zayas's novel, is richly echoed in the first two stanzas of Sor Juana's poem: "You make women bad, indeed you expose yourselves to a thousand dangers to make them bad, and then you go about telling everyone that women are bad. You never consider the fact that if you're the ones who keep them from being good, how, then, can you expect them to be good?" (238). The link between Sor Juana's "¿por qué queires que obren bien / si las incitáis al mal?" ("how can you wish that they refrain / when you incite them to their wrong?") (7-8) and Zayas's text demonstrates both authors' desire to antagonize potential love interests – a prevalent theme among many women authors of the Baroque period. In fact, Stephanie Merrim smartly argues that "the terrain of amorous complaint . . . would be the launching pad for women's literary activism" (*Early* 52).

Continuing with the buoyant structure of "Hombres necios," the speaker delivers her entertaining criticism of men with the precocious couplet "de vuestro parecer loco, / al niño que pone el coco" ("your sense is no less senseless than / the child who calls the boogeyman") (14-15). The juvenile comparison and the disyllabic words "loco" and "coco" underscore the immature behavior of these hypocritical men and continue the ad-hominem attack featured in the poem's first line. The speaker does not simply come off as an aggrieved woman venting her frustration. The following stanza employs classical allusions to demonstrate the speaker's ethos and illustrates the age-old double standard she seeks to destroy. She accuses men of wanting Lucrece as a wife but desiring Thais as a lover. The nun's pagan allusions to ancient Greek and Roman figures cast the men as un-Christian heathens and allow the speaker to demonstrate the ability of women to pass down their own history within the patriarchy's canon. Thais, a famous courtesan, represents men's lustful desires to enjoy easy sexual conquests. Because the majority of the poem discusses men's desire to turn all of their love interests into casual sex partners, the speaker implies that the men do not necessarily want a professional prostitute on the side – they simply want to make women whores for their base pleasures. Having made women replicas of Thais, however, the speaker notes that the men then hypocritically deride these women for their easiness: "¿por qué queréis que obren bien / si las incitáis al mal?" ("how can you wish that they refrain / when you incite them to their wrong?") (7-8). Lucrece, better known as Lucretia, is the celebrated Roman noblewoman who was raped by Tarquin and then committed suicide to defend her honor despite the retribution her family was able to exact on her rapist. Superficially, the choice of Lucrece as the woman men want to wed implies that men want the perfect, virtuous wife.

Sor Juana also cleverly uses a feminine heritage to provide herself with ammunition against her detractors. Following in the footsteps of perhaps the first female participant in the *querelle des femmes*, Christine de Pizan (1364-1430), Sor Juana employs Thais and Lucrece as legendary female figures to show a continuum of women who inform her arguments. Pro-woman participants in the *querelle* often "cited exemplary women who belie and defy misogynistic constructions of the female sex" (Merrim, *Early* xv). Sor Juana's allusions to these women further solidify Virginia Woolf's oft-cited contention in *A Room of One's Own*: "For we think back through our mothers if we are women. It is useless to go to the great men writers for help, however much one may go to them for pleasure" (610).

The social complex of women who are damned if they do and damned if they don't, a virgin/whore complex prevalent throughout Western literature, continues to express itself in the parallel structure found in the seventh stanza's final two lines: "quejándoos, si os tratan mal, / burlándoos, si os quieren bien." ("if they love, they are deceived, / if they love not, hear you complain") (27-28). The assonant rhymes of the first words in each line with similar suffixes create an aesthetically pleasing parallel that enhances the see-saw balance that permeates the poem as the speaker contrasts the man's hypocritical judgment against his initial desires. The limited options of women who engage with men are highlighted as negative choices that Sor Juana circumvented in her personal life in her literature as restrictive and damning for women who are not careful about their relationships with men. Sor Juana's attempt to educate women outside the convent about the pitfalls of dealing with deceitful men emphasizes her awareness of the limited potentials for women in New Spain: the domestic home, the viceregal court, and the convent. Because these spheres were ultimately controlled by men, women had to acquiesce within each one. Nonetheless, Sor Juana's assertion that "ninguna gana" ["no woman wins"] (29) demonstrates her desire to warn women about the outcome of dealing with men who are ungrateful regardless of what a woman does.

Throughout the poem the speaker employs antitheses to express the combative scene of an embattled woman publicly criticizing men. If we take "men" and "woman" as the initial binary in the first stanza, we recognize that the pluralized nature of the "misguided men" illustrates them as a common group that can be stereotyped, while the "woman" is left in the singular form so as to highlight her individuality. The classical allusions to Thais and Lucrece also function as an embodied binary of morals wherein Thais is a negative example of a prostitute servicing myriad men and Lucrece remains a faithful woman. The binaries continue throughout the poem with "mal" and "bien" (22-23), "no os admite" and "y si os admite" (31-32), and "malas" and "buenas" (47-48) in order to underscore the dichotomy that exists between men and women when the double standard is applied by the patriarchy. Sor Juana's mastery of Baroque *culteranismo* reaches its apex in the thirteenth stanza when she uses phonetic homonyms to create a double meaning in asking who is more at fault: "la que cae de rogada, / o el que ruega de caido?" ("She who errs and heeds his pleading, / or he who pleads with her to err?" (50-51). A literal reading of the first line finds the woman suffering because she acquiesces to the man's pleading. However, when read aloud, the line's phonetic pun arises in "de rogada," which sounds like "derogada," meaning abrogated or abolished. The woman's purity will be abolished for having agreed to the man's desire for a courtly love (an illicit one that exists outside of marriage).

Likewise, the second line exploits the oral pronunciation of the last two words, "de caido," to create the word "decaído," which means someone who is in despair and unwilling to do anything. Hence, the man is begging because he has nothing better to do but tarnish the woman's reputation. Although the man may be so wealthy that he need not worry about working, Sor Juana is most likely latching on to the tradition of proud Spaniards of noble descent who refuse to admit their impoverished state during the economic turmoil and inflation engendered by the flood of riches from the Americas, similar to the protagonist's impoverished Toledo master in the third chapter of the picaresque classic *Lazarillo de Tormes*. To further exhibit Sor Juana's virtuosity, she gilds the lily in Baroque fashion with the stanza's concluding line, which invokes the image of the man on his knees begging for the woman's body, thus leaving him in a spatially inferior position. Fleshing out his mortality, Sor Juana utilizes the judgment inherent in the *retruecano*'s syntax to characterize the man as sinful and bound for destruction. Like a moralizing didact, Sor Juana employs her Christian beliefs to inoculate women against men's tricks and to scold men for their deceitful ways.

Sor Juana reaches the zenith of verbal dexterity in the three stanzas that directly question hypocritical men and places their deceit in the limelight through the use of *retruecanos* – chiastic puns. These three stanzas, which precede the poem's penultimate one, ask who is guiltier – the man who deceives a woman or the woman who is deceived. By employing the chiastic structure of this alliterative *retruecano*, Sor Juana makes it clear who should take the blame. For example, "¿O cuál es más de culpar, / aunque cualquiera mal haga: / la que peca por la paga, / o el que paga por pecar?" ("Whose is the greater guilt therein / when either's conduct may dismay: / she who sins and takes the pay, / or he who pays her for her sin?") (53-56). This stanza best exemplifies the two similar stanzas that flank it because the speaker attempts to level the playing field, "when either's conduct may dismay," to dismantle gender expectations and place both sexes as equals. Adhering to the guidelines of a Catholic nun whom society anticipates will preach against premarital and extramarital sex, Sor Juana criticizes women who partake in such activities.

Nonetheless, cognizant of the persuasive power that men with economic, social, and cultural capital possess, Sor Juana molds the poem's structure to lay the blame on the men. In a typical Baroque employment of structure, Sor Juana uses the *retruecano*'s reversal of expectations to make the reader understand that men are more at fault. The power of the *retruecano* rests in the first line, which the second line opposes. To illustrate, the first line "she who sins and takes the pay" lays the groundwork for the reader's perception of options. Another successful consequence of utilizing the *retruecano* is that Sor Juana's assumably female speaker establishes an authoritarian tone that poses questions to men but does not allow them to answer the prompts. By monopolizing the discourse, Sor Juana usurps men's privilege and asserts the woman's clever juxtaposition of language as the code for deciphering the moral conundrums she presents. The chiastic structure then reverses the order of words, "or he who pays for her sin," so that the monetary object received by the women at the end of the first line is moved up in the second line and the sin of the woman is a consequence of the man's payment. Although the English translation works well to mimic the patent and latent meaning of the Spanish original, the alliteration, repetition of consonants, and the visual and aural congruities between "peca" ("sin") and "paga" ("pay") create a Christian-Marxist condemnation of prostitution and the mixture of sex and money in the Spanish original. Hence, we once again see Sor Juana working within the strictures of her vows upholding the teachings of Christ to create a feminist discourse that stresses the faults of powerful men in forcing women to sin.

Sor Juana employs her vow of poverty and a Christian message that rejects materialism in other poems. For example, after she was awarded two hundred pesos for her work in the design of ceremonial arches constructed to celebrate the arrival of the new viceroy in 1680, Sor Juana responded with four décimas that highlight her ambivalent relationship with money. In the first stanza she explains that money and art do not always mix well: "Esta grandeza que usa / conmigo vuestra grandeza / la está bien a mi pobreza / pero muy mal a mi musa / . . . / pues quien me da tanta plata, / no me quiere ver poeta" ("Décima" 251) ["This greatness that uses / with me your greatness / fits well my poverty / but very badly my muse / . . . / therefore whoever gives me so much money / does not want to see me a poet"]. We must recognize that Sor Juana accepted the money and lived comfortably in her convent thanks to the support she received from her patrons. Likewise, she penned this poem after reaping her reward, thus implying that her protests are simply something for her patrons and the public to consider. Her attitude toward money reflects most convents' relationship with financial profits: "their economic activities were directed toward a purpose that transcended the personal (their community, their Church), which in turn was governed by values not of this world. But their religious focus did not, of course, prevent the wealth of the convents from being reflected in the beauty and magnificence of the buildings and in the breaking and relaxing of rules" (Paz 119). More importantly, we see Sor Juana anxiously cognizant of her role as producer of art that is consumed by a burgeoning capitalist society diametric to her community's non-literal vows of poverty.

Returning our focus to "Hombres necios," we follow the series of highly enjoyable *retruecanos* to the poem's final two stanzas as they bring the theme back to the here-and-now. The speaker presents an ideal situation where men abandon their fraudulent wooing and receive the admiration of women they desire through more honorable means. This utopian culture is rejected in the poem's ultimate redondilla: "Bien con muchas armas fundo / que lidia vuestra arrogancia, / pues en promesa e instancia / juntáis diablo, carne y mundo" ("But no, I deem you still will revel / in your arms and arrogance, / and in promise and persistence / adjoin flesh and world and devil") (65-68). Ironically, this stanza permeated with a sense of futility occurs when the speaker uses the first-person voice for the first time. Again, we come into a dilemma of translation because the original text has the speaker preparing arms for battle, "muchas armas fundo," instead of the man reveling in his arms. The English translation de-emphasizes the speaker's agency, but still forcefully injects the speaker into the conversation by unambiguously stating her existence. As Stavans notes in his discussion of Sor Juana's awareness of the necessity to prepare herself for maneuvering through a male-dominated world, "She understood early on that to excel she would need to arm herself with a sense of security and self-esteem that precluded all possible doubts about her character" (xxvi). A more symbolically accurate translation would illustrate Sor Juana's bold speaker smelting the metal of the armory with which she would shield herself.

This poem's delayed employment of the first-person narrator articulates its political purposes if we consider Margo Echenberg's assertion that Sor Juana removes a poem's emphasis on the first-person speaker in order to allow herself to "make her most acute statements while protecting herself and her reputation" (29). By removing herself from the reader/listener's gaze, Sor Juana forces them to focus their attention on the speaker's argument. As an anonymous speaker, the woman can be anyone the male reader imagines, hopefully a woman they sympathize with such as a mother, daughter, or sister, so that they can recognize the woman's earnest and well-grounded complaint. In respect to the social constraints placed on Sor Juana as a nun and a woman who writes for a wide audience, this postponement of the first-person voice allows her to humbly submit that "she has no justification for speaking out based solely on who she is. Instead, she can only imply who she is through her creative endeavors, all the while complying with the social and moral restrictions of her time" (Echenberg 30). Therefore, having already convinced readers of men's illicit deceit and taken their eyes off her as a writer, Sor Juana's impassioned persona can no longer restrain itself, and so she transgresses social decorum by inserting the speaker squarely in the debate. The deferred entrance of the first-person voice then functions as a personal embodiment of the situation. As the woman, Sor Juana, puts on her armor we can envisage the warrior nun engage in a battle on behalf of women and feminist Christians everywhere.

Despite the problems with the translation, in both cases, even in the face of the rightfully outraged and intelligent speaker, the man will persist in his devious ways. The connotations of the words "flesh," "world," and "devil" in the final line allow the poem to transcend its corporal framework and enter a more spiritual plane. The "flesh" evokes images and homilies about Christ's mortal body, and the "world" connotes sinful worldliness. Because men were "associated with the soul, spirit, and reason, and wom[e]n with the body, carnality, and sinfulness" in "both learned and popular sectors of Spain and Spanish America" (Ibsen 1), Sor Juana's positioning of the man as the epitome of body ("flesh"), carnality ("world"), and sinfulness ("devil") demonstrates her ability to reverse the discourse of characteristics attributed metaphorically, figuratively, and literally to the sexes in order to advance a feminist critique of the double standard. As Marie-Cécile Bénassy-Berling describes this final line, "Discreetly but firmly, the nun performs a small Copernican revolution in the last line as she assigns men . . . the role of object, object of desire, object of scandal" (qtd. in Merrim, 66).

Having argued extensively about secular matters of the heart and body, Sor Juana returns to the expectations of her home in the convent to continue Christ's warnings against sin. The employment of "diablo, carne y mundo" is no coincidence as Sor Juana realigns the gendered power structures that posit life as a battle between "World, Devil, and Flesh on the one hand, and Church, Mary, and Soul on the other" (Arenal and Schlau 11). Taking square aim at the Church's and secular society's perverse amalgamation of natural carnal desire with sin, Sor Juana pragmatically refocuses her target not on dismantling the entire conflation but on vitiating women's guilt and augmenting men's responsibilities in sexual relationships. As such, Sor Juana toes the line as a nun who has taken a vow of chastity, but also advances her feminist concerns. Because the men addressed in this poem receive the speaker's disapproval of the demonic alchemy of the flesh, the world, and the devil, we see Sor Juana merge her secular and religious dialectic concerns in a manner that does justice to both by utilizing each other's ethos.

The double standard that this poem assails also stands in for other forms of sexism that Sor Juana and her literary oeuvre have had to deal with - namely, her designation by male peers as the "Tenth Muse" and as the "Mexican Phoenix." If female muses have been credited for inspiring male writers since time immemorial, then why would a female writer be deemed a muse? Did she inspire herself? If so, she is an anomaly, and that is what this backhanded compliment seems to imply, whether it is bestowed on Sor Juana, Zayas, Bradstreet, or the original Tenth Muse - Sappho. As a phoenix, Sor Juana was implied to be *sui generis*, a monstrous *rara avis*. Quevedo's famous early seventeenth-century poem "La fénix" depicts a hermaphroditic bird that has no ancestors and no descendants, an anomalous woman of undeterminable sex. Merrim argues as much when she says that "even the most hyperbolic panegyrics of the writer's work . . . [view] her as an anomaly of her gender" ("Toward" 16). Although twenty-first century readers are well aware of the number of female peers with whom Sor Juana wrote contemporaneously, each woman's isolation from the other, doubled with Sor Juana's physical isolation in a convent in the New World, could have easily made her feel like she was Judith slaying Holofernes. Her confident tone allows us to see her as assured that history would be on her side. Nevertheless, the pressures put on her by male authority figures weighed heavily on her mind, especially toward the end of her life.

"La respuesta": Feminist Theology Made Flesh

Because of the aforementioned pressure we see parallels between the strong-willed speaker of "Hombres necios" and the self-assured narrator of Sor Juana's 1691 quasi-autobiography, "Respuesta de la poetisa a la muy ilustre Sor Filotea de la Cruz" ("The Poet's Answer to the Most Illustrious Sor Filotea de la Cruz"), commonly referred to as "La respuesta" ("The Answer"). Sor Juana wrote this text in response to a letter written by Bishop Manuel Fernández de Santa Cruz under the pseudonym of Sor Filotea. The letter rebukes Sor Juana, already criticized for previous literary efforts such as "Hombres necios," for penning the "Athenagoric Letter," which was Sor Juana's theological contestation with the Portuguese Jesuit António Vieira's sermon about the reasons for Jesus's washing of his disciples' feet. Unbeknownst to Sor Juana, Fernández privately printed and distributed her theological letter. Now thrust into the spotlight for engaging in theological debates, a literary realm that was barred to nuns, Sor Juana was endangered by the wrath of church authorities buoyed by the Inquisitorial zeal of the Counter-Reformation – especially in New Spain where the Church's political tug-of-war with the viceregal court often found the Church victorious – as illustrated in the Church's ability to rouse enough opposition to the viceroyalty of the Marquis of Gelves and force the viceroy "to flee for his life" during the "tumult" of 1624 (Elliott199). Although one may conjecture that Fernández sought to protect Sor Juana by scolding her before higher authorities did worse, there is no concrete evidence either way. Subsequently, propelled into focus and publicly reprimanded, Sor Juana took up her pen and employed her Baroque sensibility to defend herself.

Similar to her ability in combining feminist and spiritual concerns in "Hombres necios," Sor Juana exploits the formulae of women's spiritual autobiography for the purpose of asserting her identity and independence. She successfully appears obedient to Church authorities and the patriarchy in "La respuesta" by adhering to the literary framework used by a series of nuns who penned their *vidas*, most famously Santa Teresa de Ávila, through the usage of such traditional tropes as "the rhetoric of humility and obedience, her repugnance toward writing on demand, the use of positive female models, [and] the paradigm of Christ and her own martyrdom" (Ibsen 137). Amidst these strategies, she peppers her text with employments of Church tradition to excuse herself for her supposed faults as an intellectual woman. For example, in a response to those who confront her about her dishonorable desire to write, she constructs herself as a meek and humble servant: "I have never written save when pressed and forced and solely to give pleasure to others, not only without taking satisfaction but with downright aversion" (47).

Sor Juana then simulates cowering from the brute force of the Church by denigrating her intellect: "as for me, I want no trouble with the Holy Office, for I am but ignorant and tremble lest I utter some ill-sounding proposition" (47). In an argument that's perfect for reading between the lines, Sor Juana claims that she "does not study in order to write" or "teach," "but simply to see whether by studying I may become less ignorant" (47). Assuredly knowing that she and her audience recognize the relatively wide circulation of her writings and their feminist, political, and educational agenda, she writes tongue-in-cheekly about the purpose of her studies and writing. Cleverly, at the very moment when Sor Juana expresses a passive form of hubristic pride, she reverts to her status as a nun engaged in the works of God to protect herself from further criticism:

> My writing has never proceeded from any dictate of my own, but a force beyond me. . . . For ever since the light of reason first dawned in me, my inclination to letters was marked by such passion and vehemence that neither the reprimands of others (for I have received many) nor reflections of my own (there have been more than a few) have sufficed to make me abandon my pursuit of this native impulse that God Himself bestowed on me. (47)

Selectively borrowing from a stream of religious Spanish writers that cite spiritual reasons for their writing, devotion, and actions, Sor Juana positions God as the unquestionable authority figure in her life. One need only read Sor Juana's religious poetry and drama to see that her faith informed all manners of her thinking since she often uses her position as a nun and her belief in Christ's message of peace, love, and equality to combat sexism. Nancy Pineda-Madrid asserts that even though Sor Juana "used her vast intellectual knowledge as the authoritative basis for the theological claims she made, the themes of her scholarly writings reflect her knowledge of mystical experience. She espoused the contemplative life, drawing frequent allusions to mystical union in her writings" (179).

In a poignant allusion to the budding strains of the Enlightenment in the Hispanic world, Sor Juana employs the Scholasticism-inspired term "the light of reason" as a syncretic amalgamation of religion (God's light) and science (reason) to explain her actions. The "reprimands of others" acknowledges the various male Church figures, Archbishop Francisco de Aguiar y Seijas, Antonio Núñez de Miranda (Sor Juana's confessor), and Fernandez, who chastised her for her readings and writings. Although this admission functions as one of guilt, it also operates as a boast about her literary prowess. Despite the popularity of saints' and nuns' *vidas*, few works by nuns were published in their own lifetimes. Sor Juana highlights her anomalous position as a nun whose works were published both in the provincial colony and in the European metropolis.

In fact, thanks to the ties her patron the Condesa de Paredes shared with a noble community of nuns in Portugal, Sor Juana wrote for and within a transatlantic community of women: the Casa del Placer. Literate nuns in various convents throughout Portugal, especially in Lisboa, were aficionados of Sor Juana's romances, redondillas, and sonnets – especially because she was a nun like them. Antonio Alatorre asserts that the Portuguese nuns reached out to the Portuguese Duchess of Aveiro who in turn communicated with her cousin, the Spanish Countess of Paredes, to relay the nuns' petition desiring more work from Sor Juana. This network of women writers and readers testifies to the skilled literacy of nuns and noblewomen and their desire to create academias on par with that of secular men in Madrid and Lisboa. The Casa del Placer's literary output included Spanish- and Portuguese-language texts written by Sor Juana's transatlantic ecclesiastical sisters. Stephanie Kirk's careful study of early modern convent life in Mexico brought her to the conclusion that the Casa del Placer acted as a liberating outlet from the male-dominated hierarchy to which nuns had to submit: "with the formation of the Casa del Placer and its creation of an autonomous female textual space, the nuns were reproducing community in an ideal form, different from the reality they actually lived" (144).

The culmination of these transatlantic communications was the 1695 Portuguese publication of *Enigmas ofrecidos a la discreta inteligencia de la Soberana Assemblea de la Casa del Plazer*. The enigmas are written by Sor Juana, but the prefatory materials written by various nuns and noblewomen is what underscores the importance of this book as a dialectic textual conversation between early modern women. The book begins with Sor Juana's Dedicatory and Prologue and is followed by laudations such as Sóror Mariana de Santo António hailing Sor Juana as "Décima insigne Musa" ["Tenth famous Muse"], a romance by Condesa de Paredes, the former vicereine of Mexico who calls herself "particular aficionada de la Autora" ["particularly fond of the author"], and two censures not by the Royal Crown but by two different women religious, Feliciana de Milão from the convent of Odivelas and Maria das Saudades of the convent in Vialonga. It is only after all these women have lauded one another that the enigmas are then offered.

As mentioned in other chapters, the convent was neither an ideal space nor a utopian retreat. Nonetheless, it was a safe alternative for women who eschewed pressures to be assimilated by the heteronormative world and its gendered expectations of females. Convents also served as a means to an end. Textual expression was a freedom granted to some nuns. By penning their thoughts and ideas, religious and profane, writing-nuns managed to rise above their expected station in life as women; their names and their ideas could enter a discourse stream of like-minded women, and, in the case of Sor Juana and a few others, forcefully engender a co-ed dialogue in the testosterone-laden field of normative communication that outlived their bodies and cultures.

The fact that Sor Juana wrote this letter epitomizes her reluctance to acquiesce to the "hombres necios" of the Church. Rather than submissively accepting Sor Filotea/Fernández's admonition to be silent, she pens a lengthy letter replete with as many classical allusions, enlightened rational proofs, and examples of literary finesse and verbal dexterity as her secular poems exhibit. Additionally, Sor Juana employs the expectations of her avowed profession by citing God and using Him as a guardian of her intellectual impulses. By "subvert[ing] forbidden practices" and "revealing the mechanisms of power that restrain her" (Ibsen 139), Sor Juana manages to offer a powerful textual defense for women's learning. Sor Juana's subversion functions as an assault on the day's misogyny as she positions herself as a warrior nun replete with "muchas armas" to deflect criticism of her intellectual, literary, and political audacity.

Although Sor Juana is responding to a letter via the same medium, her decision to rebuff her detractor with a classic epistolary genre known for combining personal narration and logic-based argumentation strengthens her ethos as a female religious. She employs rational statements to support women's right to education. In the vein of the bellicose repudiation of the double standard in "Hombres necios," "La Respuesta" is a rhetorically tight and politically vivid treatise that was ostensibly written to defend her theological writings. However, it worked double-duty as an early modern vindication of the rights of all of women to be literate and educated in both secular and spiritual letters. By configuring theology as an elite field of learning to which one must gain admittance, Sor Juana cleverly excuses her profane learning as a necessary means to the end: "directing the course of my studies toward the peak of Sacred Theology, it seeming necessary to me, in order to scale those heights, to climb the steps of the human sciences and arts; for how could one undertake the study of the Queen of Sciences if first one had not come to know her servants?" (19). The feminine, monarchical personification of theology demonstrates Sor Juana's practical approach in writing to effect change as she conflates femininity with knowledge but keeps it within a palatable, monarchical framework that espouses authoritarianism and divine rights. Scholars have noted that Sor Juana's connection between profane disciplines and theology employs a "consistent rhetorical device" that "in order to avoid the imperative" uses the more forgivable and inquisitive "interrogative" (Kirk 132).

As her biography attests, of course, her enclosed life allowed Sor Juana to flourish artistically and intellectually. The convent served sundry functions as an oasis from the stress of marriage, the pains of childbirth and childrearing, and the social ostracism of being an unmarried spinster; as an architectural safe haven of shelter, food, and safety; and as an intellectual salon that allowed her to be a relatively comfortable intellectual. In it, Sor Juana felt confident enough to defend not only her own right to write, but that of all women.

For centuries many critics took the confessional tone and apologetic content of "La respuesta" at face value without considering Sor Juana's subtle criticisms and sly wit. Deciphering her criticism and acknowledging her keenness unearths Sor Juana's subversive employment of quasi-hagiographical, *vida*-like texts that highlights the female author's obedience and repentance. Sor Juana fulfills such textual expectations but undercuts any notion of genuine regret with a string of defensive *and* offensive remarks regarding her role as a nun and a female intellectual. As Kristine Ibsen has noted, though "everything addressed to the bishop in the letter implies full acceptance of her subordinate role and intention to remain silent, the autobiographical passages of the essay underscore a different perspective on silence: that of a strategy of resistance" (138). Likewise, Paz asserts in his biography of Sor Juana that "La respuesta" was "an examination of conscience, Sor Juana emerged from that examination unrepentant. . . . Although its language is cautious and abounding in reservations and parentheses, the final impression is clear: she is not ashamed of what she is or has been" (415).

From the onset of the letter, the tenor of Sor Juana's addresses to her reader, the fabricated Sor Filotea, wraps itself in an aura of hyperbolic modesty that borders on mockery. Sor Juana effulgently praises Sor

Filotea: "Yours was a kindness, finally, of such magnitude . . . a kindness exceeding the bounds of appreciation, as great as it was unexpected . . . . To such a degree as to impose silence on the receiver" (3). Her praise is laughable when one knows of "La Respuesta"'s impetus: Sor Filotea's chiding of Sor Juana's secular writings. Sor Juana employs the conventional niceties expected of her and then exaggerates them by describing Sor Filotea's "kindness" as unappreciable, hence unappreciated. Likewise, she acknowledges that her alleged peer asked for "silence" rather than more talk. But by responding to her hidden reader, the Bishop of Puebla, Sor Juana rejects his request and transforms the framework and expectations of the *vida* into an overture that enables Sor Juana's response and an engagement in the *querelle des femmes*. Sor Juana reminds her readers of her social standing as a "humble nun, the lowliest creature of the world" (5), before detailing her penchant for intellectual inquiry and the path that led her to the convent.

Sor Juana ingeniously shields her desire for learning and wisdom behind her veil. By utilizing the tropes of confessionals penned by women religious at the behest of their confessors, Sor Juana cites divine inspiration for her actions: "my inclination towards letters has been so vehement, so overpowering, that not even the admonitions of others . . . have been sufficient to cause me to forswear this natural impulse that God placed in me" (11). One would expect that Sor Juana would employ the divine as the reason for being a nun as well, but, surprisingly, such explanations are reserved for her cerebral urges. When she explains her reasons for professing as a nun, she candidly admits that the physical conditions of the life religious were "most repugnant" to her nature, but such feelings did not supersede "the total antipathy" she had for marriage (17). Sor Juana was the real-life counterpart to the fictional, non-conformist characters of early modern literature, such as Cavendish's Lady Happy and Zayas's assembly of women afraid of marital life, keen to embrace the opportunities afforded to nuns.

Faced with the inescapable and all-too-real specter of the Holy Office and its Inquisition, Sor Juana quickly couches her decision to enter the convent in more palatable terms: "I deemed convent life the least unsuitable and the most honorable I could elect if I were to insure my salvation" ("La respuesta" 17). Although she pays respect to the early modern world's preoccupation with salvation in the afterlife, Sor Juana still posits the convent as the "least unsuitable" option available to her. She might have been a faithful Catholic, but even within a realm known for worshipping the feminine divine via the Virgin Mary, Sor Juana still felt limited and enclosed. Critics have noted that Sor Juana's repeated and exaggerated use of describing the deity in the feminine ("Deidad, Deidades"), in comparison to the masculine God ("Dios") in her *Allegorical Neptune*, reflects how ineludible her feminist beliefs were from her religious faith and work (Arenal 188).

The consistency with which she dismantles rather than reifies sexist notions about women's mental agency renders her a recidivist intellectual radical for the early modern world. Sor Juana accomplishes as much not only through the authorial attitude she holds for her assumed and implied readers (the Bishop of Puebla and ecclesiastical authority figures, respectively), but also through the celebratory autobiographical vignettes she offers. Although Sor Juana's spiritual devoutness and allegiance to Catholicism are indelible elements of her persona, one can easily question her commitment to humility when she recounts/brags about her accomplishments or compares Christ's agony to the suffering she endures from the slings and arrows of envious opponents. Illustratively, she discusses crests studded with iron barbs that are placed on the temples of those like herself who are "the target of envy and the butt of contradiction" because of "whatever eminence, whether that of dignity, nobility, riches, beauty, or science" (33). She then alludes to Christ's Passion: "the sacred head of Christ and His divine intellect were the depository of wisdom . . . . A head that is a store house of wisdom can expect nothing but a crown of thorns" (35). Sor Juana is mindful of the fine line she walks between self-aggrandizement and humility, so she covers her bases by asserting her genuine intent in discussing her tribulations: "I do not wish to say (nor is such folly to be found in me) that I have been persecuted for my wisdom, but merely for my love of wisdom and letters, having achieved neither one nor the other" (39).

In several instances, Sor Juana recognizes that she has gone too far in celebrating her abilities or criticizing those that would censor her writings and limit her autonomy. Readers witness this masterful writer having it both ways. She does "not wish to say" that she is attacked for her wisdom, yet by mentioning it she allows readers to imagine the scenario. She goes on to say that she is attacked for her "love *of* wisdom and letters" (emphasis mine); her usage of the prepositional phrase "of" demonstrates her own parsing of language and meaning. Consequently, she highlights that her desires, more than her actions, are the target of her enemies. Because Sor Juana enacts these desires, her defense of her wishes symbolically speaks for the intellectual agency of all women. After accomplishing this task, she subsequently slides back to a humble pose and states that she has not achieved any of her goals. This balancing act is a motif throughout Sor Juana's writing as she straddles the divide between her monastic obligations and her profane aspirations. Whereas in "Hombres necios" she enacts a balance through rhetorical flourishes, in her autobiographical writing she employs the traditional tropes of humility and resignation for transgressive, feminist purposes.

Although Sor Juana opted out of marriage, she understood that the domestic sphere was a woman's domain in the early modern world. A brief allusion to the culinary arts in her letter demonstrates her feminist sensibilities appropriating the sphere as one that should be more highly regarded. Her reclamation of the domestic sphere begins within the wall of her home, the convent. In a vague allusion to what was probably her short tenure with the Discalced Carmelites, Sor Juana criticizes an Abbess who believed "study was a thing of the Inquisition" and commanded her not to follow her intellectual pursuits (39). The Abbess's proscription proved a boon for Sor Juana, who turned her restless mind to study "all the things that God had wrought, reading in them, as in writing and in books, all the workings of the universe" (39). Sor Juana carefully frames her investigations of life as occurring under God's watch and, seemingly, with His permission. By equating the knowledge found in books with that found from observing the non-literate world, Sor Juana follows a traditional argument that finds God's glory in all of creation to buttress the figurative library of information that illiterate women have at their disposal. Like an academic imbibing the wisdom of scholarly books on geometry and architecture, Sor Juana reads the confines of her convent's dormitory walls to infer that "visual lines run straight but not parallel, forming a pyramidical figure. I pondered whether this might not be the reason that caused the ancients to question whether the world were spherical. Because, although it seems, this could be a deception of vision, suggesting concavities where possibly none existed" (41). After establishing her keen observations and erudite awareness of a Western history of spatial theory, Sor Juana moves to a woman's unquestioned domain within the household: the kitchen.

With tongue firmly planted in cheek, Sor Juana addresses rhetorical questions to her alleged female peer, Sor Filotea, knowing full well that a man is her adversarial correspondent: "And what shall I tell you, lady, of the natural secrets I have discovered while cooking? . . . But, lady, as women, what wisdom may be ours if not the philosophies of the kitchen?" (43). Sor Juana's love of humor and irony shines through her attempt to create a sororal bond with her allegedly female reader. After discussing her observations on how using different ingredients changes the constitution of eggs while being cooked, Sor Juana opines that "had Aristotle prepared victuals, he would have written more" (43). Citing an occasion on which she suffered from an upset stomach and her physicians ordered her not to study, Sor Juana argues that one's spirit is "consumed more greatly in a quarter of an hour than in four days' studying books" (43). Following this line of reasoning, Sor Juana convinced her doctors to approve her return to books – a more physically passive and lethargic activity.

By juxtaposing the wisdom gained from the kitchen or from studying the walls of one's room with traditional scholarly pursuits, Sor Juana disseminates the virtues of domestic life, a room of one's own, and a woman's ability to educate herself to a level equal to, if not surpassing that of men allowed to learn from books written by other learned men. By privileging a woman's personal experience and domestic space over experiential knowledge gained from access to the university, the public square, and political life, Sor Juana follows the era's acceptance of women's "more personalized relation to religion and knowledge," especially by women religious who "were instructed by their confessors to analyze every thought, action, and dream as part of their daily routine" by writing them down (Ibsen 10). Consequently, Sor Juana explains that she employs the domestic-like, confessional genre because she has "written nothing except when compelled and constrained, and then only to give pleasure to others" (11).

Sor Juana rounds out this section reclaiming a woman's space by naming mythological, ancient, and contemporary women of renown so that she can demonstrate her familiarity with history and place herself in a line of women from Minerva and Zenobia to Queen Isabel (King Alfonso the Wise's wife) and Swedish Queen Christina Alexandra. Sor Juana demonstrates she was not the *rara avis* her contemporaries made her out to be, but was a cultural descendant inheriting a rich legacy. Her employment of rhetoric is also part of a tradition of female separatism: "*La respuesta* is a rhetoric of belonging in the way it displays the symbolic vocabularies used when people join or dissociate from others. *La respuesta* is also a woman's rhetoric, attentive to the specific concerns of the female body and female literacy" (Bokser 7).

Of course, Sor Juana's power rested on her connection to the vicegeral court and on maintaining the public's perception of her as a sacrosanct and unassailable nun. Hence, Sor Juana demonstrates her argumentative finesse by segueing into a discussion about women's role in theology. She references a theological doctor's citation of Saint Paul's sexist prohibition against women speaking in the church from 1 Corinthians 14:34 and his reference to women "teaching well" in Titus 2:3. By pointing out this Biblical contradiction about a woman's role in the church, à la Geoffrey Chaucer's Wife of Bath in her prologue, Sor Juana follows Scholastic paradigms that value the citation of the Bible and venerable Patristic writings to conclude with Doctor Juan Díaz de Arce that "teaching publicly from a University chair, or preaching from the pulpit, is not permissible for women; but that to study, write, and teach privately not only is permissible, but most advantageous and useful" (49). Sor Juana guards her argument behind that of a male theologian so she can safely advance her cause while simultaneously toeing the line. She continues to align herself with the church hierarchy when she uses a maxim about knowledge versus wisdom – "he who does not know Latin is not a complete fool, but he who knows it is well qualified to be" (49) – to assert that only women whom God has "granted special virtue and prudence" might answer the call for private teaching (49). Strategically reifying Counter-Reformation ideologies that demonize Protestantism, Sor Juana refers to Martin Luther as the paragon of knowledge unpaired with wisdom: "the Divine Scriptures in the possession of the evil Pelagius and the intractable Arius, of the evil Luther, and the other heresiarchs . . . To these men, wisdom was harmful" (49). By placing herself in opposition to such heretical men, Sor Juana ensconces herself within the Catholic Church's political arm.

Imagining herself as a peer of her male adversaries, Sor Juana then argues for the education of girls by older women – a traditional activity in the conventual world. Confident that she is following male-approved teachings, Sor Juana inserts her own theological interpretation of Paul's epistle to the Romans (Roman 12:3): "And in truth, the Apostle did not direct these words to women, but to men; and that *keep silence* is intended not only for women, but for *all* incompetents" (51). Although both the Wife of Bath and Sor Juana find it easy to appropriate, twist, and highlight logical fallacies in Saint Paul's writings, Pamela Kirk astutely observes that Sor Juana also engages with Saint Paul not only because he is the most commonly cited Patristic writer for limiting women's rights but also because of the similarities the two authors share. He was a known persecutor of Christians before he converted, and Sor Juana continued to nurture her connections with the courtly life she left behind by writing about profane topics and constantly welcoming secular visitors into the convent's locutory (119). Consequently, both figures were questioned as to the authenticity of and genuine devotion to their religious profession.

Sor Juana was acutely aware of her competing interests and sought to balance them lest she draw the ire of ecclesiastical authorities. Having already claimed that she did "not study to write, even less to teach" (11) because it would be a mark of unseemly pride, Sor Juana championed the right of other women to teach by looking retrospectively and insisting "how much injury might have been avoided in our land if our aged women had been learned" (53). Her concern about male teachers possibly corrupting young girls plays into a mindset that fetishizes a woman's virginity. She does so to not only appeal to her implied male readers but also to gain some support in enhancing women's access to education. As always, Sor Juana attempts to make an inroad by swallowing some of her pride and realizing that she must carefully balance her monastic obligations and her humanist impulses.

Trials of a Noble House

Not all of Sor Juana's works are overtly polemical. She also expressed sociopolitical themes more subtly in the majority of her artistic works. The dramatic *comedia* was one of the hallmarks of the Spanish Golden Age. Sor Juana's few forays into secular theater offer the world some of the final poignant texts from this epic era of playwriting. This chapter's discussion of her most skilled dramatic secular work, *Los empeños de una casa* (*The Trials of a Noble House*), presents this book's analytic framework with a rich counterpart to previously discussed fictional works. In this instance we encounter a real nun writing about the same issues explored in the works of secular authors who use fictional nuns as conduits to interrogate gendered power structures, a woman's role in society, and other themes of the *querelle des femmes*. By employing the tried and true staples of comedic drama, known in Spain as *comedias de enredo* (mistaken identity, clandestine affairs, young lovers overcoming impediments, lower-class characters humorously mirroring the upper-class characters of the main plot), Sor Juana engages in issues that delve into the double standard, women's sexual agency, and the utilization of male relatives and spatial figurations to protect a woman's honor. This theatrical tour de force was presented not to Sor Juana's community of fellow nuns but to the full viceregal court on a night of entertainment billed as *El festejo de los empeños de una casa*, which was entirely written by Sor Juana and performed on October 4, 1683, while she remained behind the walls of her convent.

The drama's storyline offers a parallelogram of intersecting lines of desire: Leonor and Carlos love each other and plan to elope so that her father cannot choose another husband for her. But Pedro is in love with Leonor and kidnaps her as she begins her escape with Carlos. Pedro leaves Leonor in the safe-keeping of his house with his sister Ana. Carlos attempts to rescue Leonor but is delayed by Ana, who is in love with him. Ana's own devoted pursuer, the Madrileño Juan, who has followed her to

Toledo, further muddles the actions in the house, which is also crowded by the comings and goings of Celia, Ana's maid, and Castaño, Carlos's servant. In the end, Leonor is betrothed to Carlos, Juan gladly relinquishes the part of the spurned lover when Ana accepts him, and the two servants marry each other. Sor Juana punishes Pedro's violent usurpation of Leonor's agency by refusing to marry him off. The play's hijinks ensue thanks to darkened rooms, Castaño's disguise as a woman, Celia's machinations to fulfill Ana's desires for Carlos, and women covering themselves in veils that make their lovers unable to decipher which woman is which. In the midst of all the farcically entertaining entrances and exits, the audience learns of Leonor's intelligence, her frustration with living at the behest of her father's wishes, the consequences of Pedro's lust, and the patriarchal strictures that are repudiated by the lifestyles of Sor Juana and other women who choose to become Brides of Christ.

What makes this drama worth a second look is Sor Juana's balanced approach to exploding gender commonplaces and stereotypes. Men might be misguided in their attempts to win the women of their desires, but they also are portrayed as thoughtful (Don Carlos) and aware of the precarious nature of gender expectations (the witty servant Castaño). With the same candid characterization, women are seen as navigating public perceptions of their honor (Doña Leonor) and foolishly chasing uninterested lovers (Doña Ana). These actions are contested within specific physical settings that reflect intimate links between gender and space.

Neither the play's entertainingly convoluted plot nor its subtle feminist themes are unheard of for the time period. For example, earlier *comedias de enredo* such as Tirso de Molina's *Don Gil de las calzas verdes* (1615) and Ruiz de Alarcón's *Verdad sospechosa* (1634) feature similarly humorous and complex plots. Nonetheless, *Los empeños* is part and parcel of Sor Juana's concern for broadcasting women's voices and exploring her relationship with the secular world from within the confines of her convent. The speeches of the play's protagonist, Leonor, are often read autobiographically as expressions of Sor Juana's frustration over her identity as a learned and beautiful woman who is hemmed in by the patriarchy. As a playwright, Sor Juana buttresses Leonor's feelings by surrounding her and the drama's other women within the walls of a single house throughout the length of the production. The *comedia*, which humorously reads like a comedy in the contemporary sense, also employs the trope of disguised characters and mistaken identities to comment upon the elasticity of gender and, as in her poetry inspired by her time at the viceregal court, the superficial nature of most men's amorous desires.

Writing for a secular, noble audience outside the convent, Sor Juana was aware of her celebrity and makes explicit references to convents throughout the play. By doing so she not only focuses attention on the absent playwright who could not attend the extraconventual performance of the drama, but also reminds the audience of how limited women's choices were: the home or the convent. Leonora is kidnapped from her own home and then taken to another. Fearful over both what might become of her reputation and her father's remedy to the situation, which is marrying her off to the perpetrator in order to uphold the family name, Leonor breathlessly asks to be put away in a convent:

> My friend, my intention is
> that you help me
> to escape from this house,
> so that when my father returns
> he does not find me here
> and force me to the altar.
> I will go from here,
> and in a convent cell
> seek a corner to bury myself,
> where I may weep of my sorrows
> and lament my misfortunes
> for what remains of my life. (3.1.64-76)[6]

This stark depiction of the convent as a burial chamber reflects Sor Juana's own ambivalent relationship with the secluded life. If we remember Sor Juana's admission of deciding to become a nun because marriage was such an abhorrent prospect, the fact that Leonor seeks to escape marriage in the convent exemplifies art imitating life.

Nonetheless, the convent offers some consolation to Leonor and other women who face untenable scenarios in the heteronormative marriage marketplace. Because Leonor has already been taken from the safety of her familial home, her honor is at stake, and so, following the expectations of non-tragic dramas that will end with marriages, Sor Juana has her protagonist enclosed once again within four walls so she can be safely married at the end. Sor Juana constructs Ana and Pedro's house as a secular quasi-convent wherein Leonor can take refuge. Consequently, whether a woman escapes to a house or a convent, Sor Juana posits that society's myopic vision of women always casts them as safe only when

---

[6] English language quotes from *Los empeños* come from Catherine Boyle's translation of the play for the Royal Shakespeare Company.

enclosed. Julie Greer Johnson argues as much when analyzing the play in the context of New Spain's gender politics: "Respectable women were destined to remain 'indoors' whether confined at home with family members or cloistered in a convent as a servant of God. Even those who frequented the court were there at the behest of royal officials or other gentlemen of the viceroy's entourage" (par. 3).

Embodying this concept, once Leonor and her honor have been safely ensconced in Ana and Pedro's house, although Ana runs the household more so than Pedro, she gains Ana's and the audience's respect through her long monologue that establishes her nobility, beauty, intelligence, and virtue. Her first reference to her beauty, "I suppose I am allowed to say / that I was born beautiful, / for your eyes bear witness / to what my efforts have enhanced" (1.2.103-06), smacks of a vanity that would have been unbecoming for the reportedly beautiful Sor Juana to have expressed about herself. If the autobiographical nature of the speech is not automatically apparent to the audience, it becomes so when Leonor boasts of a precocious intellectual acuity that creates a verisimilitude to Sor Juana's reputation as an intellectual: "From a very young age / I was inclined to studying / with such burning fervor, / with such extreme diligence / that long and difficult tasks / were conquered with consummate ease" (1.2.119-24). Sor Juana creates her dramatic doppelgänger and imbues her with a vainglorious self-assurance that contrasts with the nun's assumed humility. In this act of creative self-fashioning, Sor Juana employs sensual language, "ardiente" ("burning fervor"), traditionally reserved for courting or, following the footsteps of St. Teresa of Ávila that Sor Juana usually circumvented, spiritual consummations with the divine. By reserving such passionate language for intellectual stimulation, Sor Juana supports not only Leonor's but also her own aspirations.

Despite the adulation that the playwright bestows on Leonor, who is worshiped and adored as a "deity" by the public (1.2.135), the character informs the audience that female intellectuals do not last long as cerebral celebrities in sexist climates:

> Through gossip my fame travelled abroad,
> and safe distance from the truth
> grave credence to the false reports.
> ...
> Midst such acclaim,
> reeling from the attention,
> and unable to find
> a sure target for my love,
> I could love no-one. (1.2.136-62)

Leonor's fame attracts countless suitors and false rumors that cause her to be vigilant about her honor's reputation. She reports how fortunate she is to have met the noble Don Carlos and how, her plans to elope being marred by Pedro's actions, she now sits in Ana's house "bereft of reputation, / honour or consolation; / breathless, helpless, / and awaiting my death sentence / in the sentencing of Don Carlos" (1.2.285-89). Without any concrete evidence of Sor Juana's love life while at the viceregal court, many biographers have speculated that Sor Juana entered the convent as a betrayed and/or jaded lover. Whatever the case may be, Pedro's depositing of Leonor in his household under the care of Ana resembles many a "ruined" woman who was left in a convent supervised by a Mother Superior. The convent and the matriarchal household are once again designated as safe havens for women like Sor Juana who straddle the boundaries of independence and decorum. Hemmed in by her father's legal prerogative to choose her husband and close to losing all prospects of a respectable marriage because of Pedro's violent machismo, Leonor can find safety only with other women and in an enclosed spatial environment that echoes her virginal purity.

Sor Juana designs the two most loquacious male characters, the noble Don Carlos and the uneducated Castaño, as foils to female characters so that the male sex can serve as a complement to the feminist strains of her drama. The buffoonish servant Castaño supplements the play with witty and dry remarks that invite the audience to analyze a woman's situation in society. His humorous comments to Carlos and entertaining cross-dressing at the end of the play break any tension audience members might have about reconsidering a woman's role in society, since Sor Juana's ideologies are delivered through a comedic conduit. Because he is a member of the lower class, Castaño's observations about luxuriant surroundings are meant to highlight his socioeconomic background and make the audience feel privy to the material wealth of the upper-class. Safely ensconced in such a role, Castaño tells Carlos that he would have preferred falling in love with the rich Ana instead of Leonor, "who's got nothing to offer / but a few measly degrees" (1.3.70-71). Carlos's rebuke, "God, but you're despicable!" (1.3.72), invites laughter and directs derision at Castaño's material obsession.

Consequently, as in "Hombres necios" Sor Juana amalgamates her anti-materialist vows with a feminist credo that supports a woman's right to learn. Later on when Castaño implies that Carlos could be romantically involved with Ana, Carlos rebuffs Castaño's invitation to betray his love for Leonor, and asserts that only "young and arrogant men / . . . seduce women / and then judge them slatterns; / who, in their misguided malice, /

only judge women honourable / when they are aloof . . ." (2.1.50-55). Once again, the echoes of "Hombres necios" ring clearly in this play as Sor Juana recruits men to fight for women's sexual agency. Engaged in a centuries-long and transatlantic *querelle des femmes*, we can see similarities between Sor Juana's male character and Thomas Middleton and Thomas Dekker's female character Moll Cutpurse in 1611's *The Roaring Girl*, who reproaches the Castaño-like gallant Laxton by claiming he is one of those men "That thinks each woman thy fond flexible whore; / If she but cast a liberal eye upon thee," (3.1.74-75). Carlos's logic is consistently lauded throughout the play, and Sor Juana breaks with Golden Age tradition by having him turn away from unfounded jealousy – "It takes a very low man / to assume without reason / that the woman he loves / has betrayed him" (2.5.43-46) – and rejecting useless violent revenge in order to focus on rescuing Leonor so that they can be reunited.

As the drama approaches its climax, Sor Juana employs Castaño so that the audience considers gender as a performance while simultaneously laughing during the play's most humorous scenes, when we see Castaño dress up as a woman. After Carlos orders Castaño to deliver a letter to Leonor's father, Don Rodrigo, which explains that he attempted to elope with Leonor and not Don Pedro in order to prevent Rodrigo from marrying off Leonor to Pedro to save her honor, Castaño decides to dress as a woman so that a wrathful Rodrigo will not lash out at him for abetting Carlos. Metatheatrically referencing the "Calderónian twist of the plot" (3.4.16), Castaño removes his cape, sword, and hat and ekphrastically describes how he is becoming a beautiful woman. His soliloquy to the audience pokes fun at the superficial concerns of vain women and expresses realistic reflections on how the construction of a lady is an artificial and contrived enterprise:

> First, to trap my locks –
> it'll take years off me
> . . .
> Now for the skirts.
> Sweet Jesus, what beautiful material.
> It suits me perfectly –
> I'm so dark that blue looks divine on me.
> . . .
> I'm not quite the perfect lady yet.
> Gloves, definitely, to hide my hands:
> . . .
> Good grief, how well this silk cloth conceals! (3.4.28-68)

The humorous lines are followed by a commentary on the foolish men who are enraptured "not with the beauty that I am, / but with the beauty they think I am" (3.4.82-83). The meticulousness of his disguise sends up the conventions of beauty and shows that feminine beauty is an artificial performance that can be played even by a mestizo servant from the New World.

This section of the play also echoes one of Sor Juana's famous sonnets, "En perseguirme, Mundo" ("In my pursuit, World"). In this sonnet she once again utilizes her prerogative and persona as an anti-materialist, chaste, and impoverished nun to stand on high moral ground in rebuking those who spend more time on shallow pursuits than in intellectual inquiry: "¿En qué te ofendo, cuando solo intento / poner bellezas en mi entendimiento / y no mi entendimiento en las bellezas?" ["In what do I offend you, when I only intend / to put beauties in my mind / and not my mind on beauties?"] (170). Despite Sor Juana's pious celebration of the authentic, undecorated self, one can read Castaño's parting comments and find a hint of the restlessness she must have felt as an enclosed nun: "Now, let's get on with being a Lady. / . . . / My beauty's wasted in these cloisters." (3.4.84-89). Just as the English translation cleverly manipulates "encerrada" ["enclosed"] to connote the cloister, the sense of women being enclosed for their own safety is an integral theme of the drama that lends itself well to seeing Sor Juana express frustration over her limited possibilities.

Núñez, Sor Juana's confessor, stated in one of his primers for female novitiates that "recreation was permitted in the convent, but as soon as it went beyond the cloistered walls, it became an unpardonable mortal sin" (Schmidhuber 18). Her confessor's prohibition did not stop Sor Juana from continuing to straddle both sides of the spiritual and secular divide. As in her poetic and epistolary efforts, Sor Juana cloaked herself with a modicum of professional decorum so that her playwriting would not veer into heretical territory even when she was espousing non-traditional beliefs about women's agency and the double standard.

Conclusion

As this chapter has established, Sor Juana's engagement with the transatlantic *querelle des femmes* was possible only because of her status as a nun with the temporal and spatial luxuries that the vast majority of women in New Spain were not afforded. Like authors who employed nuns as catalysts for conversations about gendered power structures and a woman's role in the world, Sor Juana explored such issues from the vantage point of an actual nun who succeeded in doing what fictional characters could only aspire to in terms of living a life uncommon for most women – unburdened by courting, marrying, childbearing, or childrearing, and blessed with time, space, books, money, respect, and relative autonomy.

Chapter Six

Extraconventual Escapades: Erstwhile Nuns in Erauso's and Behn's Fictions

As we conclude our examination of sympathetic literary representations of nuns in early modern English and Spanish literature, I want to close by turning our attention to two seventeenth-century texts that feature women who reject conventual life: Catalina de Erauso's *La historia de la monja alférez* (1626) and Aphra Behn's *The History of the Nun* (1688). The first is the memoir of a real-life novice-cum-soldier, and the second is a work of sensationalist fiction. In this chapter I examine how these two authors from diametrical ends of the Iberian-Anglo divide employ imaginative literature to portray women who entered the convent at a young age and left it by their own volition. Each author's construction of the life religious and retirement from such a life is expressed through personal narratives that negotiate desire, social pressures, and religious convictions, or lack thereof.

La monja alférez begins almost immediately with Catalina plotting to leave her community of nuns. Despite the narrative's brief temporal glimpse of the convent, Catalina's role as a former "nun" is integral to not only the novelty of the autobiography but also her travels, adventures, and the respect she earns from the public, the crown, and the Papacy. Her ties with the religious community are tenable and tenuous. At one point she even tells the archbishop of New Granada that she has neither "Orden ni religión." Yet her ability to survive transcontinental voyages with her honor unscathed is enabled by her upbringing as a novice, her vouched-for virginity, and the care that the nuns and bishop of Guamanga show her.

Behn's protagonist, Isabella, wrestles with her attractions for a man, Henault, soon after she takes her vows. This plotline is typical of Protestant rhetoric about the implications of placing a young girl in a convent. She eventually elopes with him. Although her tale is fraught with melodramatic incidents such as bare-bones poverty, hunger, family estrangement, death, bigamy, and murder, Behn offers a complex rendering of Isabella that belies the story's allegedly moralist ending. Is

Isabella punished for breaking her vows and leaving the convent? Is she rendered morally weak and a murderous sociopath due to the Church's sexist views of women? The answers are not obvious.

Both women feel constrained by the strictures of conventual and heteronormative life. Whereas the convent is the safe and consistent space of their youth, their extraconventual life is wrought with adventure, strife, and uncertainty. In this chapter I deconstruct how the stories of these two nuns, as portrayed in imaginative literature, reflect, respond, and inform early modern ideas about nuns with respect to the advantages and pitfalls of extracoventual life along the Catholic-Protestant socio-religious spectrum.

Channeling Catalina: History, Legend, & Fiction

Catalina's story is legendary in the Hispanic world; her name is taught to Chilean children, it resonates in Mexico, and it is increasingly being said with pride in her native town of San Sebastián, Spain. Her memoir blurs the lines between the genres of conquistador narrative, *capa y espada* (sword-and-dagger) comedy, and a queer coming-of-age novel. Much like many twenty-first-century memoirs have been challenged for their authenticity, Catalina's text and life have been scrutinized for historical accuracy. It is these dubious claims to authenticity that plague and enrich studies of Catalina's memoir. With respect to the work of this study, the controversy makes the text all the more conducive to contrasting it with Behn's fictional novella in our consideration of how the early modern literary world, be it via travel narrative, closet drama, poetry, or romance novel, conceived of nuns, convents, and a woman's place in society.

Before addressing how the Catalina of the memoir creates and portrays her own subjectivity, we must begin with a few facts: In 1592 Catalina de Erauso y Pérez de Galarraga was baptized in San Sebastián, part of Spain's Basque region. Sometime before the age of five she was placed in the Dominican convent of San Sebastián el Antiguo where three of her sisters took vows to become nuns: Mari-Juan (1605), Isabel (1606), and Jacinta (1615). Records show that as late as March 1607 their father, Manuel, deposited forty ducats for the care of Catalina. This is the last reference to Catalina in the convent's records.

In 1624, a soldier named Catalina de Erauso returned to Spain from the New World with the nickname of *la monja alferéz* (lieutenant nun). As this cross-dressed woman sought to receive remuneration for her service to the Spanish Empire, she shared her story with people that she encountered. Her fame spread via printed *relaciones*, a self-authored memoir, and a play by the popular dramaturgist Juan Pérez de Montalbán. In 1630, with the alleged permission of the King of Spain and Pope Urban VIII, Catalina returned to the New World to live the rest of her life in Mexico dressed as a man. Legend has it that she lived out her final days as an itinerant mule-driver.

The existence of documents such as church records, royal manuscripts, and contemporaneous popular literature has created not only a legend but also an ever-growing academic field into understanding just who Catalina de Erauso was. This chapter concerns itself primarily with her memoir. While I question how much of a hand Catalina had in penning the entire memoir, I have little doubt that she existed and that the story recounted in the memoir is *mostly* true. However, even if she were a work of fiction, the way with she captured and continues to capture the public imagination meshes well with this study's examination of how literature of the day portrayed early modern nuns.

Reading Catalina's memoirs, one is struck by how many chapters sound like the typical exploration narratives penned by the Spanish conquistadors of the New World. Save for the author's sex, not many of the stories included in her memoir would stand out from the pack. It is obvious that the memoir's noteworthiness comes from the fact that Catalina was a woman disguised as a man. What makes the narrative all the more novel, however, is Catalina's relationship with the religious world. She was described as a nun in popular lore and in the titles of the texts written about her. Catalina knew why she was famous and shrewdly employed the moniker of lieutenant nun. The fact that Catalina never professed as a nun is almost inconsequential. Having lived eleven years as a postulant, she might as well be a fully veiled nun by the lay population's standards.

Catalina's fame is constructed by that unique amalgamation that makes an individual a celebrity: she is both familiar and foreign. She is a nun. She is a soldier. Nuns and soldiers were familiar in the early modern landscape, but their professional settings (convents and New World battlefields, respectively) were foreign to the average citizen. Conceptions of these two unique lifestyles anticipate that never the twain shall meet. They did with Catalina. To become a soldier she needed to leave the convent. Strikingly though, she did not give up the image of herself as a nun or, at least, nun-like throughout the latter part of her journey. At different instances in her narrative she distances herself from her period as a postulant or as a model of piety, but even that estrangement implies a conflicted personal relationship that requires negotiating. When Catalina embraces her identity as a nun, she does so to protect herself more than for religious reasons. However, there is some kind of religiosity expressed in the memoir that finds Catalina working with and against the traditions of female monastic writing. Given her swashbuckling ways as a conquistador, her transparent ego makes it almost impossible for her to write a penitential confession – if she wanted to. Yet she remains a woman religious, or, at the very least, a religious woman, who invokes the help of nuns, friars, bishops, and even the pope. As we will see, Catalina's fickle style of Catholicism is more modern than early modern.

Losing My Religion: Catalina as a Nun

Readers are provided with little information about Catalina's time as a novice in the convent. Despite living there for eleven years, Catalina simply states she was "in training for the day when I would profess myself a nun"[1] without any details as to what this preparation entailed (3). The references to rising at midnight to perform matins, nuns in the choir room, and keys to various cells in the city-like community of a convent are credible enough, but also common enough as to be easily inserted into a narrative by an author who never lived in a convent. Shakespeare similarly spends little time discussing Isabella's conventual life, as the audience receives only a glimpse of the door to the convent in *Measure for Measure*, while authors such as María de Zayas, a woman in a Catholic nation-state with more access to such communities, provide us with more details about the culture of convent life.

The absence of details may add fuel to the fire for those who consider Catalina's story to be fictional. More importantly for this study, however, is the idea that the absence of details is less significant than readers knowing she was raised in a convent and, for all intents and purposes, was a nun, nun-like, or a quasi-nun. Her time in the convent marks her as having been part of that community of *others within* – those women who are removed from, by choice or not, the world of courting, marrying, and child-rearing. The sisterhood in which she existed was a different realm even from that of a girl who is relegated solely to the domestic sphere under the care of a watchful mother, aunts, and maids.

The memoir's relation of Catalina's early years provides readers with dates that do not line up with the "real" Catalina's dates. In her text she

---

[1] All quotes come from the invaluable *Lieutenant Nun: Memoir of a Basque Transvestite in the New World*. Eds. Michele Stepto and Gabri Stepto. Boston: Beacon Press, 1996.

claims to have been born in 1585, however, according to parochial records, her baptism occurred in 1592, which, by Catholic custom, would have been celebrated a few days after her birth. The convent's records show her father paying for her keep as late as 1607, which makes her claim that she left in 1600 inaccurate. It is hard to imagine that she set off on her picaresque adventure at the age of eight like a female version of Lazarillo de Tormes. If she waited to escape the convent until she was fifteen to avoid becoming a fully professed nun, that would have occurred in 1607. This guess makes the most sense as it is the last record we have of Catalina in the convent. Of course, like many celebrities who fudge the details of their biographies to make their story more legendary and memorable, Catalina could have chosen 1600 as a momentous year, the beginning of a new century, to mark her entrance to the New World. Whatever the case may be, Catalina's story is more important than the facts. She lived in a convent and decided to leave the cloistered world behind.

Although we are bereft of details as to what daily life in the convent was like for a Catalina that we can easily imagine as being precocious, independent, and confident, she shares with us the straw that broke the camel's back: "I got in a quarrel with one of the sisters, doña Catalina de Aliri . . . She was a big, robust woman, I was but a girl—and when she beat me, I felt it" (3). So much for this book's earlier analyses of how the convent offered women a respite from the violence of the extraconventual world! Although recorded instances of nun-on-nun physical hostility are rare, they are not unheard of. For example, the French Franciscan convent of Mont-Sainte-Catherine-lès-Provins experienced a community-wide dispute about the 1663 election of the convent's abbess, which led to a legal case in both ecclesiastical and secular courts. The factionalism that developed within the convent because of the lawsuit grew so strong that by 1666, life within the community's wall grew "increasingly hostile" and "degenerated towards violence" (Tuttle 14).

One can sympathize for the abuse Catalina suffered. Perhaps there were instances of violence in the past, but the void of such stories allows us to see her as fiercely resolute in rejecting such treatment. The speed with which she mentions the convent and then abandons it (within three paragraphs) foreshadows the alacrity with which she sets out for the New World, making a name for herself on the battlefield as a perpetrator of violence on others. When Catalina asks to be excused from choir duties by feigning an illness so she can escape, the last thing she hears is the "nuns singing the psalms in a mournful tone" (4). The only temporal setting that Catalina provides for the convent is in the middle of the night – we never see the convent filled with natural light. Thus far the convent has been described as violent, funerary, and opaque. The vivid imagery of later chapters will only reinforce the idea that the convent is a solemn and dark place where abuse abounds.

In 2001 José Barrado Barquilla published a history of the Dominican convent of San Sebastián el Antiguo. As the convent's most famous resident, Catalina dominates several pages in the book. Barrado is touchingly sympathetic to Catalina's situation: "Su paso por aquellos claustros y su estancia entre sus paredes la suponemos forzada . . . era un convento de monjas y para monjas, y ella se sentía varón" ["We suppose that her passage through those cloisters and her stay inside those walls were forced . . . it was a convent of nuns and for nuns, and she felt like a boy"] (84). The convent changed locations in the nineteenth century. Remarkably, the sole indicator of its former site is a bust of Catalina – the world's only known statue of her.

If we take a moment to consider popular conceptions of Catalina created through literature, we must turn our attention to a text I found in the archives of Biblioteca Nacional de España in Madrid in 2012. The nineteenth-century Spanish scholar Pascual de Gayangos owned a large collection of manuscripts featuring four *relaciones* about Catalina. These *relaciones* were printed between 1616 and 1625 in both Madrid and Sevilla. *Relaciones* are chronicles written by Spaniards and subjects of the Spanish Empire to document the cultures, lifestyles, and politics of the Americas. These shortened versions of Catalina's story, mostly based on her conversations with the bishop of Guamanga, predate the publication of her memoir. The 1618 edition's frontispiece depicts her as a nun dressed as a man. The opening page recounts what Catalina told the bishop, including the report "que es Monja professa del Covetode S. Sebastián el antiguo" ["she is a professed nun of the Convent of San Sebastián"] (Capitulo 1). Thus, word would have spread about her being a fully professed nun, at sixteen years old according to the *relación*, before she made the truth clear in her 1625 memoir that she never took vows. In his study of *relaciones*, Robert Folger argues that the writers of these texts obey the laws of the colonial enterprise wherein the writer as a subject "establishes individual agency" and is subjugated "to become subject to a regime of power" while reporting his life and that of others (4). The fact that four different reports were written and circulated about Catalina not only demonstrate her anomalous status but also her importance as a subject of the Spanish Empire – one that may be gawked at, derided, and scolded, but one who is part of the hegemonic imperial discourse of conquest, production, and submission to church and state. These *relaciones* testify for the authenticity of her memoir, but what is more important is that she is embraced as an oddity. She is sent home to the New World metropolis because of her merits and services as a solider despite her transvestitism.

This *relación* also offers an illustration of Catalina. The frontispiece contains three images in a triptych layout wherein two individuals flank a nautical scene (See Figure 1). The figure on the left is a soldier, whose long hair, akimbo stance, and crossed legs imply that it could be a woman. This is likely the first published illustration of Catalina.

An equally rich primary source of information about Catalina is the "Traslado de merced a Catalina de Erauso" from the *Registro de Reales Disposiciones de la Cámara de Indias, Nueva España Cámara, 1624 hasta 1629* files, which are housed in the Archivo General de Indias in Sevilla, Spain. This traslado asks for the Spanish Crown to pay Catalina for her services as a soldier. Both the text of the manuscript and the marginalia refer to her as "El Alférez Doña Catalina de Erauso" without any reference to her having been a nun or employing the popular, gendered moniker "la monja alférez" ("the lieutenant nun"). The writer does make note that Catalina was dressed "de baron por particular inclinación que tuvo de exercitar las armas en defensa de la fe Católica" ["as a boy because of her particular inclination to use arms in defense of the Catholic faith"] (163). Here we see the typical admixture of church and state blended with a justification for crossdressing. Catalina's transgender identity is mentioned as if to explain why the Spanish Crown would pay a soldier with the woman's name "Catalina." The straightforward explanation understates the transgressive nature of Catalina's crossdressing and does so by privileging her Catholicism. The memoirs demonstrate a different relationship between Catalina and her faith, but an official government document would require less ambiguity. Perhaps Catalina's status as a sometime-nun would have been too complicated for the bureaucratic prose of this document that is simply a means to a remunerative end. The petition goes on to recount Catalina's service "en las guerras de las provincias de Chile" ["in the wars of the Chilean provinces"] where she was rewarded with the title "Alférez" ["Lieutenant"] for the great harm she caused enemies, demonstrated through "valor de hombre . . . en muchas Batallas . . . que se tubierón con los Indios" ["manly valor . . . in many battles . . . they had against the Indians"] (163). The military prowess that Catalina boasts about in her memoir is supported by this documentation, which one assumes was written by a male, military superior – perhaps Don Fernando Luis de Contra – who shows nothing but respect and admiration for Catalina's tenacious spirit and martial expertise. In this document, Catalina is different but she is not an oddity to be gawked at. There is no talk of her profession as a nun. She is a soldier who has earned the rank of Lieutenant and should be rightfully compensated by the Spanish Empire for her efforts.

According to the memoir, a few years went by before word came from Spain that she had only been a novice nun. Thus, it would make sense that the 1618 *relación*, which most helped spread her fame in the New World as well as in Spain, identifies her as a nun. Although she clears up her status in *La monja alférez*, the *relación* includes some information that the memoir does not. For example, it relates that Catalina was in San Sebastián with her sisters, whereas the memoir fails to mention them living with her there.

Because there is no mention in the memoir of Catalina's biological sisters having lived in the convent with her, one can conclude that her experience in the convent was so harrowing that she omits references to a familial sisterhood so as to highlight her inability to find a supportive spiritual sisterhood at San Sebastián el Antiguo. Catalina "once again . . . donned the veil" (66) to re-enter the convent years later, probably around 1617, when she confessed her true story to the Bishop of Guamanga, Fray Agustín de Carvajal, who then placed her in the nunnery of Santa Clara. Since she would not have worn a veil as a postulant, I venture that here we see Catalina embrace her dubious identity as a nun for two reasons: to survive and to spread her fame. After all, the bishop is incredulous of her story and has Catalina examined by "old women" who report that she is an "intact virgin" (66).

The news of Catalina's physical purity "touched His Eminence" (66); still in possession of her virginity, Catalina technically still embodied at least one of the three vows a nun takes. By claiming to be nun-like and even feeling comfortable enough to trade her armor for a habit, Catalina assures herself of a safe passage from the garrulous life she leads in the New World. Although she once sought the adventures of a conquistador's life, the increasing number of times wherein she finds herself on the brink of death becomes too close for comfort.

Unaware of her full biography, nuns "bearing lighted candles" welcome Catalina into the convent as she is "carried in procession to the choir" (66-67). In a show of humility, Catalina kisses the abbess's hand before embracing and being embraced by the other nuns. This report follows Catalina's emotional expression about her confession to the bishop: "all the while I was speaking, I felt a calm sweeping over me, I felt as if I were humbled before God, that things were simpler than they had seemed before, and that I was very small and insignificant" (64). The humility with which she portrays herself in the memoir's final chapters is a sharp contrast to the pride she exhibits in the majority of her tale. Although we do not get details about the confession she makes in anticipation of taking the sacraments from the bishop, her journey from folly to salvation follows the path of many saints' lives and even the tropes of the confessional literature of Spanish women religious.

Catalina did not have the same spiritual inclinations of Saint Teresa of Ávila. However, Joaquín María Ferrer, who edited a popular 1800s edition of Catalina's memoir, imagined what Catalina may have achieved had she received a formal education and used the saint as model: "¿Quién sabe si cultivado su ingenio por la educación, no habría sido dirigida por la piedad una Santa Teresa?" ["Who knows if she would not have been directed by the piety of a Saint Teresa if her talents had been cultivated by an education?"] (32). Because Catalina pens a secular memoir rather than a spiritual one, the reader does not expect such details. Keeping a popular audience in mind, Catalina skips minutiae about conventual life and divine transcendence. This is not to say, however, that she doesn't portray herself as being on a spiritual journey prior to encountering the bishop.

En route to Tucumán through the Andes Mountains after accidentally killing her brother in a duel, Catalina faces death when she and two other deserters run out of food and water. Her companions die one day after the other. At one point, fearing that she will share the fate of her comrades, she prays in a moment of despair: "I propped myself against a tree and wept—for what I think was the first time in my life—I recited the rosary, commending myself to the Most Holy Virgin and to her husband, glorious Saint Joseph" (27). Catalina survives and the next morning comes across a group of "Christians" as "the heavens seemed to open before [her]" (27). Despite her escape from the convent and her warring ways, Catalina maintains some kind of a Catholic identity with her prayers. Readers who do not consider themselves particularly pious, even in the early modern era, would be able to identify with Catalina as a peer who prays only in times of need. Her affiliation with Catholicism—be it described as casual, utilitarian, or convenient— mirrors the religious identity of many.

In fact, this unconventional relationship with the Church reaches levels of outright heresy when she is sentenced to death for killing a Portuguese man in Piscobamba who attacked her at night in revenge for losing to her in a card game. In preparation for her execution, a priest arrives to confess Catalina, but she refuses (42).

CAPITVLO
DE VNA DE LAS CARTAS QVE diuerſas perſonas embiaron deſde Cartagena de las Indias a algunos amigos ſuyos a las ciudades de Seuilla y Cadiz.

En que dan cuenta como vna monja en habito de hombre anduuo gran parte de Eſpaña y de Indias, ſiruiendo a diuerſas perſonas. Y aſsi miſmo como fue ſoldado en Chile y Tipoan, y los valeroſos hechos y hazañas que hizo en cinco batallas q entrò a pelear con los Indios Chiles y Chambos: y como fue deſcubierta y la recogio don Fray Aguſtin de Carauajal Obiſpo de la ciudad de Guamanga.

EN SEVILLA

Por Iuan Serrano de Vargas en frente del Correo mayor, Año de 1618.

Figure 1. This frontispiece of a 1618 *Relacion* offers what is perhaps the first illustration of Catalina (on the left). It was published in Sevilla, Spain and is courtesy of the Biblioteca Nacional de España.

Her refusal is surprising given her earlier prayers and the fact that when her brother begs for a priest when he is dying, Catalina runs to the Franciscan church and dispatches two friars to take his confession (24). When the scaffold appears before her, Catalina rebuffs such ecclesiastical assistance: "A priest arrived to confess me, and I refused—he insisted, and I held my ground. After this, it rained priests, I was drowning in them—me, a self-professed Lutheran!" (42) Up to this point, there has been no mention of Catalina embracing or even mentioning Protestantism. Her exclamation is strange and unexpected. The rest of this scene details her perturbation with the priests: "They rode me out of the jail and down a series of unfamiliar back streets, all the while trying to keep clear of the priests—and I arrived at the gallows, half out of my mind with the priests' shrieking and flailing" (42). Admittedly, the image of a mob of priests caterwauling about Catalina is risible, but it is also perplexing that she does not take their help. It seems as if at this point in her journey, Catalina is ready for death.

In what can easily be described as humorous, when the hangman finds it difficult to put the rope around her neck she yells, "You drunk! Put it on right, or don't put it on at all—I've got my hands full with these priests!" (43). Perhaps her claim of being a Lutheran marks her as giving up hope. The sheriff seems to concur as much when in the sight of priests crying and pleading for her life "he told them if I wanted to go to hell, that was my business, he didn't give a damn" (42). Catalina does not contradict him. Because Martin Luther was the epitome of the Protestant Reformation, citing his name and the Christian denominations that sprung up because of him makes sense to grab readers' attention. Intriguingly enough, if one visits the website for the Dominican convent of San Sebastián el Antiguo today, the page mentions that the Papal Bull calling for the construction of the convent was issued in 1564, "año de la muerte de Lutero, cuya heterodoxia se infiltraba en Guipúzcoa" ["the death year of Luther, whose heterodoxy was infiltrating Guipúzcoa"] (Santo, par. 2). Whatever the reason may be for Catalina's Protestant outburst, she cannot help but be in constant contact with the Catholic Church's laity, clergy, and political power.

Her memoir is not a spiritual confession but rather a narrative of identity formation. As Pedro Rubio Merino has argued, "La Monja Álferez no alardeó nunca de su condición de persona creyente, pero actuó siempre en función de tal" ["The lieutenant nun never boasted about the nature of her personal faith, but she always acted in the function of it"] (43). That is to say that she never identifies herself as uniquely pious or sanctimonious. As Rubio notes, she went to Mass often even after she left the convent.

However, this didn't stop her from being sacrilegious by fighting in church or disobeying the Ten Commandments. Her Catholicism was informal, practical, and, in terms of how it meshed with her public persona, honest.

When Catalina arrives in Lima after the death of the Bishop of Guamanga who first offered her shelter, she is asked by the Archbishop of Lima, Bartolomé Lobo Guerrero, to decide in which of the city's convents she will live. After settling on a convent of the Order of Saint Bernard, she lives for more than two years with nearly two hundred women in the mixed community of black-veiled nuns, white-veiled nuns, novices, patronesses, and servants. The sizable population of the convent and the varied statuses among the women there is a fair representation of the convents that could be found in large cities during the early modern era. After all, at one point Sor Juana Inés de la Cruz's mother gifted her a slave to help her in the convent. Furthermore, if Catalina knew enough about the differences between women in the convent so as to note the degrees of nuns, she was knowledgeable enough to have known that she should have described herself more honestly as either a postulant or a novice rather than a nun. Her decision to not clearly define her stage of professional religious development shows how aware she was of the buzz that her status as a nun would generate in the reading public, which, for the most part, would probably not care much about such distinctions.

Readers do not get any more details about Catalina's life in this New World convent. It is enough that she was there and once again passing as a nun. Passing, in fact, is an appropriate term since she bids a "sad farewell" to her companions when they learn that she never was a professed nun. On her way back to Spain she stops in Guamanga to say goodbye to the nuns who befriended her in the convent of Santa Clara. In one brief sentence Catalina implies that she found a comforting sisterhood among these women: "they held me up there for eight days, during which we enjoyed each other's company and exchanged many gifts and finally, when it was time for me to go, many tears" (69). Nonetheless, a conventual life was not for her. When she is in New Granada, the archbishop asks her to take up residence in a convent of her order. She replies that she "had no order, and no religion" and was "simply trying to get back to [her] country" (69). At this point, Catalina's relationship with religion is almost schizophrenic, or, at least, opportunistic. She may enjoy life in certain convents, but only for a period. Like the protagonists of Zayas's stories, Catalina can find refuge and solidarity in a convent, but she has also encountered abuse. If one thinks of the convent as a jail, as Catalina might have in her early days, then her peripatetic entrances into and departures from convents mark her as a recidivist that can't quit the habit. Ultimately, she creates a new identity for herself with the help, ironically, of the pope himself.

As her fame spreads, she makes her way to the King of Spain who grants her a commission for her services to the Spanish Crown in the New World. She then travels to Rome to meet Pope Urban VIII. Catalina matter-of-factly describes the dispensation he gave her: "His Holiness seemed amazed to hear such things, and graciously gave me leave to pursue my life in men's clothing" (78). Much has been written about the transgressive nature of cross-dressing in the early modern era and about the reasons for which individuals, particularly women, did this with respect to safety, power, authority, income, and education.[2] The point behind such academic writing has been to argue how our contemporary ideas about the fluidity of gender and sexuality are not strictly modern. The early modern era had a slew of brave individuals who crossed gender lines freely, and, like Catalina, sometimes without penalty. Catalina's claim that the pope signed off on this gender-bending surprises many readers. The conservatism of the Catholic Church when it comes to matters of gender norms is well-known, and when non-academics or undergraduate students imagine what this conservatism might have been like in the 1600s, they are bewildered that such a dispensation could have occurred. Yet there it is, if one believes her story, and no one is more proud of such an achievement than Catalina, who recounts her success with a nonchalance befitting the bravura of a *mujer virago* (virile woman) of the Spanish Golden Age.

Like A Virgin: Catalina's Sexuality

As I have demonstrated in previous chapters, if one of the most important expectations for a nun is her chastity, we must not ignore literary portrayals of nuns' sexuality. Prurient texts and illustrations play on salacious desires and damaging stereotypes. However, the imaginative literature under examination in this book counters such juvenile approaches to the sexuality of women religious. The virginity of Shakespeare's Isabella attracts Duke Vincentio; Cavendish creates an enclave wherein early modern femme and butch lesbians can kiss one

---

[2] See Stephen Orgel's *Impersonations: The Performance of Gender in Shakespeare's England*, Dympna Callaghan's *Shakespeare Without Women: Representing Gender and Race on the Renaissance Stage*, and Susan Zimmerman's *Erotic Politics: Desire on the Renaissance Stage*.

another; Zayas has characters discuss genderless, Neo-Platonic love in the company of nuns; and Sor Juana's amorous poetry is scrutinized to find links with her close relationship with the vicereine. In line with such non-heteronormative expressions of sexuality, Catalina's memoir is unabashedly queer in the way she never mentions men as potential love interests and the intimate manner in which she interacts with women.

One of the first instances in which we learn about Catalina's sexuality finds her master trying to arrange her marriage to his mistress, Beatriz de Cárdenas, in order to solve several personal and professional conflicts. Catalina goes along with the plan at first. She sneaks into Beatriz's house at night where the mistress caresses Catalina and asks her to stay with her. Catalina plays coy until Beatriz becomes fed up with her hesitation: "Finally one night, she locked me in and declared that come hell or high water I was going to sleep with her—pushing and pleading so much that I had to smack her one and slip out of there" (13). The smack cannot be simply read as Catalina's internalized homophobia manifesting itself through violence. As readers continue with the memoir, they find her expressing more clear-cut same-sex desires.

When Catalina moves to Lima and works with Diego de Solarte, she runs into trouble when Solarte finds her cavorting with his sisters-in-law: "I had become accustomed to frolicking with them and teasing them—one, in particular, who had taken a fancy to me . . . one day . . . I had my head in the folds of her skirt and she was combing my hair while I ran my hand up and down between her legs" (17). The sexual play and desire expressed in these lines are palpable. Although the woman does not know that Catalina is a woman, we do. The dramatic irony creates the same kind of humor one would experience while seeing Olivia fall for Viola in Shakespeare's *Twelfth Night*, but the reader's excitement is amplified because Catalina knowingly enjoys being so intimate with another woman. The difference between this and a character in a cross-dressing comedy working off the entanglements of mistaken identity is essential. There is no metaphor, feint, or symbolism here. Catalina desires women. This memoir, billed as that of a nun, includes carnal same-sex interactions. Catalina is, characteristically, unapologetic about it. If she does make full confessions about her behavior, including that of Church-designated "unnatural" acts, we never hear of her being reprimanded for it by authority figures in the Church.

Descriptions of Catalina engaging in such physically intimate behavior are not isolated. When Catalina works as a soldier for her brother in Concepción, she visits his mistress's house without him. There are no details about what occurs during these calls, but when after a warning from her brother Catalina is caught there again, she says "he lit into me with his belt, wounding me in the hand" (19). Readers would not imagine this violent reaction was due to anything other than sexual contact between Catalina and the mistress. In another instance of same-sex relationships, when Catalina is staying in Tucumán with a woman who rescues her from starvation, the woman offers Catalina her daughter in marriage. Expressing a racist remark about the daughter, Catalina once again underscores her attraction to women: "a girl as black and ugly as the devil himself, quite the opposite of my taste, which has always run to pretty faces" (28). Catalina plays the two as fools by pretending to be interested in the betrothal for two months during which she enjoys "full run of the house and the lands" (28). In fact, Catalina turns out to be quite the eligible bachelor when the bishop's vicar-general in the area also wants to arrange a marriage between his niece and Catalina. Despite the dowry she would receive from this marriage, Catalina declines.

If Catalina is an early modern lesbian, why does she turn down the chance to marry a woman? Surely she knows that the ruse would be up soon enough. Also, she does not want to be tied down – not by the Church and certainly not by another woman. If Catalina does hold one thing in common with nuns it is with their rejection of corporal marriage, even if it were to be a queer one. As the memoir continues, there are fewer references to Catalina being attracted to or intimate with other women. However, her preference for women or at least for being single must be known by many since even when she returns to Europe as a woman, there are no questions about her marital status. No one expects a woman as cavalier as Catalina to marry a man.

Far before the advent of queer theory, nineteenth-century scholars of the text were unable to ignore Catalina's same-sex attractions. For example, Ferrer notes Catalina's penchant for skirt-chasing and explained away her desire by saying it was because "llegó a hacerse illusión de que era hombre" ["she was under the illusion that she was a man"] (20). Ferrer asserts that her intimacies with women were a ploy for dissembling her true sex to the public. Ferrer discounts the possibility of Catalina's lesbianism, which is par for the course during the time in which he wrote, but the fact that he observes and analyzes Catalina's actions rather than glosses over them underscores the novelty of her narrative and its candid portrayal of same-sex desires. Whether individual early modern readers saw such activities as titillating, illicit, or abominable depends on their perspectives as much as our own interpretations do on ours. The fact that Catalina is self-marketed as a nun only adds to the need to better understand how the early modern world conceived of women's sexuality.

For surely Catalina was not alone in her desires. No doubt there was probably a reader or two out there who could identify with Catalina's construction of her identity as a nun gone wild.

With respect to believability, I find that two questions often pop up in class discussions about Catalina's memoir: 1. How did she escape notice as a woman all those years, especially when she was arrested and stripped in jail? 2. How could the old women who examined her have concluded that she was still an "intact virgin" given the strenuous physical activity in which she engaged, including riding horses? We cannot claim suspension of disbelief if this memoir is to be read as an accurate rendering of her life. Perhaps her claim of virginity in the memoir is a nod to early modern conceptions about women's sexuality that rendered the possibility of same-sex relationships as invisible in law and unspeakable in public. It is difficult to answer such questions, but the more important element to focus on is her honest expression of same-sex desire that neither questions its morality, normalcy, nor realness.

Admittedly, Catalina's entire story is difficult to believe. Like many exploration narratives, her memoir contains elements that are so clichéd that their commonness is both hackneyed and an assurance of its authenticity. Like many exploration narratives, her memoir contains enough near-death experiences and amazing escapes to make her a poster child for literary embellishments and improbabilities. However, unlike any exploration narrative that came before it, *La monja alférez* is a journey of identity fueled by the surprise inherent in its portrayal of a non-normative woman religious. As Catalina fashions herself a soldier on the battlefield and a man-to-be-feared on the streets, she distances herself from her conventual past. When her secret is out, she employs her time as a novice to save her life. For a woman as independent, savvy, and uncomfortable with the expectations and limitations of the feminine gender as Catalina, the convent is convenient only when she can so freely enter and leave it. As discussed in the opening chapter of this book, such freedom was rare after the Council of Trent.

In the strictest sense, Catalina was never a nun. She never professed as one. She escaped as a postulant or a novice. But her eleven years of living in a convent with all the religious education it entails marked her as set for the life of a woman religious, one which she rejected. Ultimately, though, through a candid and embellished account of her life and confessions to priests, Catalina is able to establish her transgender identity with the permission of the Catholic Church. Even though the conventual life would have been too restraining for her, the Church still offered her refuge.

Isabella Revisited: Aphra Behn's *History of the Nun; or, The Fair Vow Breaker*

As we come full-circle in this book and retrain our gaze on yet another Isabella, we can see that by the late seventeenth century English authors express decidedly more mixed, if not negative, views of how conventual culture could influence and warp the sensibilities of early modern women. Aphra Behn's *The History of the Nun; or, The Fair Vow-Breaker* was published in 1689 – the year of Behn's death. This sensationalist novella followed a long line of critically and commercially successful plays, novels, and poems by Behn, who is often heralded as being one of the first English women to make a living by way of her writing. The psychological complexity with which Behn imbues her protagonist and the narrator's explicit espousal of moral standards by which to judge Isabella allows this story to rise beyond the clichés of the amatory novella genre. Isabella's desires are active and battle with the didactic simplicity of the narrator's warnings about people's failures to reign in natural inclinations. The nun in Behn's text is scandalous, subversive, and far from sacred.

Jacqueline Pearson asserts that Behn's "use of the metaphor of the nun as a means of understanding her own dilemma as a woman writer may help to explain the novella's unconventional sympathy for the guilty Isabella, whose transgressive desire to escape from confinement finds sympathetic echoes in the woman writer" (*History* 246). I argue that this assessment of Behn's unconventional sympathies for Isabella is not so clear-cut, particularly when we consider Isabella's literary antecedent in Shakespeare's *Measure for Measure*. As we follow the novella's beguiling plot, we see Isabella as a dynamic character who struggles with a complex amalgamation of society's moral standards and personal convictions. Isabella's decision to leave the convent is made after much contemplation, but, as we will see, Behn creates a protagonist whose time as a nun has plagued her with anxieties, fears, and ethical lapses that counter libertine notions of independence and sensual appreciation for corporal desires.

The narrator's perspective of heteronormative relations posits that "women are by nature more constant and just than men" until they are "taught by the lives of men to live up to all their vices" (4). The construction of women's propensity for infidelity is a double-edged sword. On one hand, it acknowledges that gender roles are created and perpetuated by a patriarchal society rather than being innate. On the other hand, it robs women of their free-will. Before the narrator focuses on sacred vows and conventual life, she generates a framework that invites readers to consider the damning effects that men and the patriarchy can have on women who are born to be "more constant." As a novice, Isabella is tempted by the secular world but rejects it – too soon, the narrator argues. Yet, the ways in which Isabella betrays her friendship with Sister Katerinna and the ways she deals with unexpectedly becoming a bigamist do not sound like the moral righteousness of Shakespeare's Isabella. However, if we consider Catalina's story then we may not be surprised that Isabella, even as the professed nun that Catalina never was, is subject to moral failures – even murder. Behn does not offer us an idealized vision of nuns or convent life.

The narrator's attempt to paint Isabella's tale as a cautionary one is ironically subverted by Behn's preface to the novella – a dedication to a woman who broke her wedding vows and enabled King Charles II to break his.[3] *The History of the Nun* is sensational and problematic but undeniably fun to read. Behn's works were popular during her lifetime with multiple reprintings of her texts. Likewise, just as Catalina's story was chronicled not only in contemporaneous *relaciones* and Montalbán's play but also as children's literature in future centuries,[4] Behn's *History of the Nun* was dramatized (without due credit) by Thomas Southerne in 1694, which was in turn adapted by David Garrick in 1757.[5] The reason for the popularity of this story of a nun who escapes the convent merits closer attention.

---

[3] The novella is dedicated to Hortense Mancini, an Italian duchess who left her cruel and authoritarian husband in 1666 by moving to London where she became a mistress to King Charles II. In Toivo David Rosvall's *The Mazarine Legacy: The Life of Hortense Mancini, Duchess Mazarine*, Hortense's husband, Armand-Charles de la Meilleraye, is seen as a religious hypocrite.

[4] My research in the Biblioteca Nacional de España revealed a popular twentieth-century tradition of retelling Catalina's story to children throughout Spain and Latin America via picture books and comic strips. Examples include María del Carmen Ochoa's 1970 *La monja alférez* and Armonía Rodríguez's 1975 *De monja a militar*.

[5] Southerne's dramatization is entitled with a more sensational flavor than Behn's, *The Fatal Marriage; or, The Innocent Adultery*, whereas Garrick's is simply named *Isabella*. Pearson's article details the ways in which the simplification of Isabella's innocence and psychological stability in these adaptations diverge from Behn's more complex portrayal of Isabella. Pearson asserts that these modifications of Behn's text demonstrate a backlash against the feminist ideology espoused by Behn in her writing.

Return to Innocence: Isabella's Trajectory

Isabella feels constrained by conventual vows and, eventually, marital vows. She eschews familiarity with the former only to suffer the foreignness of the latter. Whereas the convent was the safe and consistent space of her youth, her marital home is wrought with strife and uncertainty. This change from security to anxiety mirrors the paths of most individuals, even in the early modern era, as they become increasingly independent with age. Ironically enough, Behn's employment of the womb-like symbol of the convent is more detailed than the one offered by Catalina, who actually lived in not one but several convents. The complexity of the conventual life in Behn's novella, however, is one indebted to the artistic license inherit in works of fiction. When Behn labels it a "History," though, she vouches for its authenticity and asks readers to imagine that this novella is not so much a fiction as it is an accurate view into the lives and minds of women religious. As one Behn scholar notes in surveying the typological battle between the labels of "novel," "history," and "true history" in her work, Behn desired "to insist on the truth of the narrative and the eye-witness authority of the narrator" (Pearson 191). Although we have no explanation as to how the narrator knew Isabella, her first-person confession of once having lived in a convent enables her to guarantee the validity of Isabella's story and the passions she endures as a woman religious. The narrator intrudes when she offers personal stories, makes judgment calls, and expresses biases – just as the narrators of Zayas's novellas do, which inspired many of Behn's dramas and novels.[6]

Zayas's "The Vanquished Impossible" can be compared to Behn's work with respect to the plot of a woman having two husbands, which was a popular narrative both in novel form and in oral storytelling due to the frequency of wars to which women lost or thought they lost their husbands. Zayas, the Catholic author, does not feature the nun as a protagonist. Behn, the ostensibly Protestant author, uses the idea of the nun as a conduit through which to comment upon the barriers that women encounter when they exert agency in their lives. Isabella affirms her independence by fleeing the convent. Her physical transgression

---

[6] Dolors Altaba-Artal's *Aphra Behn's English Feminism: Wit and Satire* traces intertextual ties between Behn's work and that of Spanish writers such as Zayas and Pedro Calderón de la Barca and highlights the long English tradition of borrowing plots from Continental writers, particularly those of the Spanish Siglo de Oro.

symbolically transforms her from a passive object to an active agent. Yet Behn does not reward her.

Despite Behn's reputation for penning works with scandalous plots that highlight the agency of women's sexual desires, this story begins with a tone more befitting a moralist: "Of all the sins incident to human nature, there is none of which Heaven has took so particular, visible, and frequent notice and revenge as on that of violated vows, which never go unpunished" (3). With all the talk of "sins," "human nature," "Heaven," and "revenge," readers may feel as if the didactic lesson is introduced within the first sentence. But why would Behn write a narrative featuring such a transparent moral lesson? The narrator goes on to describe "Cupids" as merchants of love, which sets up a scenario for a criticism of love's vagaries – from those who believe in love-at-first-sight to love that dissipates once a couple have sex or are married – that would allow the text to stand as an amatory guidebook. However, the narrator asserts that "Heaven never takes cognizance of lovers' broken vows and oaths . . . 'tis the only perjury that escapes the anger of the gods" (3). Despite the odd conflation of a seemingly monotheistic Christian Heaven and a pagan, pluralized "gods," the narrator diminishes the gravity of these broken vows when she creates a hierarchy of oaths wherein the "*Sacred Vow*, made to God only" is superior to matrimonial vows (4). The narrator makes it clear that these vows are not just promises that one makes to God in times of trouble but rather those "made by those that enter into Holy Orders," which, if broken, call for the "most severe and notorious revenges of God" (4). By arguing "I am almost certain that there is not one example to be produced in the world where perjuries of this nature have passed unpunished" (4), the narrator taps into popular Protestant ideas about the superstitious beliefs and behaviors of Catholics. The first-person voice transforms any objective narratorial distance into a subjective perspective informed by general knowledge, hearsay, rumors, and personal biases. The qualifier of "almost" creates an unreliable narrator, but, given the inability to have a global awareness of such incidents, the term makes her more relatable and believable. Such ethos is further established when she confesses that she "once was designed an humble votary in the house of devotion" (5).

The fact that the narrator left a convent due to "an obstinacy of mind" (5) allows us to draw parallels between her and Catalina. However, the narrator expresses a sense of regret about her decision when she describes the extraconventual world as "full of nothing but nonsense, noise, false notions, and contradictions" in contrast to the "innocence and quiet of a cloister" (5). The dichotomy between the secular and religious spheres seems clear enough, but the narrator offers a more complex and ambivalent view on the roles for women in both: "I could wish for the prevention of abundance of mischiefs and miseries that nunneries and marriages were not to be entered into 'till the maid so destined were of a mature age to make her own choice" (5). The narrator cites the young age and immaturity of women who make decisions to marry, either to Christ or a mortal husband, to focus on the troubles that plague both sets of vows when women have only limited options in life. Although the immaturity of the novella's protagonist, Isabella Vallary of Iper, leads readers to sympathize with her plight in the convent, as she ages and gains experience, it becomes more difficult to lay the blame on her upbringing. Yet this is the rationale the novella offers. The narrator's own inability to stay in a convent allows her to express sympathy for Isabella's dilemma, which once again calls into question if readers are supposed to take her moral exhortations as realistic guidelines by which to live or ignore them.

In contrast to a shrewd Catalina who portrays herself as being able to play the system, Behn engenders a character who the narrator implies has been played by the system. In fact, her Isabella, as Frances E. Dolan argues, "suggests that women are strangers to their own desire and never fully understand their own motives, needs, or longings because their enclosure and their vows suppress rather than develop self-awareness" (522). Such stunted development occurs despite the best efforts of characters such as Isabella's aunt, the Lady Abbess, and her father, who decides to become a Jesuit after his wife's death, when they allow Isabella to "come out" and present herself to the extraconventual world at the age of thirteen. Isabella is hounded by a "thousand persons fighting for love of her" not solely because of her exceptional looks but also "her wit" (7). Behn imbues her female characters with beauty and brains. Yet, just as Dolan argues, the origins of Isabella's misfortunes can often find their origin in her conventual upbringing. In respect to her countless suitors, Isabella decides that "she had seen nothing in the world that was worth her care or venturing the losing of Heaven for, and therefore was resolved to dedicate herself to that" (8). Isabella's age, though nearing the norm for betrothal during seventeenth-century Europe, is a detrimental factor when early modern Protestant readers decide whether she can make such a decision with clarity.

Isabella's father is portrayed as protective and respectful; he uses "all the arguments he could to make her take good heed of what she went about, to consider it well" (8). His sensible approach is to be lauded, but not without criticism. After all, he is the one who placed her in the convent at the age of two. Readers can easily surmise that her biases would have developed in favor of conventual life after eleven years of living in the community. Although the father's persuasive influence is nebulous, that of the nuns in the convent is concrete: "all the fair sisterhood contributed their cunning" (8). The determination with which they try to make Isabella a permanent member of their convent paints the nuns as religious versions of manipulative women. The Lady Abbess, who epitomizes the overbearing woman, is described as using "all her arts and stratagems to make [Isabella] become a nun" within the same line in which readers learn that she is "very loath to part with [Isabella's] considerable fortune" (6). The aunt's avaricious desires buttress Protestant criticism of the Catholic Church's vast wealth. The nuns' scheming underscores the artifice of their devotion to an honest living, one that sounds more like the noxiousness of the extraconventual world that the narrator laments. And so Isabella opts for what her father describes as "severe life, watchings, midnight risings in all weathers and seasons to prayers, hard lodging, coarse diet, and homely habit, with a thousand other things of labor and work used among the nuns" (8). Behn's litany reminds readers of the austere lifestyle nuns are expected to embody. Although the narrator rejects embracing such hardships, at least there is an implied modicum of respect that women enjoy when they make decisions to accept them.

After Isabella decides to become a nun, the narrative picks up its temporal pace as Villenoys woos Isabella. Villenoys's opinion on Isabella's decision is clear when he describes the taking of her vows as a "fatal ceremony" (8). The love-struck Villenoys cannot leave the town until the ceremony occurs and he has no chance of marrying her. Due to Behn's erratic syntax and long-winded sentences, readers are unsure whether Isabella tells Villenoys that she likes him "the best" or if she simply confesses it to herself (9). The sentence structure is frustratingly unclear. Nonetheless, there has been interaction between the two, and so hope springs eternal in Villenoys—who soon falls ill due to the "cruel" actions of the "fair young victoress" (8). Like Duke Vincentio blackmailing Isabella in Shakespeare's *Measure for Measure*, Villenoys's family pleads with Isabella to forego becoming a nun so that she might better please Heaven in curing Villenoy of the "thousand tortures" he endures because of her rejection (8). Isabella cries but does not relent. Like one of the taunting nuns in Zayas's frame narrative, Isabella communicates with the family, perhaps inspiring hope in them all, rather than closing herself off and making her intentions clear. Behn plays up the Catholic exoticism and doubt about the sincerity of Catholics' professions of faith when she describes Isabella's feelings of guilt: "she would put a severe penance on her body for the mischiefs her eyes had done him . . . she believed it a crime that ought to be checked by a virtue, such as she pretended to profess, and hoped she should ever carry to her grave" (10). This line creates an image of a stereotypical nun who engages in self-flagellation at the same time that it fuels fears and dislike for Catholics who—from a hostile Protestant perspective—are prone to lewd behavior and secrecy thereof.

As readers have seen so far, Behn's portrayal of Isabella, although riddled with caricature-like qualities, also contains enough respect for and criticism of conventual life to characterize Isabella as a realistic representative of a young nun. Just as Sor Juana Inés de la Cruz welcomed visitors in her locutory, so we see Isabella and her close friend, Sister Katterina, speak with the latter's brother, Henault. This accurate representation of the cloister's permeable walls underscores the erotic potential inherent when men visit nuns – even if such contact is through cells or bars.[7] Soon enough Isabella falls in love with Henault. She describes love as a "cruel disease" for which she seeks "a cure" (13). Irrational, gullible, and naïve are adjectives apt enough to describe a character such as Isabella who thus far, despite early descriptions of her wit and acumen, is seen as boy-crazy. Katterina's own naïveté doesn't help when she warns her friend that "some people die of the disease" (14), explaining to Isabella that she was forced into the convent after her love interest lost one of her letters and her family discovered their relationship. The narrative takes off from there in a fashion expected from the novella's title. The more Isabella attempts to conceal her "flame," the more "violently" it rages (15). Behn, not one known for subtlety in terms of plot devices, utilizes the convent as the ultimate site of forbidden love. As a literary foremother for authors of twentieth- and twenty-first-century romance novels, Behn expertly creates a nun with whom readers can sympathize. Behn's Isabella may not be as innocent as Shakespeare's

---

[7] Behn does not name the order to which this convent of nuns belongs. Such ambiguity simultaneously renders all convents ands nuns as interchangeable and allows for more artistic freedom on Behn's part. Were Behn to place Isabella in a convent of Poor Clares like her Shakespearean predecessor, she would have had to consider the strictures Saint Clare established for nuns in their communication with the extraconventual world. Saint Clare's Rule 4 on Speaking explains, "4. It is not lawful for the Sisters to speak at the Speak-house, or at the Grate without license of the Abbesse, or of the Vicaresse: and those that have leave to speake at the Speake-house, must not speake, but in the presence of two Sisters, who must hear the things spoken there" (Da Silva 25).

Isabella, who desires no one but God, but she is unaware as to how far she is about to fall.

If we compare Henault to the scheming Duke Vincentio in *Measure for Measure* or the duplicitous Prince in Margaret Cavendish's *The Convent of Pleasure*, he comes across as a far better lover than these two men. Lovesickness may cloud his vision in his overeager quest to win Isabella, but it should not excuse some of the rhetoric he employs when strategizing to win the woman who has rejected him. When speaking with Katterina, Henault asserts that "naturally (my dear sister) maids are curious and vain; and however divine the mind of the fair Isabella may be, it bears the tincture still of mortal woman" (17). In this example Henault is mimicking patriarchal discourse about a woman's innate identity. Martin Luther's 1524 letter to nuns comes easily to mind with respect to an argument like Henault's: "Though womenfolk are ashamed to admit to this, nevertheless Scripture and experience show that among many thousands there is not a one to whom God has given to remain in pure chastity. A woman has no control over herself. God has made her body to be with man, to bear children and to raise them" (141). Although Henault does not give Isabella this counsel, soon after his remarks Behn has Isabella resort to a "woman's skill" as she practices the "art" of "cunning" (17). Isabella's innocence does not prevent her from possessing and exercising feminine wiles as she devises a way to make their relationship possible without seeming to be the aggressor or culpable for the breaking of her vows.

Ironically enough, Katterina and Henault's relationship echoes that of Shakespeare's Isabella and Claudio when Katterina refuses to indulge her brother's passions any longer. Henault's cry of "And is this all, my sister, you will do to save a brother?" is rejected by Katterina with "I would not be the occasion of making a nun violate her vow to save a brother's life, no, nor my own" (19). In *Measure for Measure*, Claudio argues with his sister that "What sin you do to save a brother's life, / Nature dispenses with the deed so far / That it becomes a virtue" (3.1.136-38), to which she replies "O, fie, fie, fie! / Thy sin's not accidental, but a trade. / Mercy to thee would prove itself a bawd" (3.1.150-52). Behn's Isabella is not as rigid or strong-willed as either her Shakespearean namesake or Katterina. Such a shift from one Isabella to the other highlights changing conceptions about nuns as the seventeenth century progressed. Behn does not offer her nun as an unimpeachable representative of women religious despite the Catholic sympathies she was thought to have because of her close relationship with many Catholics such as the potential heir to King Charles

II's throne, the Duke of York, to whom she dedicated the second part of *The Rover*.[8]

Behn's penchant for unconventional portrayals of religious figures can be aligned with her affinity with the popular libertinism of the English Restoration. This cultural revival of Hedonism offered a stark contrast to the Puritan culture that preceded the House of Stuart's return to the throne. Libertinism elevated the importance of the physical senses in acquiring knowledge and understanding truths over more abstract and philosophical ideas that were incorporal. The pleasures of the body were the nexus of libertine ideology, nowhere better expressed than in the work of John Wilmot, the Earl of Rochester. Behn's appreciation for libertine culture injected a feminist strain into the male-dominated discourse about sexual liberties.[9] Ros Ballaster goes so far as to describe Behn as a "disciple of this libertine aesthetic" (172). Unlike Cavendish, who describes the potential for same-sex erotic expression in the convent, or Zayas, whose nuns are aware of and proud of their ability to sexually taunt men, Behn does not have Isabella engage in sexual relations inside the convent. The cloister is a metonymy for patriarchal control – or at least one version of it. After all, once Isabella escapes and is widowed, the motivating factor in her decision to remarry is money. In the case of *The History of the Nun*, neither a religious profession nor a marital union can allow women to be autonomous in their desires. The third option of a convent yearned for by some Protestant women is rejected by Isabella, and, although this dismissal can be superficially listed as a reason for her demise, Behn's overall framework for the novel undercuts this possibility.

Susan Staves's study of Behn's work notes that the churches in her fiction were usually Roman Catholic and typically seen as "places where men and women discover their loves and make assignations" rather than as "places of devotion" (12). Staves argues that Behn showcased her wit and cleverness in the blasphemy of such scenarios. I agree with Staves and see that while Behn could be compared to Cavendish and Zayas, who knowingly employ the convent as a transgressive site of sexual desires and

---

[8] Ros Ballaster charts Behn's writing career and observes that Behn turned her attention to fiction writing as her playwriting efforts were challenged by an economic downturn in London theaters as well as the political and ideological upheaval in the late 1670s and 1680s, most notable of which was the alleged Popish plot to assassinate King Charles II so that Catholic York could ascend to the throne.

[9] Behn's poem "The Golden Age" contains some of the best examples of her artistic expression of Libertine values.

female autonomy for reasons both poignant and puerile, Behn undercuts the narrator's moral pleas by focusing keenly on the trials and tribulations of a nun who is encloistered despite her desires – whether they be conscious or not – so as to highlight the scandalous nature of such a plot.

In fact, once Isabella decides that suppressing her feelings for Henault would be tantamount to "resisting even Divine Providence," she quickly falls down a slippery slope of moral relativism wherein she identifies not as an "angel" but as a "human" in a realm where "that sin might be as soon forgiven as another" (24). The narrator does not comment on such rationalization, but her earlier arguments about the gravity of breaking a sacred vow may lead readers to see her as casting this decision in a negative light. However, the rigid didacticism of the novella's opening chapter is absent at this point as the narrator offers us a glimpse into Isabella's mind teeming with ideas about living "to repent" and choosing the "least" of "two evils" (24).

Once Isabella has escaped the convent, the novella's pace quickens. Like Cavendish's Lady Happy, Isabella has inherited money from a deceased parent. Unlike Lady Happy who uses her wealth to start a convent of pleasure, Isabella rejects any trappings of the community in which she lived and funds her and Henault's countryside home. Isabella suffers a miscarriage when Henault informs her that he is joining the military to regain his father's approval. She considers entering a monastery while awaiting his return. However, growing "pale" with the memory of a convent that interfered with their relationship, he refuses to leave until she makes a "vow" to never "go again within the walls of a religious house" (29). To make matters even more salacious, Behn has Henault meet Villenoys as the two become friends. However, Henault soon dies while battling Turkish adversaries. When her aunt dies, the widowed Isabella is bereft of financial support yet rejects the possibility of entering a convent "because her heart deceived her once and she durst not trust it again" (32). Neither the narrator nor Isabella explicitly trace the former nun's woes down a chronological track starting with her time at the convent, but the damage that it has done on her psyche and heart is sufficiently documented through subtext and the narrator's opening statements. Curses befall Isabella for having broken her vow, and the readers are prodded to recognize her inexperience about the expectations of a chaste life versus the realities of women's innate desires.

If readers remember the narrator's early criticism of both sacred and matrimonial vows, then they can understand her tone when she explains that Isabella "was forced to submit herself to be a second time a wife" when she marries Villenoys (32). Although Behn may not embrace the option of being a nun as ideal or even as a safe alternative to the marriage market, she still sees it as possessing a capitalist framework. Her proto-Marxist critique is clear when she says Isabella entertains Villenoys's courtship "for interest" (32). The double-valence of interest, denoting both a personal and financial stake that someone has in something or someone, showcases Isabella's dire straits. If she continues to reject the convent, then she must come up with some form of economic sustenance with which to support herself. Unlike so many women who took all their savings into the convent, Isabella decides to invest in Villenoys, a former flame, to continue chasing her desires in the extraconventual world. This investment will pay poor dividends – neither children nor happiness – which meshes well with Staves's observation that Behn "denounces marriage for money as virtual prostitution" (16). If this novella still possesses any of the moralistic tone it does in the opening pages, then the misfortunes that will quickly befall Isabella can be traced to her rejection of the convent.

While Villenoy is away, Henault returns. Alive and well, Henault's presence has turned Isabella into an inadvertent bigamist. Panicked, Isabella reverts to moral relativism as she "resolves upon the murder of Henault . . . believing the murder the least evil, since she could live with him" (37). The steepness of her slide is apparent when she smothers Henault and then lies to Villenoy by saying that Henault died of grief when he learned that she had remarried. Isabella then asks Villenoys to get rid of the body by throwing a sack that contains Henault's body into the river. She sews "the sacks with several strong stitches to the collar of Villenoy's coat," which causes him to plummet into the river along with Henault's body (39). The men are clueless, passive objects. Behn emphasizes this naïveté when the narrator explains that Villenoy "died without considering what was the occasion of his fate" (39). Isabella may be the active and intelligent heroine, but she is one marked for a swift downfall as a villain.

After nearly escaping punishment for her crimes, Isabella is condemned to death. The engrossing if not melodramatic conclusion comes with a final moral exhortation, but this time from Isabella rather than the narrator. While imprisoned, Isabella advises the youths who visit her "never to break a vow; for that was the first ruin of her, and she never since prospered" (42). She makes a half hour-long speech on the scaffold before she is beheaded, trying as hard as she can – even to the point of death – to serve as a warning to others. Isabella may be imprisoned and subject to public scrutiny as an example of a woman gone awry, but she is neither seen as a witch nor a social outcast. Behn allows Isabella to keep her wits throughout the novella, which enables her to circumvent the plight of so many mentally unstable women who came before and after her in literature. The cause-and-effect of Isabella's demise is nowhere more clear. Given the opening pages' rigid view of the consequences for breakings one's vow, one would understand an interpretation of the novella as a cautionary tale about breaking promises to God. However, through the narrator's complex, and sometimes confusing psychological sketch of Isabella, readers are prodded to consider the taking of sacred vows as the more questionable decision.

Is this novella an attack on nuns who break their vows or a polemic against the very nature of nuns? Behn structures the tale so as to prompt readers to observe Isabella as she wrestles with balancing her desires and her vows. As the former wins over the latter, the reader witnesses Isabella's moral, spiritual, and physical decline. However, her undoing begins at an early age, and, so, even if Isabella makes Luther and other Protestants happy when she renounces the convent for a life of marriage and child-rearing, she cannot escape her misfortunes. Her tragic flaw is the warped psychological mindset she inherits from an enclosed life sheltered from the realities of secular relationships. The confinement Catalina de Erauso and Behn's Isabella experience in the convent is not concomitant with the joys that Shakespeare's Isabella, Cavendish's Lady Happy, Zayas's Beatrice, or Sor Juana Inés de la Cruz relished in a community of women religious.

Bibliography

Albers, Irene and Uta Felten. "Introducción." *Escenas de transgresión: María de Zayas en su contexto literario-cultural.* Eds. Irene Albers and Uta Felten. Madrid: IberoAmericana, 2009. Print.

Altaba-Artal, Dolors. *Aphra Behn's English Feminism: Wit and Satire.* Selinsgrove, PA: Susquehanna University Press, 1999. Print.

Alwain, Zainab. "Muslim Women's Contribution in Building Society." *Fiqh Council of North America.* n.d. Web. 11 July 2016.

Andreadis, Harriette. *Sappho in Early Modern England: Female Same-Sex Literary Erotics 1550-1714.* Chicago: University of Chicago Press, 2001. Print.

Arenal, Electa. "Sor Juana's Arch: Public Spectacle, Private Battle." *Crossing Boundaries: Attending to Early Modern Women.* Eds. Jane Donawerth and Adele Seeff. Newark, DE: University of Delaware Press, 2000. Print.

Arenal, Electa, and Stacey Schlau. *Untold Sisters: Hispanic Nuns in Their Own Works.* Albuquerque, NM: University of New Mexico Press, 1989. Print.

Armon, Shifra. *Picking Wedlock: Women and the Courtship Novel in Spain.* Lanham, MD: Rowman & Littlefield Publishers, Inc., 2002. Print.

Astell, Mary. *A Serious Proposal to The Ladies. Parts I and II.* Ed. Patricia Springborg. London: Pickering & Chatto, 1997. Print.

Augustine of Hippo, Saint. *De Bono Viduitatis. 414.* Trans. Rev. C.L. Cornish. *New Advent: The Fathers of the Church.* 2007. Web. 8 March 2009.

Auerbach, Nina. *Communities of Women: An Idea in Fiction.* Cambridge, MA: Harvard University Press, 1978. Print.

Atkinson, Clarissa W. "'Precious Balsam in a Fragile Glass": The Ideology of Virginity in the Late Middle Ages." *Journal of Family History.* 8.2 (Summer 1983): 131-43. Print.

Bailey, Derrick Sherwin. *Homosexuality and the Western Christian Tradition.* 1955. Hamden, CT: Archon Book/Shoe String Press, Inc., 1975. Print.

Baines, Barbara J. "Effacing Rape in Early Modern Representation." *English Literary History.* 65.1 (1998): 69-98. Print.

Ballaster, Ros. "'Pretences of State': Aphra Behn and the Female Plot." *Rereading Aphra Behn: History, Theory, and Criticism*. Ed. Heidi Hunter. Charlottesville, VA: University Press of Virginia, 1993. Print.

—. "Taking Liberties: Revisiting Behn's Libertinism." *Women's Writing*. 19:2 (2012): 165-76. Print.

Battigelli, Anna. *Margaret Cavendish and The Exiles of the Mind*. Lexington, KY: University Press of Kentucky, 1998. Print.

Behn, Aphra. "The History of the Nun; or, The Fair Vow-Breaker." *Popular Fiction by Women 1660-1730: An Anthology*. Ed. Paula R. Backshcheider and John J. Richetti. Oxford: Oxford University Press, 1996. Print.

Bennett, Alexandra G., ed. *Bell in Campo and The Sociable Companions*. Toronto, ON: Broadview Literary Texts, 2002. Print.

Bergmann, Emilie. "The Exclusion of the Feminine in the Cultural Discourse of the Golden Age: Juan Luis Vives and Fray Luis de León." *Religion, Body and Gender in Early Modern Spain*. Ed. Alain Saint-Saëns. San Francisco: Mellen Research University Press, 1991. Print.

Bevington, David. Introduction. *Friar Bacon and Friar Bungay*. By Robert Greene. Ed. David Bevington. *English Renaissance Drama: A Norton Anthology*. New York: W. W. Norton & Company, 2002. 129-33. Print.

Bokser, Julie A. "Sor Juana's Rhetoric of Silence." *Rhetoric Review*. 25.1 (2006): 5-21. Print.

Borris, Kenneth, ed. *Same-Sex Desire in the English Renaissance: A Sourcebook of Texts, 1470-1650*. New York, Routledge: 2004. Print.

Bossy, John. *The English Catholic Community: 1578-1850*. New York: Oxford University Press, 1976. Print.

Bowerbank, Sylvia and Sara Mendelson, eds. *Paper Bodies: A Margaret Cavendish Reader*. Toronto, ON: Broadview Literary Texts, 1999. Print.

Bowman, Jeffrey A. "Infamy and Proof in Medieval Spain." *Fama: The Politics of Talk and Reputation in Medieval Europe*. Eds. Thelma Fenster and Daniel Lorda Smail. Ithaca, NY: Cornell University Press, 2003. 95-117. Print.

Boxer, Marilyn J. and Jean H. Quataert, eds. *Connecting Spheres: Women in the Western World, 1500 to the Present*. 1st Edition. New York: Oxford University Press, 1987. Print.

Boyer, Patsy H. Introduction. *The Disenchantments of Love: A Translation of Desengaños Amorosos*. By María de Zayas y Sotomayor. Trans. H.

Patsy Boyer. Albany, NY: State University of New York Press, 1997. Print.

Bray, Alan. *Homosexuality in Renaissance England*. Viborg, Denmark: Gay Men's Press, 1982. Print.

Brown, Carolyn M. "*Measure for Measure*: Isabella's Beating Fantasies." *American Imago*. 43:1 (1986): 67-80. Print.

—. *Connecting Spheres: Women in the Western World, 1500 to the Present*. 2nd Edition. New York: Oxford University Press, 2000. Print.

Brown, Judith C. *Immodest Acts: The Life of a Lesbian Nun in Renaissance Italy*. New York: Oxford University Press, 1986. Print.

Brownlee, Marina S. *The Cultural Labyrinth of María de Zayas*. Philadelphia, PA: University of Pennsylvania Press, 2000. Print.

Byrne, Sister Mary of the Incarnation. *The Tradition of the Nun in Medieval England*. Washington, D.C.: Catholic University of America, 1932. Dissertation.

"Capitulo de una de las Cartas que diversas personsas enviaron desde Cartagena de las Indias a algunos amigos suyos a las ciudades de Sevilla y Cadiz." *Papeles varios políticos y genealógicos [Manuscrito]*. Printed by Sor Juan Serrano de Vargasen. Seville, Madrid. 1618. Print.

Casey, James. *Early Modern Spain: A Social History*. London: Routledge, 1999. Print.

Cavendish, Margaret. *The Convent of Pleasure and Other Plays*. Edited by Anne Shaver, Baltimore: John Hopkins University Press, 1999. Print.

—. *Natures Picture Drawn By Fancies Pencil To The Life*. 1656. 2nd Edition. London, 1671. Print.

—. *Orations of Divers Sorts Accommodated to Divers Places*. London, 1662. Ann Arbor: University Microfilms International. Catalog no. 1364:12.

—. *Playes*. London, 1662. Ann Arbor: University Microfilms International. Catalog no. 502:11.

—. *Plays, Never Before Printed*. London, 1668. Ann Arbor: University Microfilms International. Catalog no. 674:2.

—. *Sociable Letters*. 1664. Ed. James Fitzmaurice. New York: Garland Publishing, 1997. Print.

—. *The Worlds Olio*. London, 1655. Ann Arbor: University Microfilms International. Catalog no. 503:2.

Cervantes Saavedra, Miguel de. *Exemplary Stories*. 1613. Trans. C.A. Jones. London: Penguin Books, 1986. Print.

—. *Don Quixote*. 1605. Trans. Edith Grossman. New York: Harper Perennial, 2003. Print.

Chedgzoy, Kate. "'For *Virgin* Buildings Oft Brought Forth': Fantasies of Convent Sexuality." *Female Communities 1600-1800: Literary Visions and Cultural Realities.* Eds. Rebecca D'Monté and Nicole Pohl. Chippenham, England: Macmillan Press Ltd, 2000. Print.

Cho, Sung-Won. "Renaissance Nun Vs. Korean *Gisaeng*: Chastity and Female Celibacy in *Measure for Measure* and 'Chung-Hyang Jeon.'" *Comparative Literature Studies.* 41.4 (2004): 565-83. Print.

Cifuentes-Aldunate, Claudio. "El aspecto *kinky* del entretenimiento honesto en María de Zayas." *Escenas de transgresión: María de Zayas en su contexto literario-cultural.* Eds. Irene Albers and Uta Felten. Madrid: IberoAmericana, 2009. Print.

Clark, Ira. *Rhetorical Readings, Dark Comedies, and Shakespeare's Problem Plays.* Gainesville, FL: University Press of Florida, 2007. Print.

Clark, Sandra. *Renaissance Drama.* Cambridge: Polity Press, 2007. Print.

Cowans, Jon. *Early Modern Spain: A Documentary History.* Philadelphia, University of Pennsylvania Press, 2003. Print.

Crawford, Julie. "Fletcher's The Tragedie of Bonduca and the Anxieties of the Masculine Government of James I." *SEL: Studies in English Literature 1500-1900.* 39.2 (1999): 357-81. Print.

Cruz, Anne J. "María de Zayas and Miguel de Cervantes: A Deceitful Marriage." *Studies in Memory of Carroll B. Johnson.* Ed. Sherry Velasco. Newark, DE: Juan de la Cuesta Monographs, 2008: 89-106. Print.

Daichman, Graciela S. *Wayward Nuns in Medieval Literature.* Syracuse, NY: Syracuse University Press, 1986. Print.

Daly, Mary. *The Church and The Second Sex.* New York: Harper & Row, 1968. Print.

D'Assumpção, Lino. *Frades e Freiras: Chroniquetas Monasticas.* Lisboa: Companhia Nacional Editora, 1893. Print.

Da Silva, Marcos. *Primeira parte das chronicas da ordem dos Frades Menores. The life of the glorious virgin S. Clare. Together with the conversion, and life of S. Agnes her sister, and of another S. Agnes, daughter to the King of Bohemia. Also the Rule of S. Clare. And the life of S. Catharine of Bologna. Translated into English. Marcos da SILVA, Bishop of Oporto.* S. Omer: English College Press, 1622. Print.

Davidson, Peter. "Recusant Catholic Spaces in Early Modern England." *Catholic Culture in Early Modern England.* Eds. Ronald Corthell, Frances E. Dolan, Christopher Highley and Arthur F. Marotti. Notre Dame, IN: University of Notre Dame Press, 2007. 19-51. Print.

Defourneaux, Marcelin. *Daily Life in Spain in the Golden Age.* Stanford, CA: Stanford University Press, 1970. Print.

Desens, Marliss C. *The Bed-Trick in English Renaissance Drama: Explorations in Gender, Sexuality, and Power.* Newark, DE: University of Delaware Press, 2004. Print.

D'Monté, Rebecca. "Mirroring Female Power: Separatist Spaces in the Plays of Margaret Cavendish, Duchess of Newcastle." *Female Communities 1600-1800: Literary Visions and Cultural Realities.* Eds. Rebecca D'Monté and Nicole Pohl. Chippenham, England: Macmillan Press Ltd, 2000. Print.

Dogget, Nicholas. *Patterns of Re-use: The Transformation of Former Monastic Buildings in Post-Dissolution Hertfordshire, 1540-1600.* Oxford: Archaeopress, 2002. Print.

Dolan, Frances E. *Whores of Babylon: Catholicism, Gender, and Seventeenth-Century Print Culture.* Ithaca, NY: Cornell University Press, 1999. Print.

Dolan, Frances E. "Why Are Nuns Funny?" *Huntingdon Library Quarterly.* 70.4 (2007): 509-35. Print.

Dopico-Black, Georgina. *Perfect Wives, Other Women: Adultery and Inquisition in Early Modern Spain.* Durham: Duke University Press, 2001. Print.

Du Molin, Peter. *The Ruine of Papacy: Or, A Clear Display of the Simony of the Romish Clergy.* London: Robert Harford, Angel in Cornhill, 1678. Print.

Echenberg, Margo. "Self-Fashioning through Self-Portraiture in Sor Juana Inés de la Cruz." *Feminist Interventions in Early American Studies.* Ed. Mary C. Carruth. Tuscaloosa, AL: University of Alabama Press, 2006. Print.

Edelman, Lee. *No Future: Queer Theory and the Death Drive.* Durham, NC: Duke University Press, 2004. Print.

Elliot, John H. *Empires of the Atlantic World: Britain and Spain in America, 1492-1830.* New Haven: Yale University Press, 2006. Print.

Ennes, Antonio. *As Ultimas Freiras, Com Uma Carta.* Porto: Livraria Portuense de Lopes & C. Editores, 1894. Print.

Erauso, Catalina de. *Lieutenant Nun: Memoir of a Basque Transvestite in the New World.* Eds. Michele Stepto and Gabri Stepto. Boston: Beacon Press, 1996.

Erler, Mary C. *Reading and Writing During the Dissolution: Monks, Friars, and Nuns 1530-1558.* Cambridge: Cambridge University Press, 2013. Print.

Ferrer, Joaquín María, ed. *Historia de la Monja Alférez, Doña Catalina de Erasuo*. Paris: Imprenta de Julio Didot, 1829. Print.

Fish, Simon. *A Supplication for the Beggars*. 1529. Southgate, London. 1878. Print.

Folger, Robert. *Writing as Poaching: Interpellation and Self-Fashioning in Colonial relaciones de méritos y servicios*. Leiden, Netherlands: Brill Publishing, 2011. Print.

Forell, George W. "Luther and the War Against the Turks." *Church History*. 14.4 (1945): 256- 71. Print.

Forker, Charles R. "Masculine love,' Renaissance Writing, and The 'New Invention' of Homosexuality: An Addendum." *Journal of Homosexuality*. 31.3 (1996): 85-93. Print.

Friedman, Michael D. "'O, let him marry her!': Matrimony and Recompense in *Measure for Measure*." *Shakespeare Quarterly*. 46.4 (1995): 454-64. Print.

Froide, Amy M. "The Religious Lives of Singlewomen in the Anglo-Atlantic World: Quaker Missionaries, Protestant Nuns, and Covert Catholics." In *Women, Religion, and the Atlantic World (1600–1800)*. Ed. Daniella Kostroun and Lisa Vollendorf. Toronto: University of Toronto Press, 2009: 60–78. Print.

García, Susan Paun De. "Zayas as Writer: Hell Hath No Fury." *María de Zayas: The Dynamics of Discourse*. Eds. Amy R. Williamsen and Judith A. Whitenack. Madison, NJ: Fairleigh Dickinson University Press, 1995. 40-51. Print.

Gee, Henry and William John Hardy, eds. *Documents Illustrative of English Church History*. New York: Macmillan, 1896. Print.

Gibson, Joan. "The Logic of Chastity: Women, Sex, and the History of Philosophy in the Early Modern Period." *Hypatia*. 21.4 (Fall 2006): 1-19. Print.

Gorfkle, Laura J. "Reconstituting the Feminine: Travesty and Masquerade in María de Zayas's 'Amar sólo para vencer.'" *María de Zayas: The Dynamics of Discourse*. Eds. Amy R. Williamsen and Judith A. Whitenack. Madison, NJ: Fairleigh Dickinson University Press, 1995. 75-89. Print.

Goodstein, Laurie. "American Nuns Vow To Fight Vatican Criticism." *The New York Times*. 1 June 2012. 1A. Print.

—. "U.S. Nuns facing Vatican Scrutiny." *The New York Times*. 2 July 2009. 1A. Print.

Greer, Margaret R. "The M(Other] Plot: Psychoanalytic Theory and Narrative Structure in María de Zayas." *María de Zayas: The Dynamics of Discourse*. Eds. Amy R. Williamsen and Judith A.

Whitenack. Madison, NJ: Fairleigh Dickinson University Press, 1995. 90-116. Print.

Gregorian, Dareh. "Art 'Cheat': Nunsense." *The New York Post*. 20 Feb. 2009. Web. 7 Sept. 2009.

Gross, Jane. "Months to Live: Sisters Face Death With Dignity and Reverence." *The New York Times*. 8 July 2009. A1. Print.

Groves, Beatrice. *Texts and Traditions: Religion in Shakespeare 1592-1604*. Oxford: Clarendon Press, 2007. Print.

Gubar, Susan. "'The Blank Page' and the Issues of Female Creativity." *Writing and Sexual Difference*. Ed. Elizabeth Abel. Chicago: University of Chicago Press, 1982. Print.

Haigh, Christopher. *English Reformations: Religion, Politics, and Society under the Tudors*. Oxford: Clarendon Press, 1993. Print.

Hampton-Reeves, Stuart. *Measure for Measure: A Guide to the Text and Its Theatrical Life*. New York: Palgrave MacMillan, 2007. Print.

Halberstam, Judith. *In a Queer Time and Place: Transgender Bodies, Subcultural Lives*. New York: New York University Press, 2005. Print.

Hibbard, Caroline. "A Cosmopolitan Court in a Confessional Age: Henrietta Maria Revisited." *Catholic Culture in Early Modern England*. Eds. Ronald Corthell, Frances E. Dolan, Christopher Highley and Arthur F. Marotti. Notre Dame, IN: University of Notre Dame Press, 2007. 117-34. Print.

Hibbert, Francis Aidan. *The Dissolution of the Monasteries as Illustrated by the Suppression of the Religious Houses of Staffordshire*. London: Sir Isaac Pitman & Sons, Ltd. 1910. Print.

Holmes, Michael Morgan and Jessica Slights. "Isabella's Order: Religious Acts and Personal Desire in *Measure for Measure*." *Studies in Philology*. 95.3 (1998): 263-91. Print.

Homan, Sidney. *When the Theater Turns to Itself: The Aesthetic Metaphor in Shakespeare*. Lewisburg, PA: Bucknell University Press, 1981. Print.

Homem, Eduardo. *The English College: Convento dos Inglesinhos*. Lisboa: Chamartín Imobiliária, 2007. Print.

hooks, bell. *Feminism is For Everybody: Passionate Politics*. Cambridge, MA: South End Press, 2000. Print.

Hull, Suzanne W. *Chaste, Silent & Obedient: English Books for Women 1475-1640*. San Marino, CA: Huntington Library, 1982. Print.

Ibsen, Kristine. *Women's Spiritual Autobiography in Colonial Spanish America*. Gainesville, FL: University Press of Florida, 1999. Print.

Ife, B.W. and Trudi L. Darby. "Remorse, Retribution and Redemption in *La fuerza de sangre*: Spanish and English Perspectives." *A Companion to Cervantes's Novelas Ejemplares*. Ed. Stephen Boyd. Woodbridge, Suffolk, UK: Tamesis, Boydell & Brewer Ltd. 2005. Print.

James I, King. *Letters of King James VI & I*. Ed. G.P.V. Akrigg. Berkeley, CA: University of California Press, 1984. Print.

Jankowski, Theodora A. *Pure Resistance: Queer Virginity in Early Modern English Drama*. Philadelphia: University of Pennsylvania Press, 2000. Print.

Johnson, Julie Greer. "Engendered Theatrical Space and the Colonial Woman in Sor Juana's *Los empeños de una casa*." *CiberLetras*. 5 (August 2001). Web. 7 August 2009.

Jonson, Ben. *Volpone*. *English Renaissance Drama: A Norton Anthology*. Ed. David Bevington. New York: W.W. Norton & Company, 2002. 673-773. Print.

Juana Inés de la Cruz, Sor. "Décima 115." *Obras Completas De Sor Juana Inés de la Cruz: Lírica Personal*." Ed. Alfonso Méndez Plancarte. Mexico City: Fondo de Cultura Economica, 1951. Print.

—. "En perseguirme, Mundo." *Poems, Protest, and a Dream*. Trans. Margaret Sayers Peden. New York: Penguin, 1997. 170. Print.

—. "Hombres necios." *Poems, Protest, and a Dream*. Trans. Margaret Sayers Peden. New York: Penguin, 1997. 148-51. Print.

—. "La Respuesta." *Poems, Protest, and a Dream*. Trans. Margaret Sayers Peden. New York: Penguin, 1997. 1-75. Print.

—. "Que dan el Colirio merecido a un Soberbio." Trans. Margaret Sayers Peden. New York: Penguin, 1997. 156-57. Print.

—. "Respondiendo a un Caballero del Perú, que le envoi unos Barros diciéndole que se volviese hombre." *Poems, Protest, and a Dream*. Trans. Margaret Sayers Peden. New York: Penguin, 1997. 136-43. Print.

—. *Los empeños de una casa (House of Desires)*. Trans. Catherine Boyle. London: Oberon Books, 2004. Print.

Kirk, Pamela. *Sor Juana Inés de la Cruz: Religion, Art, and Feminism*. New York: Continuum, 1998. Print.

Kirk, Stephanie. *Convent Life in Colonial Mexico: A Tale of Two Communities*. Gainesville, FL: University Press of Florida, 2007. Print.

Knowles, James. "Richard Flecknoe c.1605-c.1677" *Royalist Refugees: William and Margaret Cavendish in the Rubens House: 1648-1660*. Eds. Ben Van Beneden and Nora De Poorter. Antwerp: Rubenshuis & Rubenianum, 2006. Print.

Kraman, Cynthia. "Communities of Otherness in Chaucer's Merchant's Tale." *Medieval Women in their Communities*. Ed. Diane Watt. Toronto: University of Toronto Press, 1997. 138-54. Print.

Kristeva, Julia. *Tales of Love.* New York: Columbia University Press, 1987. Print.
Kuhns, Elizabeth. *The Habit: A History of the Clothing of Nuns.* New York: Doubleday, 2003. Print.
Lalanda, Maria Margarida. *Vida religiosa e trabalho: Freiras de clausura nos Açores no século XVII.* Ponta Delgada, Portugal: n.p., 2008.
Leggatt, Alexander. "Substitution in *Measure for Measure.*" *Shakespeare Quarterly.* 39.3 (Autumn 1988): 342-59. Print.
Lehfeldt, Elizabeth A. *The Permeable Cloister: Religious Women in Golden Age Spain.* Hampshire, England: Ashgate Publishing, 2005. Print.
—. "Ideal Men: Masculinity and Decline in Seventeenth-Century Spain." *Renaissance Quarterly.* 61.2 (Summer 2008): 463-94. Print.
Lilly, Kate. "Blazing Worlds: Seventeenth-Century Women's Utopian Writings." *Women, Text and Histories 1575-1610.* Ed. by Clare Brant and Diane Purkiss. London: Routledge, 1992. 102-33. Print.
Luciani, Frederick. *Literary Self-Fashioning in Sor Juana Inés de la Cruz.* Lewisburg, PA: Bucknell University Press, 2004. Print.
Luis de León, Fray. *Obras del M. FR. Luis de León.* Transcribed by Antolin Merino. Madrid: Hija de Ibarra, 1805. Print.
Luther, Martin. *Luther on Women: A Sourcebook.* Trans. and Eds. Susan C. Karant-Nunn and Merry E. Wiesner-Hanks. Cambridge: Cambridge University Press, 2003. Print.
Magedanz, Stacy. "Public Justice and Private Mercy in *Measure for Measure.*" *SEL: Studies in English Literature 1500-1900.* 44.2 (2004): 317-32. Print.
Makowski, Elizabeth. *Canon Law and Cloistered Women: Periculoso and Its Commentators, 1298-1545.* Washington, D.C.: Catholic University of America Press, 1997. Print.
Margonelli, Lisa. "Tapped Out." *The New York Times.* 15 June 2008. BR 1. Print.
Marks, Peter. "Shakespeare Theatre's Latest Play Doesn't 'Measure' Up to Its Prologue." *The Washington Post.* 24 Sep. 2013. Web. 2 August 2016.
McNamara, Jo Ann Kay. *Sisters in Arms: Catholic Nuns through Two Millennia.* Cambridge, Massachusetts: Harvard University Press, 1996. Print.
McKanna, Mary Lawrence Sister. *Women of the Church: Role and Renewal.* New York: P.J. Kennedy & Sons, 1967. Print.
Mendelson, Sara. "Playing Games with Gender and Genre: The Dramatic Self-Fashioning of Margaret Cavendish." In *Authorial Conquests:*

Essays on Genre in the Writings of Margaret Cavendish, edited by Line Cottegnies and Nancy Weitz. Madison: Fairleigh Dickinson University Press, 2003. Print.

Merrim, Stephanie. *Early Modern Women's Writing and Sor Juana Inés de la Cruz*. Nashville, TN: Vanderbilt University Press, 1999. Print.

—. "Toward a Feminist Reading of Sor Juana Inés de la Cruz: Past, Present, and Future Directions in Sor Juana Criticism." *Feminist Perspective on Sor Juana Inés de la Cruz*. Ed. Stephanie Merrim. Detroit, MI: Wayne State University Press, 1991. Print.

Middleton, Thomas and Thomas Dekker. *The Roaring Girl. English Renaissance Drama: A Norton Anthology*. Ed. David Bevington. New York: Norton, 2002. Print.

Mourão, Manuela. *Altered Habits: Reconsidering the Nun in Fiction*. Gainesville, FL: University Press of Florida, 2002. Print.

Mutschmann, Heinrich and Karl Wentersdorf. *Shakespeare and Catholicism*. New York: Sheed and Ward, 1952. Print.

Newton, William. *London in the Olden Time. Being a topographical and historical memoir of London, Westminster and Southwark, accompanying a pictorial map of the city and suburbs, as they existed in the reign of Henry VIII., before the dissolution of monasteries. Compiled from ancient documents and other authentic sources by W. Newton*. London: Bell & Daldy, 1855. Print.

O'Brien, Eavan. *Women in the Prose of María de Zayas*. Woodbridge, England: Tamesis Books, 2010. Print.

O'Hara, Edwin. "Poor Clares." *The Catholic Encyclopedia*. Vol. 12. New York: Robert Appleton Company, 1911. Web. 15 Aug. 2008.

Oliger, Livarius. "Friar." *The Catholic Encyclopedia*. Volume 4. 1909. New York: Robert Appleton Company. Web. 9 March 2008.

Paz, Octavio. *Sor Juana or, The Traps of Faith*. Trans. Margaret Sayers Peden. Cambridge, MA: Harvard University Press, 1988. Print.

Peacock, Judith. "Writing for the Brain and Writing for the Boards: the Producibility of Margaret Cavendish's Dramatic Texts." *A Princely Brave Woman: Essays on Margaret Cavendish, Duchess of Newcastle*. Ed. Stephen Clucas. Bodmin, Cornwall: Ashgate Publishing Company, 2003. Print.

Pearson, Jacqueline. "*History of* The History of the Nun." *Rereading Aphra Behn: History, Theory, and Criticism*. Ed. Heidi Hunter. Charlottesville, VA: University Press of Virginia, 1993. Print.

—. "The Short Fiction (excluding *Oroonoko*)." *The Cambridge Companion to Aphra Behn*. Ed. Derek Hughes and Janet Todd. Cambridge: University of Cambridge Press, 2004. Print.

Persons, Robert. *Relacion de un sacerdote ingles, escrita a Flandes, à un caballero de su tierra ... en la qual le da cuenta de la venida de su Magestad a Valladolid, y al Colegio de los Ingleses, y lo que alli se hizo en su recebimiento.* Trans. Tomas Eclesal. Madrid: Pedro Madrigal, 1592. Print.

Perry, Henry Ten Eyck. *The First Duchess of Newcastle and Her Husband as Figures in Literary History.* Boston: Ginn and Company, Publishers. 1918. Print.

Pineda-Madrid, Nancy. "On Mysticism, Latinas/os, and the Journey: A Reflection in Conversation with Mary Engel." *Journal of Feminist Studies in Religion.* 24.2 (Fall 2008): 178-83. Print.

"Pink Smoke Declares 'Priestly People Come In Both Sexes'." *National Catholic Reporter.* 29 April 2005. Print. 3.

Purkiss, Diane. "Material Girls: The Seventeenth-Century Woman Debate." *Women, Text and Histories 1575-1610.* Eds. Clare Brant and Diane Purkiss. London: Routledge, 1992. 96-101. Print.

Raber, Karen. *Dramatic Difference: Gender, Class, and Genre in the Early Modern Closet Drama.* Newark: University of Delaware Press, 2001. Print.

Raylor, Timothy. "Samuel Hartlib and the Commonwealth of Bees." *Culture and Cultivation in Early Modern England: Writing and the Land.* Eds. Michael Leslie and Timothy Raylor. Leicester: Leicester University Press, 1992. Print.

Rees, Emma L. E. *Margaret Cavendish: Gender, Genre, Exile.* Manchester: Manchester University Press, 2003. Print.

Richmond, Velma Bourgeois. *Shakespeare, Catholicism, and Romance.* New York: Continuum. 2000. Print.

Robbins, Jeremy *The Challenges of Uncertainty: An Introduction to Seventeenth-Century Spanish Literature.* Lanham, MD: Rowman & Littlefield Publishers, Inc., 1998. Print.

Rubio Merino, Pedro. *La Monja Alférez: Doña Catalina de Erauso [Texto impreso] : dos manuscritos inéditos de su autobiografía conservados en el Archivo de la Santa Iglesia Catedral de Sevilla.* Sevilla: Cabildo Metropolitano de la Catedral de Sevilla, 1995. Print.

Ruggiero, Guido. *Binding Passions: Tales of Magic, Marriage, and Power at the End of the Renaissance.* New York: Oxford University Press, 1993. Print.

Sabra, Adam. *Poverty and Charity in Medieval Islam: Mamluk Egypt, 1250-1517.* Cambridge: Cambridge University Press, 2006.

Saint Augustine. Trans. Henry Bettenson. *The City of God.* 1467. London: Penguin Books, 1984. Print.

—. Trans. Edward Bouverie Pusey. *The Confessions of Saint Augustine.* 4th Century. New York: E.P. Dutton & Co., 1900. Print.

Saint Jerome. *Commentariorum in Epistolam ad Ephesios* III, 5 in *PL* 26, col. 567.

Saint-Saëns, Alain. "A Case of Gendered Rejection: The Hermitess in Golden Age Spain." *Spanish Women in the Golden Age: Images and Realities.* Eds. Magdalena S. Sánchez and Alain Saint-Saëns. Westport, CT: Greenwood Press, 1996. Print.

Sánchez, Magdalena S. *The Empress, The Queen, and The Nun: Women and Power at the Court of Phillip III of Spain.* Baltimore: John Hopkins University Press, 1998. Print.

"Santo Domingo, San Sebastián." *Dominicos.* Orden de Predicadores, n.d. Web. 8 September 2012.

Schulenburg, Jane Tibbetts. "The Heroics of Virginity: Brides of Christ and Sacrificial Mutilation." *Women in the Middle Ages and the Renaissance: Literary and Historical Perspectives.* Ed. Mary Beth Rose. Syracuse, NY: Syracuse University Press, 1986. 29-72. Print.

Schmidhuber, Guillermo. *The Three Secular Plays of Sor Juana Inés de la Cruz: A Critical Study.* Trans. Shelby Thacker. Lexington, KY: University Press of Kentucky, 2000. Print.

Schons, Dorothy. "Some Obscure Points in the Life of Sor Juana." *Feminist Perspective on Sor Juana Inés de la Cruz.* Ed. Stephanie Merrim. Detroit, MI: Wayne State University Press, 1991. 38-60. Print.

Shakespeare, William. *Measure for Measure.* 1603. Eds. Ivo Kamps and Karen Raber. Boston: Bedford/St. Martin's, 2004. Print.

—. *Twelfth Night, Or, What You Will.* 1600. Ed. Bruce Smith. Boston: Bedford/St. Martin's, 2001. Print.

Shaw, Anthony N. "*The Compendium Compertorum* and the making of the Suppression Act of 1536." PhD thesis, University of Warwick. 2003. Web. 6 January 2016.

Las Siete Partidas. Volumes 1-5. Trans. Samuel Parsons Scott. Ed. Robert I. Burns, S.J. Philadelphia: University of Pennsylvania Press, 2001. Print.

Smith, Hilda L. "Margaret Cavendish, Duchess of Newcastle (1623-73)." *Women's Political & Social Thought.* Eds. Hilda L. Smith and Berenice A. Carroll. Bloomington, IN: Indiana University Press, 2000. Print.

Stavans, Ilan. Introduction. *Poems, Protest, and a Dream.* By Sor Juana Inés de la Cruz. Trans. Margaret Sayers Peden. New York: Penguin, 1997. Print.

Staves, Susan. "Behn, Women, and Society." *The Cambridge Companion to Aphra Behn*. Ed. Derek Hughes and Janet Todd. Cambridge: University of Cambridge Press, 2004. Print.

Stevenson, Jane. "Women Catholics and Latin Culture." *Catholic Culture in Early Modern England*. Eds. Ronald Corthell, Frances E. Dolan, Christopher Highley and Arthur F. Marotti. Notre Dame, IN: University of Notre Dame Press, 2007. 52-72. Print.

Surtz, Ronald E. *Writing Women in Late Medieval and Early Modern Spain: The Mothers of Saint Teresa of Avila*. Philadelphia: University of Pennsylvania Press, 1995. Print.

Taylor, Scott K. *Honor and Violence in Golden Age Spain*. New Haven, CT: Yale University Press, 2008. Print.

Terry, Arthur. *Seventeenth-Century Spanish Poetry: The Power of Artifice*. Cambridge: Cambridge University Press, 1993. Print.

Tomlinson, Sophie. "'My Brain the Stage': Margaret Cavendish and the Fantasy of Female Performance." *Women, Text and Histories 1757-1610*. Eds. Clare Brant and Diane Purkiss. London: Routledge, 1992. 134-63. Print.

Tovey, Barbara. "Wisdom and the Law: Thoughts on the Political Philosophy of *Measure for Measure*." *Shakespeare's Political Pageant: Essays in Literature and Politics*. Eds. Joseph Alulis and Vickie Sullivan. Lanham, MD: Rowan & Littlefield Publishers Lanham, 1996. Print.

"Traslado de Merced a Catalina de Erauso." *Registro de Reales Disposiciones de la Cámara de Indias, Nueva España Cámara, 1624 hasta 1629*. Archivo General de Indias. Indiferente, 451, L.A11, F.162V-164V. 1628-6-26. Manuscript.

Traub, Valerie. *The Renaissance of Lesbianism in Early Modern England*. Cambridge: Cambridge University Press, 2002. Print.

Tuttle, Leslie. "From Cloister to Court: Nuns and the Gendered Culture of Disputing in Early Modern France." *The Journal of Women's History*. 22.2 (Summer 2010): 11-33. Print.

"Two Groups of Nuns Call For End to Iraq War." *National Catholic Reporter*. 16 Sept. 2005. Print. 5.

Van Beneden, Ben and Nora De Poorter, eds. *Royalist Refugees: William and Margaret Cavendish in the Rubens House: 1648-1660*. Antwerp: Rubenshuis & Rubenianum, 2006. Print.

Velasco, Sherry M. "María de Zayas and Lesbian Desire in Early Modern Spain." *Reading and Writing the Ambiente: Queer Sexualities in Latino, Latin American, and Spanish Culture*. Eds. Susana Chávez-

Silverman and Librada Hernández. Madison, WI: University of Wisconsin Press, 2000. Print.

Vigil, Mariló. *La vida de las mujeres en los siglos XVI y XVII.* Madrid: Siglo Veintiuno Editores, 1986. Print.

Vives, Pío Fray. "Approbación del Maestro Fray Pío Vives, Prior de Santa Catalina Mártir, De Barcelona." *Desengaños amorosos: parte segunda del sarao y entretenimiento honesto.* Ed. Agustín G. De Amezúa y Mayo. Madrid: Real Academia Española Biblioteca Selecta de Clásicos Españoles, 1950. 5. Print.

Vollendorf, Lisa. *Reclaiming the Body: Maria de Zayas's Early Modern Feminism.* Chapel Hill, NC: University of North Carolina Press, 2001. Print.

—. "'No Doubt It Will Amaze You': Maria de Zayas's Early Modern Feminism." *Recovering Spain's Feminist Tradition.* Ed. Lisa Vollendorf. New York: Modern Language Association of America, 2001. Print.

Walker, Lenore E. "Who Are the Battered Women?" *Frontiers: A Journal of Women Studies.* 2.1 (Spring 1977): 52-57. Print.

Ward, Jennifer C. "English Noblewomen and the Local Community in the Later Middle Ages." *Medieval Women in Their Communities.* Ed. Diane Watt. Toronto: University of Toronto Press, 1997. 186-203. Print.

Waterworth, J., Ed. and Trans. *The Canons and Decrees of the Sacred and Oecumencial Council of Trent.* London: Dolman, 1848. Print.

Weaver, Elissa B. "The Convent Wall in Tuscan Convent Drama." *The Crannied Wall: Women, Religion, and the Arts in Early Modern Europe.* Ed. Craig A. Monson. Ann Arbor, MI: University of Michigan Press, 1992. Print.

Wheeler, Richard P. *Shakespeare's Development and the Problem Comedies: Turn and Counter- Turn.* Berkeley, CA: University of California Press, 1981. Print.

Whetstone, George. *Promos and Cassandra.* New York: AMS Press Inc., 1970. Print.

Whitaker, Katie. *Mad Madge: The Extraordinary Life of Margaret Cavendish, Duchess of Newcastle, the First Woman to Live by Her Pen.* New York: Basic Books, 2002. Print.

Wickham, Chris. "Fama *and the Law in Twelfth-Century Tuscany.*" *Fama: The Politics of Talk and Reputation in Medieval Europe.* Eds. Thelma Fenster and Daniel Lorda Smail. Ithaca, NY: Cornell University Press, 2003. 15-26. Print.

Williams, L. Susan. "Trying on Gender, Gender Regimes, and the Process of Becoming Women." *Gender & Society.* 16.1 (February 2002): 29-52. Print.

Williamson, Marilyn L. *Raising Their Voices: British Women Writers, 1650-1750.* Detroit, MI: Wayne State University Press, 1990. Print.

Wilson, Bee. *The Hive: The Story of the Honeybee and Us.* New York: Thomas Dunne Books/St. Martin's Press, 2006. Print.

Wiseman, Susan. *Drama and Politics in the English Civil War.* Cambridge: Cambridge University Press, 2000. Print.

Woodward, G.W.O. *The Dissolution of the Monasteries.* New York: Walker and Company, 1966. Print.

Woolf, Virginia. "A Room of One's Own." *Selected Works of Virginia Woolf.* London: Wordsworth Editions, 2005. 561-633. Print.

Wray, Grady C. "Sacred Allusions: Theology in Sor Juana's Works." *Approaches to Teaching the Works of Sor Juana Inés de la Cruz.* Eds. Emilie L. Bergmann and Stacey Schlau. New York: MLA, 2007. Print.

Zayas y Sotomayor, María de. *The Disenchantments of Love: A Translation of Desengaños Amorosos.* Trans. H. Patsy Boyer. Albany, NY: State University of New York Press, 1997. Print.

—. *Desengaños amorosos: parte segunda del sarao y entretenimiento honesto.* Ed. Agustín G. De Amezúa y Mayo. Madrid: Real Academia Española Biblioteca Selecta de Clásicos Españoles, 1950. Print.

—. *The Enchantments of Love: Amorous and Exemplary Novels.* Trans. H. Patsy Boyer. Berkeley, CA: University of California Press, 1990. Print.

INDEX

academias, 112, 113, 117, 172
Alfonso the Wise, King of Spain, 26, 120-121, 123, 178
Anglican Church, 18, 64
Behn, Aphra, 28, 187-188, 204-215
Boccaccio, Giovanni, 32, 109, 116, 144
Boniface VIII, Pope, 9, 10
Catalina de Erauso, 2, 28, 132, 187-208, 215
Cavendish, Margaret, 2, 8, 12, 23-27, 44, 69-110, 141, 149, 154, 162, 175, 200, 211-213, 215
Cervantes Saavedra, Miguel de, 109, 117, 119-120, 126, 129-130, 135
convents, 1, 2, 5-16, 22-28, 33-37, 40-61, 69-215
  locutories, 113, 158, 179, 210
Council of Trent, 9, 13, 21, 62, 139, 203
Disenchantments of Love, 2, 6, 26, 93, 109, 110-116, 125-135, 144, 147, 163
  Lisis, 26, 109, 110-120, 125-147, 163
dissolution of monasteries, 9, 13, 14-19, 89, 115, 141
Elizabeth I, Queen of England, 5, 18, 67, 80, 102
Franciscans, 12, 16
Halberstam, Judith, 25, 31, 97
Henrietta Maria, Queen Consort of England, 74, 75, 80
Henry VIII, King of England, 8, 14, 16, 19, 23
James I, King of England, 24, 31, 49, 54, 62-66, 86, 102

Jankowski, Theodora, 22-23, 46, 57, 59, 89-90, 94, 97-98, 139
Jesuits, 22, 73, 84, 159, 170, 208
Jonson, Ben, 34, 76
  Volpone, 34-36, 76
Lisboa, Portugal, 20, 172
Luther, Martin, 8, 85, 179, 198, 211
Measure for Measure, 2, 5, 8, 13, 23, 24, 31-93, 190, 204, 209, 211
  Angelo, 8, 24, 32-65, 92
  Claudio, 32, 33-45, 48, 50, 53, 54, 55-58, 63-66, 121, 138, 211
  Duke Vincentio, 24, 32-35, 39, 40, 42, 44, 45, 46, 47, 49, 52, 54-69, 142, 200, 209, 211
  Isabella, 2, 5, 8, 9, 13, 23-67, 80, 92-93, 149, 154, 190, 200, 204-205, 209, 211
Merchant of Venice, 61, 78
Mexico City, 151, 154, 155, 160, 163
New Spain, 150, 151, 170
nuns
  chastity, 6, 7, 22, 25, 33-40, 45, 46, 48, 51, 88, 98-99, 107, 116, 127, 132-134, 152, 164, 169, 184, 212
  poverty, 23, 83, 166, 213, 214
  vows, 1, 3, 10, 12, 21, 23, 28, 35, 46, 48, 51, 57, 97, 140, 155, 157, 167, 184, 188-189, 193, 194, 204-209, 211, 213, 215
Ovid, 101, 136
Paul II, Pope, 12
Periculoso, 9- 11, 13, 21, 62
Phillip II, King of Spain, 19, 120, 124

Poor Clares, 5, 12-3, 24, 32, 38, 41, 46-48, 50, 57, 60, 84, 102, 210
Protestantism, 1, 4, 5, 7- 9, 13-31, 34, 36, 38, 47, 48, 53, 61, 67, 69, 72, 79, 80, 82, 84-93, 99-100, 108, 179, 188, 198, 206-215
queer theory, 2-3, 24-25, 31, 45-46, 57, 59, 65- 67, 94, 97, 104, 107, 127, 134-135, 188, 201, 202
querelle des femmes, 2-3, 26, 58, 69, 71, 81, 92, 111, 113, 132, 143-144, 147, 150, 162, 164, 175, 180, 185-186
Reformation, 5, 8, 15-18, 19, 21, 49, 72, 74, 84-86, 89, 94, 102, 170, 179, 198
Saint Augustine, 9, 42, 44-46, 51, 99
Saint Catherine of Alexandria, 160
Saint Clare, 12
Saint Francis, 50
Saint Jerome, 9, 10, 49, 91
Saint Paul, 78, 84, 153, 178, 179
Saint Teresa of Ávila, 79, 150, 153, 156, 158, 170, 195
Sevilla, Spain, 20, 124, 160, 192, 193, 197
Shakespeare, William, 2-5, 8-9, 13, 24, 27, 31- 37, 40, 41, 43, 45-55, 59-66, 76, 78-80, 89, 95, 100, 104, 105, 114, 121, 149, 154, 182, 190, 200-201, 204-205, 209-211, 215
Sor Juana, 2, 5-6, 23, 27, 149-201, 210, 215

"Hombres necios", 27, 150, 152, 161-167, 170, 173, 177, 184, 185
"La Respuesta", 27
Los empeños de una casa, 27, 150-151, 180-182
Spain, 2, 5, 7, 12-14, 19-20, 22, 26, 109, 111, 115, 117, 120-127, 130, 140-142, 145, 147, 150-154, 156-164, 169, 180, 183, 186, 188-189, 193, 194, 199-200, 205
Spanish Empire, 2, 20, 189, 192, 194
The Convent of Pleasure, 12, 23, 25, 26, 44, 69, 70-72, 75, 77-78, 82, 84, 95- 98, 100, 106, 107, 111, 211
    Lady Happy, 12, 23, 25, 27, 44, 69, 72, 77, 78, 79-91, 92, 95, 97-108, 149, 154, 175, 213, 215
The History of the Nun
    Isabella, 188, 204, 205, 206
Twelfth Night, 52, 58, 95, 100, 201
Virgin Mary, 7, 50, 61, 101, 131, 132, 134, 139, 175
Wales, 13, 18, 19
widows, 27, 47, 49, 62, 117, 127, 134, 141
Woolf, Virginia
    A Room of One's Own, 23, 27, 149, 158
Zayas, María de, 2, 3, 5, 6, 9, 26-27, 93, 109-169, 175, 190, 199, 201, 206, 209, 212, 215